# FAMOUS CRICKETERS
## OF
# HAMPSHIRE

—

# FAMOUS CRICKETERS
## OF
# HAMPSHIRE

by

## DEAN HAYES

**Foreword by**
**Mark Nicholas**

## SPELLMOUNT LTD
### Tunbridge Wells

In the Spellmount/Nutshell Cricket list:

*The Test Match Career of Geoffrey Boycott*
by C D Clark
*The Test Match Career of Sir Jack Hobbs*
by Clive W Porter
*Cricket Anthology*
by Samuel J Looker
*Cricket at Hastings*
by Gerald Brodribb
*The Test Match Career of Walter Hammond*
by Derek Lodge
*Kent Cricketing Greats*
by Dean Hayes
*The Test Match Career of Ted Dexter*
by Derek Lodge
*Gloucestershire Cricketing Greats*
by Dean Hayes
*The Army's Grace*
*Brig-Gen R M Poore*
by Jeremy Lonsdale
*The Cricket Masters 1890–1991*
*England v Australia*
by Derek Johnson
*Famous Cricketers of Essex*
by Dean Hayes
*Famous Cricketers of Middlesex*
by Dean Hayes
*The Lord's Test*
by Steven Lynch

First published in the UK in 1993 by
*Spellmount Ltd*
12 Dene Way, Speldhurst
Tunbridge Wells, Kent TN3 0NX

British Library Cataloguing-in-Publication Data
A Catalogue record for this book is available from the British Library

ISBN–0–946771–76–6

Design by David Morley-Clarke
Typeset by Kudos Graphics, Slinfold, West Sussex

Printed and bound in Great Britain by
Biddles Ltd, Guildford and King's Lynn

# FAMOUS CRICKETERS OF HAMPSHIRE

Famous Cricketers of Hampshire is a unique survey of some of the players who have moulded the game in the county since 1864.

From the talents of Harry Baldwin and Alex Bowell right up to present players like Malcolm Marshall and Robin Smith, the author analyses the contribution made by 59 Famous Cricketers of Hampshire – names like Philip Mead, Jack Newman, Alec Kennedy, George Brown, Lionel Tennyson, Stuart Boyes, Derek Shackleton, Peter Sainsbury, Bob Cottam, Barry Richards and Gordon Greenidge.

With the help of up-to-date statistics and new research, Dean Hayes has selected the fifty-nine cricketers carefully and, by means of a biographical sketch and a discussion of each player's merits, he has placed each within the context of Hampshire cricket as a whole.

*Questions*

1. Who is the only first-class cricketer to have taken part in three tied Championship matches?
2. Who has scored the fastest century for the County, his hundred coming after only 45 minutes?
3. Who in a match against Gloucestershire, bowled a ball that struck a butterfly in flight and killed it?
4. Which Hampshire bowler spent 7 years in the Palestine Police Force before returning to England to play county cricket?
5. Who took a hat-trick in a Lambert and Butler seven-a-side floodlit tournament at Ashton Gate, the home of Bristol City F.C.?
6. Who at the age of forty was the last man to perform the 'double' for Hampshire?

*Answers*

1. Desmond Eagar
2. E M Sprot v Gloucestershire at Bristol in 1911
3. Charlie Knott in 1951
4. Vic Cannings
5. David Turner!
6. Jim Bailey

# CONTENTS

# ACKNOWLEDGEMENTS

I am greatly indebted to the following for their help in the compilation of this book.

The officials of Hampshire County Cricket Club for their selection of the fifty-nine players for inclusion in the book, and especially Mike Taylor (Marketing Manager), Neil Jenkinson (Curator) and Victor Isaacs (Scorer and Statistician) for their 'extra' assistance.

To Mark Nicholas who has kindly written the foreword and to Peter Stafford (ex-Bolton League Secretary) for his continued support. The illustrations were kindly provided by Hampshire County Cricket Club and Patrick Eagar.

# SELECT BIBLIOGRAPHY

H S Altham, John Arlott, E D R Eagar, Roy Webber: *The Official History of Hampshire County Cricket Club* (Phoenix House, London) 1957

*John Arlott's Book of Cricketers* (Lutterworth Press) 1979

Association of Cricket Statisticians: *Hampshire Cricketers 1861–1982* by Victor Isaacs

Philip Bailey, Philip Thorn, Peter Wynne-Thomas: *Who's Who of Cricketers* (Newnes Feltham) 1984

Benny Green: *Wisden Book of Cricketers Lives* (Macdonald Queen Anne Press) 1986

Christopher Martin-Jenkins: *Wisden Book of County Cricket* (Queen Anne Press) 1981

John Nyren: *The Young Cricketer's Tutor* (Effingham Wilson) 1833

Roy Webber: *Who's Who in World Cricket* (Hodder and Stoughton) 1954

Peter Wynne-Thomas: *The History of Hampshire County Cricket Club* (Christopher Helm) 1988

plus various Cricketer Magazines; Wisden Cricket Monthlies: Wisdens: and Hampshire Yearbooks.

# FOREWORD

Why is it that Hampshire cricket attracts such romance? The mixture of poetry and patois I suppose and the variables that keep even the most devoted supporters on their toes. The players have ranged from the desultory to the delectable, neither more appealing than the other for everyone has his favourite. There are tales too that have inflated the legends of the Marshalls, the Smiths and Shackleton and reach back as far as Mead, Sprot and Tennyson.

In many ways the Hon L H Tennyson engineered much of the romance and humour that set the style. He had characters under him who allowed such expression. Once when 'Lofty' Herman came in to bat under strict instructions to appeal against the light as things were dire for the County, Tennyson exclaimed from the non-striker's end 'the light Herman, the light'. 'I hear you my Lord' said 'Lofty' 'but I don't see you.'

Mention of 'Lofty' reminds me that his son Bob, who opened the bowling in the Championship side of 1973, is not included in this illustrious list. Nor for that matter is David O'Sullivan who took nearly 50 wickets in August securing the pennant. Also missing are David Gower and C B Fry, two men touched by magic whose charm and style enhance the Hampshire story.

There have been stroke-makers and stodgers, speed merchants and spinners. Richards and Greenidge; Horton and Gray; White and Roberts; Newman and Knott. Some who did play for England and others who might have done Cottam, Brown and Terry; Turner, Rogers and Sainsbury.

If Lionel Tennyson started Hampshire's flirtation with the Gods, no one more personified its character than Colin Ingleby-Mackenzie. In bringing Hampshire its first County Championship title he refused to compromise himself encouraging fun and bonhomie as eagerly as runs and wickets. He sneaked the title from under the noses of wide-eyed Yorkshiremen and numbed Londoners. Some would say that Colin has lived since in its memory – certainly Hampshire cricket has no greater ambassador.

And so the dreams go on: of Harry Baldwin's stature and Desmond Eagar's authority; of Sam Pothecary and Johnny Arnold; and of the record breakers Leo Harrison and Bobby Parks. How well I remember Jim Bailey who loved everyone and whom everyone loved, who played snooker like a wizard and who once achieved the elusive double. How the Members must have loved to watch Phil Mead, who made more runs for Hampshire than anyone, as he nudged the ball off his toes and scurried down the pitch crying 'more coal for the winter Walter' as he passed Livsey, Tennyson's batman, butler and wicket-keeper.

And lastly, how the Members have loved Arthur Holt, the timeless custodian of so much of the Hampshire legend.

May this book personify it.

MARK NICHOLAS

# INTRODUCTION

Hampshire cricket, though not exactly born in the cradle of the game, has records and history splendid and old enough to link the county closely enough to Hambledon.

Through the writings of John Nyren, who chronicled the affairs of the Hambledon Club and its cricketers, we have a charming insight into those days on Broadhalfpenny Down. Nyren was not alone in writing with rich distinction of the Hambledon era, for the Reverend James Pycroft came on the scene in time to interview the last major surviving cricketer, William Beldham. Also, the writings of Arthur Haygarth and the reminiscences of the Reverend John Mitford are a delight.

The earliest extant reference to cricket in Hambledon is dated 1756, when the following notice appeared in the *Reading Mercury* of 8 September that year: 'Lost at the Cricket Match on Broadhalfpenny on Wed Aug 18, a dog'. In the same year as the lost dog, Dartford played three matches against a team which is reported to be Hampton or Hambledon. It is a further eight years before the next authentic notice of the Hambledon team appears, when a game between the gèntlemen of Hambledon called Squire Lamb's Club and the gentlemen of Chertsey was played at Laleham Burway.

As regards the establishment of the 'Hambledon Club', as opposed to a team representing the village, there is a wide selection of dates to choose from! Whatever the speculation regarding the date of formation, there can be no arguing that the 1770s and early 1780s were the great days of Hambledon.

The majority of players were qualified for Hampshire both by birth and residence and so Hambledon did field a team that was either 'Hampshire' or 'Hampshire with 1 or 2 given men'. Therefore supporters of Hampshire County Cricket Club, are quite justified in calling most Hambledon teams 'Hampshire'.

Between 1772 and 1788, Hambledon opposed England in thirty-seven eleven-a-side matches, winning twenty-one and losing only fifteen, the remaining match being drawn. Their best year was 1779 when the Club beat England four times. Of all the players in that year, pride of place without doubt goes to Richard Hyre, described by his son as: 'the chosen General of all matches, ordering and directing the whole.' Others who played in the games of 1779 include John Small senior, the best batsman, whose innings of 136 against Surrey on Broadhalfpenny Down in 1775, was it is believed the highest score in a major match to that date.

Indeed, he was acclaimed 'the best cricketer the world ever produced'. Another good batsman was Richard Veck, whilst Thomas Sueter was the wicket-keeper. David Harris, who is credited with inventing or perfecting 'length' bowling was for a time, the premier bowler in England. He began playing for Hambledon in 1782, though in later years, he suffered from gout and would arrive at matches on a pair of crutches!

Of all the other players to have represented Hambledon, William Beldham was the best known. Nyren referred to him as 'a most venomous hitter' and he was certainly one of England's best batsmen.

The decline of the Hambledon Club began in the late 1780s and accelerated through the next decade. Richard Nyren who had looked after the Hambledon ground, both at Broadhalfpenny Down and then Windmill Down and whose inns, the *Bat and Ball* and then the *George* had been the Club's headquarters, left the village, as did his son.

The first recorded meeting of the Hampshire Country Crickt Club was in 1795. The actual reference in Waghorn's *The Dawn of Cricket* reads:

'Aug 17 1795. The members of the Hampshire county club will please to take notice that the anniversary meeting will be held at the White Hart Inn, Winchester on Wednesday the 26th. Dinner at 3 o'clock.'

There is a five year gap following 1798 in county cricket in Hampshire, but then from 1803 to 1807, there ensued a period of varying fortunes. The outstanding figure to appear in the Hampshire sides in this time was Lord Frederick Beauclerk. In 1805, playing as a 'given man' in his first county match, he made 68 and 129 not out as Hampshire beat England at Lord's. There were further victories in 1806 and 1807, whilst after the County's eight wicket win in 1828, a long gap occured before in 1838, *Bell's Life* mentions the creation of a County Club. This Club was organised by Thomas Chamberlayne.

He laid out a cricket ground and began to revive the game within the county, beating the MCC at Lord's in 1842 by 235 runs. The following year, Chamberlayne was a little more ambitious, with his Hampshire side playing home and away games with both the MCC and Nottinghamshire. One of the most noted players to assist Chamberlayne was Sir Frederick Bathurst, a fast round-arm bowler.

During the 1850s, when the other leading cricketing counties were beginning to build their county clubs, there was a distinct lack of enthusiasm for a County Club in Hampshire. However, in 1861, the Hampshire side returned to Lord's to play the MCC and though they were heavily beaten by an innings and 202 runs, there followed wins over the Gentlemen of Sussex and I Zingari. These victories encouraged Thomas Chamberlayne, Sir Frederick Bathurst and friends to think of laying the foundations of a new Hampshire County Cricket Club.

It was on 12 August 1863, at a meeting held in Southampton, that the county club was formed, under the chairmanship of Mr Thomas Chamberlayne and he patronage of Sir Frederick Bathurst. The first important inter-county match played by the newly formed Hampshire County Cricket Club, was against Sussex at the Antelope Ground, Southampton.

In 1875, Clement Booth was appointed as both captain and secretary. He strengthened the fixture list and set the County on the road to first-class status and with it a place in the County Championship.

In 1880, Hampshire beat the MCC twice, but they lost twice to Sussex and indeed to both Devonshire and Somerset. It was in 1882 that Hampshire began again the slow climb that was to lift them in the end to first-class status. In 1884, Hampshire made 645 in defeating Somerset, whilst Francis Lacey scored 211 out of 414 in the first innings of the win over Kent. Throughout the 1880s, Lacey was Hampshire's most outstanding cricketer. He demonstrated his batting skill in May 1885 when the new County Ground at Bannister Road, Southampton was first used, hitting 181 not out for the South of the County against the North. In 1887, Colonel James Fellowes was succeeded as secretary by Dr Russell Bencraft, the man to whom in the view of that great Hampshireman H S Altham, the county owes its greatest debt. His appointment though did not immediately solve Hampshire's problems. For the only victory of the summer was a win by an innings and 342 runs against Norfolk, with F E Lacey hitting an unbeaten 323.

Captain E G Wynyard, a young soldier emerged as a most promising batsman. He had played on and off since 1878, but in 1890, he was at home and able to play regularly, coinciding with an upturn in the county's fortunes. At the end of the 1892 season, 'Bombardier' Victor Barton topped both the batting and bowling averages. He was a very attractive batsman, hitting 161 v MCC and another hundred against Oxfordshire. In 1893, A J L Hill began a long and valuable career with the county. He was the second native of the County to appear in Test cricket. Two other bowlers whose names were to be linked with Hampshire for many years, were Harry Baldwin and Tom Soar.

In May 1895, the MCC decided that Hampshire's matches against Derbyshire, Essex, Leicestershire and Warwickshire should be regarded as first-class. However, the first half of the County's programme that season produced a disappointing record, with only one success against a weak MCC side, out of the six matches played. The month of August brought a welcome transformation. A victory againt Sussex by six wickets with just three minutes to spare came in the middle of a run of five victories in the County's last six matches and clinched their Championship status. Hampshire's first Championship match was against Somerset at Taunton in 1895, the County winning by 11 runs. In the next match, Derbyshire were beaten by an innings and 79 runs and later in the season, the County surprisingly defeated Yorcshire at Bramall Lane, to end the summer with six wins. Harry Baldwin took 102 wickets at 16 runs each, whilst Tom Soar had 89 victims at 18 runs each. Russell Bencraft retired from the captaincy at the end of that season and was succeeded by Captain Wynyard. Unfortunately, he couldn't play as often as he would have liked due to his military duties, though he played in the last Test against Australia in 1896, after he had made 268 aginst Yorkshire at Southampton. The County fell away slightly over the next two seasons, coinciding with the drop in form of Baldwin and Soar. In the latter of those two seasons, the County found another notable player from military circles in Major R M Poore. His debut was quite remarkable, in that he carried his bat through the County's innings for 49 not out in a Hampshire total of 97. He was to take the cricket world by storm in 1899, when he scored 1,399 championship runs at an average of 116.58. He and Wynyard, when they were in form, made the County a force to be reckoned with. Wynyard had a superb summer, scoring 225 against Somerset, but no one challenged Poore's 304 in the same match, as the pair added a record 411 for the sixth wicket. Others who changed the face of Hampshire cricket around this time, were the South African, C B Llewellyn and Captain J G Greig. In 1901, Llewellyn took 115 Championship wickets, whilst in the same season, Greig hit five scores of over 100, including 249 not out against Lancashire at Liverpool.

For four years from 1902, the County finished bottom of the Championship and only the tenacity of Russell Bencraft kept them going. This a result of many of the Army players Hampshire relied on away at the Boer War. The summer of 1906 started badly, though a nineteen-year-old left-handed batsman by the name of Philip Mead took 109 off the Yorkshire attack in the second game of the season. By the end of the campaign, the County had put together a string of victories to finish in eighth place in the Championship. One of the men responsible for this turn around, was John Badcock who took 92 wickets at 24.71 runs each, bringing great encouragement to E M Sprot, the captain through some depressing years.

It was around this time that Hampshire gave debuts to three outstanding cricketers – Jack Newman (1906) Alec Kennedy (1907) and George Brown (1908) – all of them playing together until the early 1930s. Also, Alec Bowell had made his debut in 1902 – playing until 1927, he had scored more runs for Hampshire when he ended his career than any other batsman except Philip Mead.

In 1909, Charles Burgess Fry, the eminent England all-rounder, left Sussex for Hampshire, though he only played in two matches the following summer, when Hampshire with 10 victories in twenty-four games, rose to sixth place in the Championsip. In 1911, Philip Mead continued his advance, scoring 1,706 runs at an average of 58.82, whilst Fry was in great form and hit 258 not out off the Gloucestershire attack. In fact, Fry ended the season at the head of the national batting averages, with Mead who finished his season with two brilliant innings, in second place.

In 1912, Hampshire beat the Australians by 8 wickets, a feat not repeated by an English county until Surrey won at the Oval in 1956. Fry was absent for this game, but ended the season with 612 Championship runs at 102.00 to help the side rise five places in the table. He topped the national first-class averages for a second successive year. The Hampshire batsmen had even improved on the previous season's showing, for A C Johnston was second and Mead third. In fact, if the bowling had matched up, the County might well have won the Championship. At the end of the season, Dr Bencraft who was by then the President of the Club, described this as the best Hampshire team he had seen in an experience going back to the 1870s. In 1913, the Hon Lionel Tennyson, had a very successful introduction to the side, though it was Mead, who not only topped the national batting averages, but also scored most runs – 2,627 at 50.51. In 1914, the County achieved a record 13 Championship wins which gave them fifth place – the highest in their history so far. So when war broke out to end first-class cricket, Hampshire were at their strongest.

During 1918, E M Sprot indicated that he didn't want to continue as captain, and so the Committee elected the Hon Lionel Tennyson – he was to captain the side until 1933. Mead soon picked up where he'd left off, scoring 1,332 runs at an average of 60.54 in 1919, whilst Kennedy was easily the County's best bowler with 164 wickets at 17.64 in 1920.

In 1921, Tennyson was chosen to captain England. He took up his appointment for the third Test against the Australians at Leeds, and though he injured his hand whilst fielding, he insisted on facing the ferocious pace of McDonald and Gregory to hit 63 and 36 one-handed.

The following season saw Hampshire gain one of the most famous of all vintories. Replying to Warwickshire's first innings total of 223, a dramatic collapse saw Hampshire dismissed for 15. Following on, the County lost six wickets for 186 and an innings defeat seemed certian. But, stands of 85 for the seventh wicket and 177 for the ninth between Brown (172) and Livsey (110*) left

Warwickshire needing 304 to win. Whereupon Kennedy and Newman went on to dismiss their opponents cheaply and Hampshire won the most incredible victory.

The season also saw an oddity in that Newman was barracked by a section of the Trent Bridge crowd for the amount of time he took in setting his field when bowling. Tennyson ordered him to stop wasting time, whereupon Newman told his captain in no uncertain manner, what he could do! Tennyson then ordered him to leave the field and in doing so, Newman kicked down the wicket – fortunately there were apologies all round and Newman was reinstated the next day.

Between 1920 and 1930, the County's average position in the Championship was a disappointing eleventh. In fact, the successes of Hampshire in those years was based too often on the efforts of individuals.

The batting averages told a now-familiar story. No one has ever made more runs in county cricket than Philip Mead did for Hampshire (48,892) and in first-class cricket, only Sir Jack Hobbs, 'Patsy' Hendren and Frank Woolley have greater aggregates than the County's outstanding left-hander. Kennedy and Newman were the main force of Hampshire's bowling. Kennedy was of medium-pace, varying inswingers and leg-cutters. In all, he performed the 'double' five times and his best season with the ball was 1922 when he took 205 wickets at an average of 16.80. Newman, though he didn't play for England, was a great off-break bowler and with the new ball, also he could be effective. The two often bowled unchanged throughout an innings. Kennedy scored 16,586 runs in all F C cricket (14,925 for Hants) and took 2,874 in all first-class cricket (2,549) wickets; Newman made 15,333 runs took 2,032 wickets Newman (13,904 for Hants) (1,946 wickts).

By 1930, the side was beginning to change. In the County's final match of the season, Brown, Kennedy, Mead and Newman took the field for the last time together. W H Livsey, wicket-keeper since 1913, had played his last game the season before. In the winter of 1930–31, Newman fell ill and retired. Younger men began to take the places of the old order, with Johnny Arnold the most promising of them.

He gained his only cap at Test level against New Zealand in 1931. An exceptional games player, he won an England international soccer cap against Scotland at Hampden Park in 1931. He developed into a very sound batsman and he and Brown formed a good opening pair. However, at the end of the 1933 season, Brown retired. For over twenty years, he had been one of the most popular players in the game. A versatile cricketer, he scored 25,649 (22,962 for Hants) runs and took over 600 catches. Just (602 for Hants) wickets. The summer had seen the likes of McCorkell, Creese, Pothecary and Herman establish themselves, but the main feature of the season was Mead's remarkable batting at the age of forty-six, his average being 68.83. (In championship cricket).

At the close of the 1936 season, it was announced that Mead had been released by the County. His career stretched back thirty-two years and saw him appear in 700 matches.

R H Moore, Hampshire's captain, was capable of brilliant things and always led by example. His great innings of 316 not out against Warwickshire in 1937 is still the highest individual score made for Hampshire. He was the last man out and batted for 380 minutes, hitting forty-three fours and three sixes. Stuart Boyes was the county's stock slow left-arm bowler - the effect of the relief he afforded was reflected in the performances of the two bowlers, Kennedy and Newman, though Boyes himself captured 1,415 wickets. When war broke out in 1939, Hampshire were fifteenth in the Championship, claiming just three victories against seventeen losses. When first-class cricket resumed seven years later, the nucleus of the Hampshire side was still there with Arnold, Bailey, Heath, Herman, Hill and McCorkell common to the pre-war and post-war sides.

In October 1945, the Committee appointed Desmond Eagar as captain and secretary for 1946. He had played occasionally for Gloucestershire before the war, but he took Hampshire to his heart immediately. He took over a side which was as unpredictable as ever, for they were the only county to beat the Champions – Yorkshire, and this they did by ten wickets. For most of their successes in this first year of peace, they owed a great debt to C J Knott, an off-spinner, later to become chairman of the cricket committee, who took 676 wickets in all first-class games – more than any amateur had done before.

Hampshire supporters were amazed by the apparent transformation of the side in the first half of the 1948 season. For by mid-July, the County were in fifth place in the Championship and with an outside chance of taking the title. Unfortunately, they fell away achieving just one more win and had to settle for ninth place. Jim Bailey enjoyed an Indian summer, to top both the batting (1,310 runs at 32.75) and bowling (109 wickets at 17.97) averages.

Also making his debut that season was a player by the name of Derek Shackleton. He was discovered when playing in Army cricket and was given a trial as a batsman, then had a spell bowling leg-breaks and finally settled on seam bowling.

By 1949, Eagar described Shackleton's advance as the best thing to have happened to Hampshire since the war – he took 92 wickets in the County Championship at 26 runs each.

For the 1950 season, the County engaged Vic Cannings, a Hampshire man by birth, who had had a season or two with Warwickshire. The aim that summer was to give youth its chance, a policy that was continued in 1951, when Hampshire finished ninth, their most successful season since the Second World War. The bowling became very much a two man attack with both Shackleton and Cannings using the seam to great effect. The batting relied heavily on the opening pair of N H Rogers (1,971 runs at 41.06) and Neil McCorkell, while both Leo Harrison and J R Gray, a Southampton-born professional completed 1,000 runs for the first time.

In 1953, the County acquired the services of both Roy Marshall and Henry Horton. A Barbadian, Marshall had toured England with the West Indian side of 1950. He scored runs in minor matches and hit a hundred against The Army and Hampshire, but it would be two years later before he began his Championship career. Henry Horton was registered from Worcestershire and his defensive batting saved many matches, but he would also attack the bowling, scoring the majority of his runs in front of the wicket by putting a great deal of power behind his 'pushes'.

There were three young bowlers who looked as if they would give good support to Shackleton and Cannings. They were Sainsbury, Heath and Burden, who captured forty-six Championship wickets in the second half of the 1954 season. In 1955, Hampshire gained sixteen Championship wins to finish third, the highest position that the County had ever achieved in what was their Diamond Jubilee year.

Roy Marshall was, by now, rated one of the most attractive batsmen in England and in 1957, he hit 100 against Kent at Southampton in sixty-six minutes. It was the fastest of the season and the fastest for the County since 1927. However, the year was a sad one for Desmond Eagar, for it was his last as captain. His successor was Colin Ingleby-Mackenzie who brought more than a touch of the tactical ingeniousness of Lord Tennyson. In 1958, his first year as captain, Marshall and Shackleton were both in great form. Heath took 119 Championship wickets at 16.32, whilst Gray's game was raised by Marshall's example, as the County finished second in the Championship. In 1959, the County played some entertaining cricket and Marshall and Shackleton were two of Wisden's Five Cricketers of the Year. In all the County's first-class matches, Horton, Gray and Marshall each reached 2,000 runs – a unique event in Hampshire's History. With eighty-three dismissals, Leo Harrison broke Livsey's wicket-keeping record for the county. The bright spot of the following season was the bowling of D W White, who took 124 wickets at 19 runs each.

It was at Dean Park on 1 September 1961 that Hampshire secured the County Championship for the first time as they beat Derbyshire by 140 runs. In that season, an experimental law had disallowed the follow-on and a skilled assessment of the alternatives was needed. So nice did Ingleby-Mackenzie's perceptions become that more than half Hampshire's wins were the fruits of clever declarations. Ten sides were caught and only two got away. Against Somerset, after being led by over a hundred, he took advantage of a superb second innings double hundred by Marshall to declare, setting the enemy a perfectly possible target, and getting them out in time. Against Nottinghamshire, he cut even finer, Hampshire winning by 15 runs with three minutes to spare.

This was a batsman's year in which seventeen of them scored 2,000 runs, but of the Hampshire heroes, Marshall (2,607) was only one; Horton (2,329) and Gray (2,034) were not far behind. Three batsmen made 2,000 and six, bringing in Sainsbury, Ingleby-Mackenzie and Livingstone (who had averaged over 100 in Club and Ground matches in 1959 and only qualified for Championship games in 1960) made 1,000.

Derek Shackleton in spite of his 158 wickets did not (though it may have appeared so) bowl at both ends. Although grey by now, he could still bowl all day and was always changing the accent of his attack. Ingleby-Mackenzie used him to influence the course of almost every game, though the maturing of 'Butch' White with 121 wickets, decided a number of matches with his explosive bursts.

It was Danny Livingstone who caught Derbyshire's Bob Taylor in the outfield and so Hampshire for the first time in their history were County Champions. It had been an exciting campaign, for by mid-season, it had developed into a three-cornered fight between Hampshire, Midlesex and Yorkshire. Hampshire eventually moved into the lead at the beginning of August, after which they were never caught.

There were memorable scenes at Bournemouth and as Ingleby-Mackenzie told the Hampshire supporters: 'This is the most wonderful occasion of all time. I would like to toast the luckiest captain, and the great men who have made this possible. I am too excited to say much more. I just hope I won't wake up tomorrow morning and find that we are twelfth in the table.'

Several disappointing seasons followed, for the County were no longer the all-conquering side of 1961. However, the summer of 1965, brought two away wins against Lancashire and Yorkshire that will linger long in the memory of those who witnessed the matches. At Middlesbrough in the middle of May, the Yorkshire side were bowled out for 23 (the lowest total in their history) with White returning figures of:

| O | M | R | W |
|----|---|----|---|
| 10 | 7 | 10 | 6 |

Hampshire won the game by ten wickets, the teams having been very close on the first innings. At Old Trafford in June, Hampshire could only muster 174 against some good seam bowling by Higgs and Statham. In contrast, Lancashire started brightly and were at one stage, 102 for 1, but then Bob Cottam produced a magnificent spell of bowling to take all the remaining wickets for the addition of 34 runs. His bowling analysis was:

| O | M | R | W |
|---|---|---|---|
| 11.1 | 4 | 25 | 9 |

– a new Hampshire record. The visitors were then bowled out cheaply, leaving Lancashire 116 to win, but White (6 for 48) and Shackleton (4 for 15) helped bring victory by 13 runs. The end of the season saw the retirement of Ingleby-Mackenzie and the end of an era for Hampshire cricket.

In 1966, Roy Marshall became the first contracted player to be appointed Hampshire's captain, whilst the following summer, Derek Shackleton overtook Kennedy's record total of wickets for the County.

The season of 1968 saw the face of county cricket altered dramatically - the decision to allow the instant registration of overseas players, led to the arrival of Barry Richards. A relatively unknown twenty-two-year-old, he announced his determination to hit 2,000 runs in the season. This he did, much to the astonishment of the cynics, scoring 2,039 runs in inter-county matches at 48.54. Cottam had another good year with the ball and both he and Shackleton took over 100 wickets. These performances went a long way in helping Hampshire finish the season in fifth place.

At the end of the year Shackleton announced his retirement, though he seemed as good as ever. In each of twenty seasons, he had taken 100 wickets, a record surpassed only by Wilfred Rhodes. In fact, when he hung up his boots, Wisden wrote: 'Hampshire without Shackleton will be like Blackpool without its tower'.

He actually reappeared against Sussex the following season, taking 5 for 58 in the second innings to ensure a Hampshire victory. In the month of June, Richard Gilliat hit four Championship hundreds, culminating in an innings of 223 not out against Warwickshire on the final day of the month. He also hit the season's fastest century in the match against Essex. In 1970, a nineteen-year-old Barbadian batsman by the name of Gordon Greenidge appeared in the Hampshire side. When he qualified in July, his appearances compensated somewhat for the fact that Barry Richards was playing in the Rest of the World side in their five-match series with England.

Barry Richards was a marvellous player and at his best, the best batsman in the world. When he and Greenidge were batting together at the start of a Hampshire innings, spectators were treated to many memorable displays.

After a couple of seasons of modest achievement, the county's prospects for 1973 did not appear to be much brighter, and in fact, the bookmakers offered sixty-six to one against them winning the Championship. The only new face was that of Mike Taylor, who had spent nine seasons with Nottinghamshire. He used to spend hours studying Shackleton's methods when the two counties met – now in effect, he had got Shackleton's place. The attack also consisted of Sainsbury, David O'Sullivan (an orthodox left-arm spinner who played for New Zealand), Tom Mottram and Bob Herman, the son of 'Lofty' Herman, though Trevor Jesty too, had some good spells.

Richards and Greenidge were probably the best opening pair in the country, certainly the most entertaining. The other batting places were filled by David Turner, Richard Lewis and Jesty, who were like the captain, Richard Gilliat, by nature, attacking batsmen. Bob Stephenson (who had been specially registered from Derbyshire in 1969) equalled Leo Harrison's county record of eight catches in a match, whilst the only survivor of Ingleby-Mackenzies' side was Peter Sainsbury, who finished second in the national bowling averages.

It is difficult to call the Hampshire side of 1973 a great team by historic standards, yet they won the title in a grand manner. At the end of July, Northants and Kent were closing the gap and had matches in hand, but Hampshire won six of their remaining eight fixtures and needed only a little more time to have taken the other two. The decisive match was against their closest challengers, Northants, who won the toss and were virtually beaten on the first morning as they lost eight wickets before lunch, and the game won by Monday afernoon. Hampshire's Championship win was surely, the most unexpected in the history of that competition! In 1974, Hampshire also had the services of the Antiguan, Andy Roberts – one of the world's fastest bowlers – at the expense of O'Sullivan their retention of the title, seemed a reasonable expectation.

Roberts took 119 first-class wickets at an average of 13.62, but with just three matches to play, the weather dealt the County a nasty blow. It began to rain in Hampshire and though the County only needed to win one of their matches and gain reasonable bonus points from the other two, they were thwarted – the title going to Worcestershire.

In 1975, the County proved the experts, who had labelled them an ideal 'one-day' team right, by winning the John Player Sunday League. They also won ten Championship matches (the same as in 1973 and 1974) but failed to win as many bonus points and had to settle for third place. In the Gillette Cup of that season, Hampshire created new records in the competition. Richards (129) and Greenidge (177) put on 210 for the first wicket. The total of 371 for four was not only the highest total in a Gillette Cup game, but the highest total ever recorded up to that date in a major limited-overs match, anywhere in the world.

In 1978, the County won the John Player Sunday League for the second time, winning four of their last five matches without Richards or Roberts, who both left the County in July with their contracts unexpired. Roberts' departure was a surprise, but Richards had said at the beginning of the season: 'When I walk off a county ground for the last time, it will be with a sense of relief.' It could be said, that he found batting too easy for his own good; it was this and the English county game that helped make his name, but also reduce him all too soon to boredom.

Hampshire were now faced with the decision of which new overseas player should fill the boots of the departed Richards and Roberts. The County chose a twenty-year-old Barbadian by the name of Malcolm Marshall. Both Greenidge and Marshall missed some games in 1979 due to their World Cup commitments, though the latter didn't play a game. It was the same story the following summer, with the West Indies touring England. Nick Pocock was appointed captain in place of Stephenson, who did the job in 1979, whilst Shaun Graf, the Victorian fast bowler and Chris Smith, a twenty-one-year-old batsman from Natal, were engaged as replacements for Marshall and Greenidge. The County also signed a third player in Steve Malone, the Essex medium-pace bowler. Neither Graf nor Malone proved successful and the side ended up bottom of the Championship – their worse record since 1905.

Nick Pocock was committed to positive cricket and in 1982, the County climbed to third place in the Championship, with the bowling of Marshall, the most outstanding feature of the season. He came second to Richard Hadlee in the national averages, but took twice as many wickets, and was the only bowler to reach the hundred mark.

The County finished in the same position in 1983. A season in which Chris Smith qualified for England and hit six Championship centuries and in which Paul Terry reached a thousand runs for the first time. After a barren 1984, Pocock made way for a new captain. Trevor Jesty who had been vice-captain to Pocock, was overlooked by the committee in favour of Mark Nicholas. This action prompted Jesty to move to Surrey, where he immediately took on the role of acting captain in the absence of Geoff Howarth.

In 1985, Hampshire were at full strength and in the running for the Championship, the Nat West Trophy and the John Player Sunday League, until well into August.

Chris Smith topped the batting averages, whilst his younger brother Robin, who had qualified as an English player at the beginning of the season, hit 1,351 Championship runs at 39.73. Marshall took 95 wickets at 17.68 runs apiece and Tim Tremlett was one of the best seam bowlers in the country. With Bobby Parks as a steadily improving wicket-keeper, the County played much cricket worthy of Southampton's centenary year, but had to be satisfied with second place in the championship, third in the John Player League and a place in the semi-finals of the Nat West Trophy.

In 1986, the County won the Sunday League for the third time and two years later reached ther first ever Lord's final when they triumphed in the Benson and Hedges Cup, defeating Derbyshire by seven wickets, with South African Steve Jeffries returning figures of 5 for 13 – this in a season when Greenidge and Marshall were unavailable for selection due to the West Indies tour.

In 1990, the County finished third in the County championship and had acquired the services of David Gower. They scored 600 for eight declared againt Sussex and won an exciting game at Southampton against Gloucestershire when set 445 to win in the fourth innings.

In 1991, Chris Smith left the County to take up a marketing position with the Western Australian Cricket Association, whilst captain Mark Nicholas had his finger broken by the pace of Surrey's Waqar Younis and missed his side's triumph in the Nat West Final. Surrey scored 240, after acting captain Gower had won the toss and put them in. There was a wonderful innings from Robin Smith before John Ayling's late contribution sealed the game for Hampshire.

In 1992, the County won the Benson and Hedges Cup for a second time, beating Kent by 41 runs to give Malcolm Marshall success in a Lord's final.

I feel the prospects for 1993 and succeeding years are rosy. For with Mark Nicholas to lead them, and promising players like Ayling, Shine and Udal to join Test stars Robin Smith, David Gower and Malcolm Marshall, Hampshire should be a county to reckon with.

Since Hampshire became a first-class county, they have produced several fine sides and more outstanding cricketers than the majority of the county clubs. This book, I hope, captures the flavour of those players.

Dean Hayes
Bolton 1993

# JOHNNY ARNOLD

Born: 30 November 1907, Cowley
Died: 3 April 1984
Played: 1919–1950

## FIRST-CLASS HAMPSHIRE RECORD

| Matches | Innings | NO | Runs | HS | Ave | 100s |
|---|---|---|---|---|---|---|
| 396 | 701 | 45 | 21596 | 227 | 32.92 | 36 |

| Runs | Wkts | Ave | Best |
|---|---|---|---|
| 1182 | 17 | 69.52 | 3-34 |

## NOTABLE FEATS

- He scored 1,000 runs in a season for Hampshire on fourteen occasions.
- In 1932, he scored 227 v Glamorgan at Cardiff.
- In 1934, he added 259 with C P Mead for the third wicket v Derbyshire at Portsmouth.
- His best season was 1934, when he scored 2,136 runs.

An Oxford man by birth, Johnny Arnold had played soccer and cricket for Oxford Schools before leaving to work in the Morris car plant at Cowley. At seventeen, he played outside left for Oxford City and the next summer, George Brown was playing in The Parks and during the evening he called at Johnny Arnold's home with an invitation to visit Southampton for a trial with the county. While he was at Southampton he called on the Saints manager and was signed on to their football staff.

The son of an Oxfordshire wicket-keeper, Johnny Arnold had a very successful season for his native county in 1929, scoring 650 runs at an average of 52.75. In scoring a splendid 62 in the vital match against Buckinghamshire, he helped his side secure the Minor Counties Championship. Also that season, though not qualified, he had played for Hampshire against the South Africans.

Johnny Arnold was Hampshire's outstanding player of the second decade of the inter-war period. He was a class batsman, at his best a fine attacker and when he found himself out of touch, good enough to be a regular scorer as a primarily defensive bat.

In 1930, Arnold in his first season as a county player, was soon promoted to open the batting with George Brown, although he was not qualified to play until the sixth match. He scored 1,186 runs at 32.05 to top the county averages ahead of the veteran Philip Mead.

He was undisturbed by pace bowling and could be hard on inswing, but his great strength was against off-spin, which he often murdered – even the best off-break bowlers in the land disliked bowling to him, for Johnny Arnold's footwork, eye and immense power made him a perfect hitter with the spin.

When the first ever Test played by New Zealand in England in June 1931 came along, the selectors had to find not only a successor as an opening batsman to Jack Hobbs, but also temporarily to Herbert Sutcliffe, and the choice fell on Arnold and Bakewell of Northants. If England's opponents had been Australia, then I'm sure veterans Holmes and Sandham would have been pressed into service, but against 'lesser' nations, it was the selectors' policy to blood youngsters. In fact, Arnold had never played at Lord's when he was called upon to face the daunting experience of a Test there. In his first innings, he made a 'duck' and 34 in the second, but he was dropped and never received another chance.

There can be no doubt, that promotion was thrust upon Arnold far too soon, for at that time, he was a painstaking defensive batsman, though as I have said, he later developed some very powerful attacking strokes. In 1932, he made his highest career score, with an innings of 227 against Glamorgan at Cardiff, sharing in three century stands. He ended the season with 1619 runs at 35.19.

He had his best ever season in 1934, scoring 2,136 runs at an average of 46.43. He hit a century for the Players against the Gentlemen and 109 not out against the Australians, which comfortably saved the game for the county.

Arnold was a cheerful, popular character, as is suggested perhaps by the fact that he was universally known as 'Johnny'.

He played first-class cricket in summer and professional soccer in winter, as outside left for Southampton and Fulham. Playing his last league game against West Ham on the Saturday before war started, he did play soccer with the Civil Defence team while he served in the National Fire Service, but a cartilage removed finally closed his career. What made him conspicuous among this company, was that he played both games for England, gaining a soccer cap in 1932–33 against Scotland. As befits a footballer, he was a very good outfielder, with a powerful throw and extremely quick between the wickets.

In 1938, Arnold for the first time for nine seasons failed to complete 1,000 runs or score a century; indeed at one time the Hampshire committee decided not to re-engage him after his efforts of that season. However, he was given the benefit of the doubt as 'Lofty' Herman had decided to go into Lancashire League cricket. His decline that summer was almost inexplicable. All his front-of-the-wicket power was lost and even his hooking had gone off, so that he seemed little more than a nudger and deflector, though against Kent, he and McCorkell put on 102 in the first innings and 100 in the second.

Happily, he recovered his form the following season, to head the county averages with 1467 runs at 34.11.

Johnny Arnold was a great team man and would open the innings or bat lower down the order as required. In 1946, he was at his most dependable, scoring over 1,500 runs, but only reaching three figures on one occasion.

In 1949, the New Zealander produced some remarkable cricket at the county ground. Hampshire were bowled out for 129 and were well adrift when New Zealand scored 430 for five wickets. Hampshire scored 409 in their second innings, mainly due to a magnificent 100 by Arnold. He played on a regular basis until late July 1950 when he was stricken by a serious illness, which ended his playing career. His loss to the county was all the more galling, for he was batting in his old form. In 15 Championship matches, he scored 997 runs at 43.34.

During a playing career which spanned twenty-one years, he scored 21,831 runs in all matches, including thirty-seven centuries and an average of 32.92.

From 1961 to 1974, he was on the first-class umpire's panel and was probably the only one to use cob nuts as counters!

# JIM BAILEY

Born: 6 April 1908, Shawford
Died: 9 February 1988
Played: 1927–1952

FIRST-CLASS HAMPSHIRE RECORD

| Matches | Innings | NO | Runs | HS | Ave | 100s |
|---------|---------|-----|------|-----|-------|------|
| 242 | 408 | 35 | 9301 | 133 | 24.93 | 5 |

| Runs | Wkts | Ave | Best |
|------|------|-------|------|
| 12595 | 467 | 26.97 | 7-7 |

NOTABLE FEATS

- He carried his bat for 70* from 139 v West Indies at Bournemouth in 1939.

- He had figures of:

| O | M | R | W |
|---|---|---|---|
| 7 | 3 | 7 | 7 |

including five wickets for five runs in 12 balls, against Nottinghamshire at Southampton in 1932.
- He added 209 with N H Rogers for the fifth wicket v Worcestershire at Southampton in 1946.
- In 1948, he performed the 'double' and v Leicestershire, scored 62 and 77 and took 11 for 70.
- He scored 1,000 runs in a season for Hampshire on four occasions.

One of the unluckiest players to play for Hampshire, Jim Bailey was found playing for Wimborne in Dorset and engaged on the groundstaff. He first appeared for the county in 1927 when he was nineteen and already a promising all-round player, yet it was twenty-one years before, in 1948 at the age of forty, he first performed the 'double' – the last man to do so for the County.

He established himself in 1931, when he scored 922 runs, making an admirable opening partner for Johnny Arnold, so that five times – twice after Hampshire had lost the toss and been put into bat – the two put on a hundred for the opening partnership. The following year saw his batting recede but his bowling advance so much so, that in June, he stood at the top of the bowling averages for the entire country. Against Nottingham-shire, he was in superb form, taking seven wickets for seven runs, including five wickets for five runs in 12 balls. Then he seemed to fall away and was dropped. He returned later in the season to bat in commanding fashion against Yorkshire, though a recovery with the bat the following season was discounted by a complete loss of his bowling.

Jim Bailey was probably the Hampshire player to suffer most from the struggle between two generations.

Unable to gain a regular place in the Hampshire side, he joined the ground staff at Lord's to serve a two-year residential qualification with Middlesex. But of course, that was the era of Compton, Edrich, Robertson and Young – tremendous com-petition and things didn't work out. In 1936 he began his three seasons with Accrington, becoming the first English professional to score 1,000 runs in a season in the Lancashire League.

In 1938, he was recalled to the county side in a desperate attempt to strengthen the batting – he scored 44 and 69 in his first two innings upon his return. He re-established himself as a county player in 1939, but then six years of war cruelly interrupted an already fragmented career.

After 1945, he took up his bowling again and despite putting a fair amount of weight on, remained both a valuable batsman and good slow left-arm bowler. In fact, in the first four post-war seasons, he was one of the best county all-rounders, reaching his peak in the summer of 1948.

Jim Bailey was a very solid batsman, very difficult to remove on a slow wicket and extremely patient. As a slow bowler, he was at his best – for he had flight, length and spin and a tremendous cricketing brain. He was certainly unlucky – his talents justified a more successful career than his figures grant him, but the county too must also be regarded as unwise in its failure to make more of his powers. In 1946, he hit the highest of his five centuries, a magnificent 133 out of Hampshire's total of 346 in the match against Worcestershire. He had problems with his leg this summer, it preventing him from bowling very much during the season.

An expert amateur billiards player, Jim Bailey played many exhibition matches in 1946–47 to aid club funds and earned for the club no less than £250 on his own.

The summer of 1948 saw him finish top of the Hampshire batting and bowling averages. Despite not scoring a century, punishing leg-side shots helped the left-handed batsman to 1,399 runs at 31.79 and his orthodox left-arm spin reaped 121 wickets at 18.13.

It was a wonderful season for him, for at the age of forty, he had realised every cricketer's dream.

In his lounge cabinet, Jim had three mounted cricket balls. One was the ball with which he took those seven wickets for seven runs against Nottinghamshire in 1932, whilst the other two bore testimony to that triumphant season. With one ball, he reached the 'double' against Warwickshire at Southampton on August 10 and with the other he turned in one of the finest pieces of slow bowling on a good wicket at Lord's. The full Middlesex side were bowled out for 207 with Jim Bailey's figures reading:

| O | M | R | W |
|---|---|---|---|
| 22 | 11 | 26 | 5 |

– his victims being Robertson, Edrich, Compton, Mann and Fairbairn. In fact, he twice dismissed Denis Compton cheaply, though Hampshire lost the match by 12 runs. Jim produced a string of fine performances during that memorable summer for him, when two other players, George Pope of Derbyshire and Northants' Vince Broderick also did the 'double'. He emerged with superb figures of 11 for 95 and 8 for 71 against Essex and Gloucestershire respectively; Nottinghamshire suffered when he took 6 for 52 in an innings, and in a remarkable spell against Warwickshire at Edgbaston, he claimed five for 63 in 42.3 overs.

He and his fellow spinner, Charlie Knott, who took 101 wickets that season, routed the all-conquering Australians at South-ampton. With Bailey taking 4 for 27 and Knott 5 for 57, the unbeaten Aussies were dismissed for 117 to trail Hampshire by 78 runs on first innings. But, as the wicket eased out, the tourists recovered to win by eight wickets. Only three other Hampshire cricketers, Charles Llewellyn, Alex Kennedy and Jack Newman have achieved the 'double' – Jim Bailey being the first from the County to reach the milestone for eighteen years.

After the 1949 season, when he scored 1,254 runs and captured 86 wickets, he retired to take up a job as the South's representative for a leading paint company. In 1952 though, at the age of forty-four, he came out of retirement briefly to bowl steadily and well to take three more wickets in 30 overs. His final figures in all matches were 9,500 runs (average 24.94) and 473 wickets (at 27.24) reasonable all-round figures which could as I have said been so much more impressive.

After his retirement, Jim Bailey served for many years on the Hampshire committee and was a regular visitor to county headquarters, summer and winter, until a few days before his death after a short illness on February 1988.

A good-humoured, modest and talented cricketer, he was in later years remembered as the epitome of the solid county professional.

# HARRY BALDWIN

Born: 27 November 1860, Wokingham
Died: 12 February 1935
Played: 1877–1905

## FIRST-CLASS HAMPSHIRE RECORD

| Matches | Innings | NO | Runs | HS | Ave | 100s |
|---------|---------|------|------|------|-------|------|
| 150 | 240 | 65 | 1863 | 55* | 10.64 | 0 |

| Runs | Wkts | Ave | Best |
|-------|------|-------|------|
| 14336 | 580 | 24.71 | 8-74 |

## NOTABLE FEATS

- He took 102 wickets in Hampshire's first year in the County Championship.
- He bowled unchanged in a completed match of two innings v Derbyshire at Southampton in 1895, taking 8 for 93.

- He took 15 for 142 v Sussex at Hove in 1898; ending with 59 wickets at 16.52 to finish eighth in the national averages.

Shown in a well-known photograph hitching up his capacious flannels around a body shaped like a rugby ball, Harry Baldwin played for Hampshire for nearly twenty years before they were any sort of power in the land.

Harry Baldwin came from Wokingham, but lived at Winchfield; he belonged to a family which could put an eleven in the field.

After making his Hampshire debut in 1877, he was conspicuous in raising the County to the first-class championship in 1895. Although he stood no more than 5ft 6ins in height, he weighed well over twelve stone. Baldwin's portly figure running to the crease for his slow right-hand bowling, or standing at point, made him one of Hampshire's most memorable characters in a side captained by Sir Russell Bencraft.

Bowling with a fastish arm action, he occasionally let the ball go early, producing a provocative slow one. He was deadly on a wicket affected by rain or badly worn, with his length and off-break with pace from the pitch. As tubby as he was cheerful and stout-hearted, he could bowl all day without losing his accuracy and often got wickets with the one that went straight on. When the ball really turned, he was quite a formidable bowler, especially to batsmen – and in those days there were many of them – who relied for defence on conventional forward play.

The highlights of the 1890 season were the County's two victories over Sussex; in the second, Baldwin took nine wickets. In the fixtures with minor counties, Baldwin had a superb all-round game against Staffordshire, not only scoring 113 but taking 14 for 99. His record for the season was most impressive – 58 wickets at 11 runs each.

In the match against Derbyshire in 1894, he proved the most diffi-cult of all the bowlers and returned match figures of 12 for 112 as Hampshire, despite several breaks for rain, won by five wickets.

During Hampshire's first year in the County Championship, he took 102 wickets at 16 runs each, including 13 for 78 against Essex as Hampshire won by 171 runs. His total wasn't matched until C B Llewellyn took 121 wickets in 1901. At home to Derbyshire, Baldwin and Soar bowled unchanged throughout both innings – Baldwin's figures being eight for 93. He had no pretensions as a batsman, but in his great match with Essex, he scored 32 in the side's second innings.

The following season, his seventy-three victims cost him over 25 runs each, yet in the last two matches of the season, showed with 19 wickets for 186, that on pitches that helped him, he was far from a spent force.

Harry Baldwin was the first Hampshire professional to have a benefit, but unfortunate in the match he selected. Yorkshire were the opponents in 1898 and so strong an opposition were they, that after a day's rain, the match was finished off between twelve o'clock and five minutes past six. He never struck much form until the month of August when he had a great match at Brighton, taking 15 Sussex wickets for 142 runs. He ended the season with 59 wickets at 16.49 runs apiece in all matches, to top the county bowling averages for the second time in his career.

He toiled manfully through the summer of 1900 to take 84 wickets at 28 runs each.

In 1904, the County's bowling was sadly weak and it was necessary to recall Baldwin from a two year retirement and gallantly throughout the season, he held an end. The following season, the bulk of the County's bowling fell on the shoulders of Harry Baldwin – now age forty-four – he was exceeding his age in waist measurement – he bowled twice as many overs as anyone else – his 67 wickets costing him 30 runs apiece.

The 1905 season was his last in the Hampshire side – his nineteen year career bringing him 580 wickets at an average of 24.71 runs apiece.

# MIKE BARNARD

Born: 18 July 1933, Portsmouth
Played: 1952–1966

## FIRST-CLASS HAMPSHIRE RECORD

| Matches | Innings | NO | Runs | HS | Ave | 100s |
|---|---|---|---|---|---|---|
| 276 | 463 | 41 | 9314 | 128* | 22.07 | 6 |

| Runs | Wkts | Ave | Best |
|---|---|---|---|
| 563 | 16 | 35.18 | 3-35 |

## NOTABLE FEATS

● He hit a hundred for the MCC against the Australians
● He took 313 catches in his career with Hampshire.

Mike Barnard became an effortlessly, fluent, fast-scoring middle-order batsman of great value to the Hampshire side, though there were occasions in his career when the County's supporters felt that he hadn't made good his early promise.

He made his first-class debut in 1952, before 'National Service' the following year. Prior to this, he had spent one summer on the ground staff, where to this day, he still has happy memories of excellent 'digs' with Ernie and Bella Knights in the Groundsman's Cottage. His duties during that 1951 season included cleaning under the terracing after matches, getting down on his hands and knees to weed the square and pulling the heavy roller every day!

Mike was also on the books for Portsmouth FC, playing in 118 First Division matches at inside-forward. After surviving one winter of First Division football unscathed, he was caught by a 'late tackle' in a pre-cricket season kick about at The County Ground and was out of action for a month!

In 1954, the Portsmouth-born player made his initial hundred against the Pakistani tourists at the age of twenty-one. It was a season in which he played other good innings and fielded magnificently. The game against Pakistan was not very exciting and in fact, is perhaps best remembered by Barnard's excellent maiden hundred. Hampshire batted first and were all out for 185, after being 47 for 4. The Pakistanis were bowled out for 163 and Hampshire's second innings, thanks to Barnard, reached 238 for 6 and despite a declaration, the tourists decided not to go for the runs.

Mike Barnard always seemed to reserve his best batting performances for matches against the tourists. For following his maiden century against Pakistan, he hit 77 against the South Africans at Southampton in 1960, 123 against the Australians also at the County Ground in 1964 and a hundred for the MCC against the Australian's at Lord's. However, he did bag a 'pair' against the South Africans on another occasion!

As I wrote earlier, there were Hampshire supporters during the county's championship-winning summer of 1961 that felt that Mike Barnard nine years after making his first-class debut had not flourished as much as they would have liked. But suddenly in the County Championship match against Warwickshire at Southampton, his play flowered in an innings of 114 which turned the game and stamped Hampshire as a Championship-winning side.

The number twenty-three must mean something to Mike Barnard, for he was a member of the Hampshire side bowled out for that total against Derbyshire at Burton in 1958 and the team that dismissed Yorkshire for the same score at Middlesbrough in 1965.

The summer of 1962 was the only one in which he passed the 1,000 run mark, scoring 1,114 runs at 27.17 – and though he hit eight fifties, he could not reach the three figure mark. He came close to achieving the feat in both 1963 (980 runs at 25.12) and 1965 (958 runs at 21.28).

A specialist slip fielder, he took 313 catches in his career with Hampshire.

During his early years wih the County, he was described as a useful right-arm medium-pace change bowler and though his sixteen first-class wickets cost him 35.18 runs each, his victims included Ted Dexter and Tom Graveney!

# ALEC BOWELL

Born: 27 April 1880, Oxford
Died: 28 August 1957
Played: 1902–1927

FIRST-CLASS HAMPSHIRE RECORD

| Matches | Innings | NO | Runs | HS | Ave | 100s |
|---|---|---|---|---|---|---|
| 473 | 806 | 43 | 18466 | 204 | 24.20 | 25 |

| Runs | Wkts | Ave | Best |
|---|---|---|---|
| 1766 | 34 | 51.94 | 4-20 |

NOTABLE FEATS

- He scored 1,000 runs in a season for Hampshire on eight occasions.
- In 1914, he scored 204 v Lancashire at Bournemouth.
- In 1921, he added 192 for the tenth wicket with W H Livsey v Worcestershire at Bournemouth (County record).

Alec Bowell was one of the earliest players recruited by Hampshire from the Oxford district – his son Norman also played for the County – he was a patient right-hand batsman, orthodox, with extremely neat footwork, who occasionally, bowled fast-medium and was a brilliant cover-point.

In 473 matches for the County from 1902 to 1927, he scored 18,466 runs and made a thousand runs in a season on eight occasions.

Alec Bowell's best stroke was the square-cut, which he executed with great wristy power – it bringing him many of his runs. In 1905, his innings of 101 helped the County defeat Derbyshire – the side's only success of the season. In 1908, he hit 160 against the Philadelphians at Southampton, whilst the following season, he and Llewellyn put on 199 in just two hours against Worcestershire as Hampshire won with just six minutes to spare.

As a batsman, he possessed every stroke in the book, though they were made from a pronounced two-eyed stance. He was at his best against slow bowling, which he played with perfect balance. He was very quick on his feet – a necessary accomplishment in those days, since every county had one or more good slow bowlers.

He was slightly less secure against fast bowling – his record though is that of a consistently useful county batsman. He had his most successful season to date in 1911, when he topped the 1,400 run mark.

In 1914, he hit the highest score of his first-class career, 204 in the match against Lancashire, with 104 of his runs coming in boundary strokes. Hampshire totalled 377 in the match which was played at Bournemouth – it being transferred from Portsmouth owing to the outbreak of the First World War. In fact, he almost carried his bat, being the last man out. In some ways though, it was a disappointing season for him, as he lost out in his benefit – the match against Sussex at Southampton, only bringing in some £425.

The season of 1920 was a season of 'nearlys' for Alec Bowell. He nearly scored 1,000 runs and against Yorkshire at Headingley, he nearly scored a century, making 95 as Hampshire amassed 456 for two declared to win the match by an innings. He also shared in Hampshire's then record first wicket partnership of 204 with George Brown in the match against Worcestershire at Portsmouth, scoring his only century of the season.

The following season, he and Walter Livsey added 192 for the tenth wicket also against Worcestershire – an achievement only rarely exceeded as a last wicket partnership in English first-class cricket. When they came together, Hampshire were 118 for nine – ending 310 all out. Alec Bowell took part in the celebrated match with Warwickshire at Edgbaston in 1922, when Hampshire after being dismissed by Howell and Calthorpe for 15 and following-on 208 behind, put together a total of 521 and triumphed by 155 runs. Bowell was one of eight men dismissed without scoring, having his stumps shattered into pieces by Howell – in the second innings, he fared much better, scoring 45.

The following summer, Bowell was in and out of the Hampshire side, scoring 786 runs at 20.83, often batting usefully. In 1924, he only came into the Hampshire side halfway through the season and batted steadily to score 571 runs at 27.19 to finish second to Mead in the county's batting averages.

After hitting 1,000 runs in 1926, he had a poor season in 1927. He was, by now, forty-six years old and after being granted a testimonial that raised him £338, he was not re-engaged for the following season. When he retired, Alec Bowell had scored more runs for Hampshire than any other batsman except Philip Mead. He made regular scores of thirties, forties and fifties rather than the type of player who mixed low scores with hundreds – having said that though, he did hit 25 centuries for the County.

A ginger-headed bow-legged, squat figure, he looked anything but an agile cover-point!

He returned to Oxford after his days with Hampshire were ended, where in retirement, he was full of memories and wisdom.

# STUART BOYES

Born: 31 March 1899, Southampton
Died: 11 February 1973
Played: 1921–1939

## FIRST-CLASS HAMPSHIRE RECORD

| Matches | Innings | NO | Runs | HS | Ave | 100s |
|---|---|---|---|---|---|---|
| 474 | 677 | 156 | 7515 | 104 | 14.42 | 2 |

| Runs | Wkts | Ave | Best |
|---|---|---|---|
| 33513 | 1415 | 23.68 | 9-57 |

## NOTABLE FEATS

- He took 100 wickets in a season for Hampshire on three occasions.
- He performed the hat-trick for Hampshire on two occasions: v Surrey at Portsmouth in 1925 and v Warwickshire at Edgbaston in 1926.
- He took 474 catches in his career with Hampshire
- He had figures of:

| O | M | R | W |
|---|---|---|---|
| 9.1 | 6 | 5 | 6 |

  v Derbyshire at Portsmouth in 1937.
- In 1938, he took 9 for 57 v Somerset at Yeovil.

Stuart Boyes was only fourteen in 1913 when Alec Bowell took him to the Hampshire secretary to be engaged on the groundstaff.

He played in five matches in 1921 and though he only took four wickets at 47 runs each, the County recognised that he had a fine action, spun the ball well and was capable in the field. Here it seemed, was the bowler Hampshire needed so urgently to support Kennedy and Newman.

County cricket attracted Boyes. He was employed in the Ordnance Survey Office at Southampton and legally was a regular soldier in the Royal Engineers. At a committee meeting in October 1921, it was 'decided to pay half of Boyes' discharge purchase from the Army'.

He did exactly the job for which he had been brought in. In 1922, he took 94 wickets at an average of 18.82, including match figures of 10 for 52 against Glamorgan and 9 for 78 against Yorkshire, and 10 for 90 v Lancs.

In the memorable match against Warwickshire that season, the Edgbaston wicket was slightly soft, enabling Boyes to turn the ball, if only slowly to take 4 for 56 as the home side were dismissed for 223. Within forty minutes – not quite nine overs – Hampshire were all out for 15. Following-on, an innings defeat seemed certain as six wickets went down for 186. Brown and Livsey put on 177 for the ninth wicket and Hampshire were 243 ahead when the uncapped Boyes joined wicket-keeper Livsey. Boyes propped up one end whilst Livsey – who had only reached double figures three times that season – went on to make the first century of his career. Boyes, who went on to make 29, then began to play strokes as the last pair added 70 for the tenth wicket. Newman and Kennedy bowling remorselessly on a length, dismissed Warwickshire for 158, Hampshire had won by 155 runs. He fell away slightly in 1923, probably in reaction from a very hard-worked first season, taking 36 wickets at 24 runs each, missing the second half of the season with knee trouble.

An intelligent slow left-arm bowler, he had a beautifully smooth action, turned the ball on any wicket and appreciated the value of flight. He was a bowler who could have been a great foil for Kennedy and Newman, if only he had been used with discretion. He spun the ball more penetratively in his earlier years than later, when experience, tactical sense and variation more or less made good the loss of 'bite'.

Sometimes his captain, Lord Tennyson, roused from his post-prandial doze at mid-off by lack of action, would grumble, 'Spin the damned thing, Boyes, spin it.' 'I'm spinning it as hard as I can my Lord,' was the answer as bowling with his left hand, he snapped the fingers of his right, 'but it won't turn on this.'

He performed the hat-trick on two occasions – against Surrey at Portsmouth in 1925 and against Warwickshire at Edgbaston the following year, when he also took 105 wickets – the first of three summers he was to achieve this feat.

In 1929, despite injuring his arm and missing quite a few matches, he took 74 wickets at 23.45 and was the first of the 'new' professionals to win a cap since the war. In 1933, he took 111 wickets and scored 617 runs as his batting began to pick up. The following summer, he bowled 480 balls in an innings against Nottinghamshire at Southampton to end up with the following analysis:

| 0 | M | R | W |
|---|---|---|---|
| 80 | 28 | 138 | 3 |

In 1933, he turned in the remarkable bowling analysis of:

| O | M | R | W |
|---|---|---|---|
| 9.1 | 6 | 5 | 6 |

against Derbyshire at Portsmouth.

In the nets, Stuart Boyes looked a good batsman; perhaps however, he lacked the combative urge, for his batting was not seriously regarded in county cricket, though in 1936, he hit his maiden first-class century, 101 not out against Lancashire at Liverpool. It was a season in which he had to miss four matches with a broken thumb, but still managed to take 90 wickets.

In August 1938, Hampshire broke new ground by playing their first County Championship match on the Isle of Wight, when they opposed Northamptonshire on the Newport Ground. The match belonged to Stuart Boyes, who not only hit 104, the highest score of his career, but provided Hampshire with an unexpected victory by taking 6 for 40 in Northants second innings – including his 100th wicket of the season, to head the county averages with 107 wickets at 21.71. It was a summer in which he also produced his best ever bowling figures, taking nine for 57 against Somerset at Yeovil.

In June 1939 when Hampshire returned to Newport with Middlesex the visitors, Boyes was again the leading wicket taker with 5 for 45. He was one of the first if not the first, of the modern type of short-leg fieldsmen. Lean, gracefully poised, he stood extremely close to the bat for the off-spin of Charlie Knott or Jack Newman, the in-swing of 'Lofty' Herman or Alec Kennedy. He watched eagerly, ducked late and clamly took some strokes off the bat when most men would have been taking cover – he had a career record of 474 catches for the county. From 1945 to 1963, he was a highly popular coach at Ampleforth College, and then was back on the Southampton ground, sociably watching matches with his colleagues, only a few months before his death.

In eighteen years, Boyes took 1,472 wickets at 23.5 runs apiece, all but fifty-seven of them for Hampshire; with guidance of wise captaincy, he could have worn England colours.

# GEORGE BROWN

Born: 6 October 1887, Cowley, Oxfordshire
Died: 3 December 1964
Played: 1908–1933

FIRST-CLASS HAMPSHIRE RECORD

| Matches | Innings | NO | Runs | HS | Ave | 100s |
|---------|---------|-----|-------|------|-------|------|
| 539 | 900 | 46 | 22962 | 232* | 26.88 | 37 |

| Runs | Wkts | Ave | Best |
|-------|------|-------|------|
| 17857 | 602 | 29.66 | 8-55 |

NOTABLE FEATS

- He scored 1,000 runs in a season for Hampshire on ten occasions.
- He took 484 catches and 51 stumpings for the County
- He took five catches in an innings on two occasions: v Somerset at Bath in 1914 and v Kent at Portsmouth in 1932.
- He carried his bat on two occasions with a best of 150* out of 294 v Surrey at the Oval in 1933.
- He scored three double centuries for Hampshire with a best of 232* v Yorkshire at Headingley in 1920.
- He added 321 with E I M Barratt v Gloucestershire at Southampton in 1920 – Hampshire 2nd wicket record.
- He added 344 with C P Mead v Yorkshire at Portsmouth in 1927 – Hampshire 3rd wicket record.
- He added 325 with C H Abercrombie v Essex at Leyton in 1913 – Hampshire 7th wicket record.

George Brown was one of the most remarkable all-round players the game has ever known.

It was in the spring of 1906, that the eighteen-year-old country lad set out from his native Cowley to the County Ground at Southampton for a trial. It was said – and George never denied it – that he walked the entire sixty-odd miles with a tin trunk holding his cricket gear, clothes and belongings on his shoulder, and without the fare back.

As a batsman, he shared in three-figure stands for every Hampshire wicket except the sixth. He could improvise, using strokes not seen in any textbook, but was strongest on the leg side either hooking or driving. He enjoyed playing fast bowling. Once when Fielder, the Kent fast bowler 'bounced' a ball at him, Brown dropped his bat deliberately, took the ball on his chest and said, 'He's not fast' and went on to make seventy. Some said he wasn't as happy against slow bowling, but in 1930, he top scored in both innings – 56 and 47 – when Grimmett twice ran through Hampshire.

Once, after a run of low scores, he opened the Hampshire innings against Essex at Bournemouth and struck the first ball from Johnny Douglas clean out of the ground!

A left-handed batsman, he opened the innings for England in 1921, when the best of England's batsmen were being swept aside by the Australian fast bowlers, Gregory and McDonald. He held his nerve and his place and never failed. Only once did either of the fast bowlers get him out; and he finished second in England's Test batting averages.

Of his thirty-seven centuries, the highest was 232 not out against traditionally the toughest county opposition, Yorkshire, at Leeds in 1920 and easily his best record in touring-side matches was against Australia. He thrived on challenge and was at his best when the battle was at its hottest.

The display for which he will always be remembered was that at Edgbaston in 1922. Dismissed for 15, the smallest total in their first-class history, Hampshire followed-on, 208 behind and seemed destined for a humiliating defeat when they had lost six wickets for 186. Then, George Brown played magnificently for 72, as Hampshire totalled 521, before Kennedy and Newman bowled Warwickshire out for 158 to give Hampshire a famous victory by 155 runs!

Although he was not Hampshire's regular wicket-keeper, he kept for England against both Australia and South Africa, and was chosen for the team which won back The Ashes at the Oval in 1926, but injured his thumb in practice and had to withdraw. His wicket-keeping was truly remarkable. In Livsey's absence and completely without practice and at a moment's notice, he would don the gloves after an interval of a year or more, and keep to Test standard. That stern judge, Alec Kennedy, described George Brown as 'unquestionably the best wicket-keeper who ever took my bowling'.

For Hampshire however, he was more often a bowler; he took over six hundred wickets for the county at a pace, which in his early days, bordered on genuine fast, and he commanded sharp late outswing.

As a fieldsman, he was incomparable. His favourite trick was to stand a little deeper than was necessary, fail to walk in with the bowler or move sluggishly to the ball, until a batsman judged that he might take a single to him. Then when a stroke was played and the ball seemed to have pased him and the batsman began to run, he would turn, leap to the ball and turn in a single movement and, before the batsmen had even crossed, without taking aim, threw the stumps down.

Nothing delighted him more than to field impossibly close to the bats of the greats. In June 1919, he is credited by Wisden with causing the unexpected defeat of Surrey at the Oval by catching Jack Hobbs off Kennedy at silly point. It was a catch so amazing that no one on the ground saw it – they were looking to the boundary when George threw up the ball – the imprint of the gilt trade mark was left on the palm of his hand !

From all his obvious talent, Brown was at times, a volatile character and this was reflected in his cricket – for his form varied from season to season and match to match.

Technically, there was nothing in the game that he could not do and do brilliantly.

The records show that he scored over twenty-five thousand runs in all matches, yet there was never a player in the game whose reputation was less beholden to statistics than George Brown.

He was a big man, physically superb, but big in impact too; just as he could pick up a split bat and tear it in two – as he once did, batting on aggressively with the spike – so he could take up a match and change its shape.

A man of mighty strength, he could tear a pack of cards across in his huge bare hands; and taking a full-grown man by the coat front, lift him off the ground with one hand and hold him out at arm's length!

For George Brown, cricket was a very personal matter. On the South African tour of 1922–23, he and another pro bowled in the nets to a certain famous amateur for a whole hour of torrid heat. At the end of it, when he was putting on his pads for a knock, the gentleman remarked, 'You don't think I'm going to bowl to you do you? – it's far too hot.' The following summer, that same amateur was bowling to Brown in a county match. Whatever temptation he put Brown's way, it was met with a calm, careful, defensive stroke, as Brown rolled the ball gently down the wicket. 'What the hell is the matter with you, Brown?' asked the bowler. 'There's nothing the matter with me: I'm just having that hour's net practice you owe me Mr . . . '

After retiring from county cricket, George Brown stood as a first-class umpire for several seasons.

Eccentric, quick-tempered, loyal, he was as lovable as he was unpredictable. He died, after being in ill health for some years, at Winchester in 1964, aged seventy-seven.

# MERVYN BURDEN

Born: 4 October 1930, Southampton
Died: 9 November 1987
Played: 1953–1963

FIRST-CLASS HAMPSHIRE RECORD

| Matches | Innings | NO | Runs | HS | Ave | 100s |
|---|---|---|---|---|---|---|
| 174 | 191 | 59 | 901 | 51 | 6.82 | 0 |

| Runs | Wkts | Ave | Best |
|---|---|---|---|
| 12559 | 481 | 26.11 | 8-38 |

NOTABLE FEATS

- He took 7 for 53 v Oxford University in 1955.
- Against Somerset at Frome in 1961, he dismissed five batsmen in 31 balls for a single run conceded – ending with his best figures of 8 for 38.

Mervyn Burden was one of a group of Hampshire-born players who emerged in the 1950s to help the county enjoy its most successful period to that time, culminating in the winning of the County Championship in 1961.

Yet, in many ways, he was an unlucky cricketer, never sure of his team place. So, he never felt that he could take a risk; throw the ball up, experiment with one tossed wide or one spun out of the back of the hand. He tried to bowl tight, leading to over-anxiety and the loose ball sent down out of tension. He spun his off-breaks, but his weakness lay in the fact that he tried to bowl the unhittable ball every time!

The odds of Mervyn Burden becoming a county cricketer must have been strongly against him. For most of his time at King Edward VI School, he was in evacuation quarters at Poole and though he did gain a place in the Under-14 cricket team, his main sporting ability lay as a footballer.

When he returned to Southampton after the war, football was still his chief sport. As a member of the ATC football team, he attended the indoor cricket school at the Cunliffe-Owen factory at Swaythling in an attempt to keep fit and in participation for some cricket the ATC boys were going to play between the soccer seasons.

It was here that Mervyn Burden's cricket career had a fairy-tale beginning. He only bowled in those nets on three evenings and on the second, solely by coincidence, County coach Sam Staples and Desmond Eagar were there talent spotting. The two of them were content that he was a worthwhile prospect for the county and asked him to join the Hampshire ground staff.

His first appearance in the Hampshire nets is marvellously told in the 1964 Hampshire Handbook and in John Arlott's 'Book of Cricketers.' I feel it is worth repeating again, for it sums up his marvellous sense of humour which made him a popular figure among the cricketing fraternity.

'I've never felt so nervous in my life. I went up and bowled my first ball and it flew clean over the top of the nets and smashed one of the windows in the old dining-room. Someone gave me another one and as I walked back to bowl my next ball, I was wondering what the dickens I should do this time. But I didn't have to worry. Johnny Arnold was batting in the next net, and as I turned to run in, he hit an on-drive. I had my back to him and never saw it coming, it caught me a terrific crack on the ankle and I couldn't bowl for a fortnight. Still, I thought I had better show willing, so I turned up the next morning to see if there was anything I could do, and they sent me out to help Ernie on the pitch. You know, I hadn't been there a couple of minutes before I kicked a bucket of whiting across the square. So they sent me home until my ankle was better.'

He topped the Club and Ground averages that year with 47 wickets, as a seam bowler. After another good season in 1948, he went to do his National Service, playing regularly for the Southern command, as an opening bowler and a No. 3 batsman!

He came back to Southampton to find his path blocked by Shackleton, Cannings and company. After a talk with Arthur Holt, he decided to try bowling off-breaks and took 20 wickets in Club and Ground and Second Eleven matches in 1951. His chance came in 1953 when he made his debut against Worcestershire at Worcester. His second appearance was against Surrey at Bourne-mouth, where tying down their batting, he took 6 for 70. In 1954, he was only introduced into the team at the beginning of July and played for the rest of the season, capturing 46 Championship wickets (including seven for 48 against Leicestershire) – a full season and he may have produced 100 wickets.

His best season was 1955, when he took 70 wickets, including 7 for 53 against Oxford University to win his county cap. It was also the season when in the match with Sussex at Eastbourne, he waited two hours with his pads on, while Sainsbury and Cannings put on 55. He went in last with the scores tied and even took guard before he realised that Sainsbury had been out to the last ball of the over. Cannings did not survive the new over, so Burden's batting in a crisis was not put to the test.

There were occasions when Mervyn Burden was a match-winner. In 1956, he took 6 for 23 against Surrey, the Champions, to set up a 28-run win for Hampshire, In 1958, when the County finished as runners-up, he effectively won the close games with Nottinghamshire at Trent Bridge and Northants at Southampton.

As a batsman, he rarely made runs, but in 1960 at Portsmouth when Warwickshire took two quick wickets, he went in as night-watchman and achieved a four off the edge that night. The next day, he batted until 5.20 p.m to score his first and only fifty in first-class cricket – as he was looking up to see it come up on the scoreboard, Ray Hitchcock came up and bowled and had him lbw!

In 1961, Mervyn Burden only played in fourteen matches, yet he took 50 wickets at 22.92 as the county won the championship. He confused Somerset in a devastating spell of 31 balls, dismissing five batsmen for a single run conceded. He ended with the best figures of his career – eight for 38. But, with typical Burden luck, he missed the £100 award for the best bowling performance of the season because Pearson took all ten in the Cambridge University-Leicestershire match.

By sheer effort and enthusiasm, he turned himself into a superb fielder and in that summer of 1961, he caught Brian Crump of Northants in both innings with two magnificent catches off strokes that seemed certain to go for six.

In 1962, he took 65 wickets in 17 matches, but played only three games in 1963, decided it was time to finish and was granted a testimonial which produed £1,000.

Seventeen seasons on the staff, with only one season – 1955 – as a regular player, yet he remained an uncomplaining and loyal professional – always splendidly good-natured and full of natural humour.

# VIC CANNINGS

Born: 3 April 1919, Brighton
Played: 1950–1959

## FIRST-CLASS HAMPSHIRE RECORD

| Matches | Innings | NO | Runs | HS | Ave | 100s |
|---|---|---|---|---|---|---|
| 230 | 294 | 103 | 1888 | 43* | 9.88 | 0 |

| Runs | Wkts | Ave | Best |
|---|---|---|---|
| 18091 | 834 | 21.69 | 7-52 |

- He took 100 wickets in a season for Hampshire on four occasions.
- He took 7 for 52 v Oxford University in 1950.
- In 1956, he took the last two Oxford wickets with the last two possible balls of the match, as Hampshire won by one run !

Owing to the Second World War – he was in the Palestine Police Force for seven years before returning to England – he did not make his County Championship debut until 1947 when he was twenty-eight years old. Playing for Warwickshire, he won his county cap after just nine weeks in the Midland side's ranks. He fell away so markedly after a fine first season, when he took 63 wickets, that the following two seasons yielded only 25 wickets at an average of 41 from 481 overs.

A right-arm medium-pace bowler, who at his best could move the ball disconcertingly, especially away from the bat, he took three wickets in four balls against Scotland at Edgbaston in 1948, whilst his top score of 61 had come a season earlier against Nottinghamshire. Released to join Hampshire, he was signed as a professional in an attempt to strengthen the county's bowling resources. He quickly became a valuable member of the Hampshire side and was awarded his county cap after only a month. In his first season for the county in 1950, he took 83 wickets at 24.32 runs apiece – it was the start of a successful bowling partnership with Derek Shackleton. One of the most accurate bowlers in the first-class game, he returned his best ever figures of 7 for 52 in the match against Oxford Univeristy. A professional who took the game very seriously – he may have joked about his batting in the dressing rooms, but at the crease, it was a different matter. In the game against Kent at Southampton in 1950, the visitors had made 162, Hampshire replying with 180. In their second innings, Kent made 170, leaving Hampshire 153 to win. The wicket was taking spin and the score progressed steadily from 17 for 2 to 101 for 6 and eventually 131 for nine – it was anybody's game. The last pair of Cannings and Knott were at the wicket with 22 runs required for victory. There were ten minutes to lunch on that last day and, perhaps the only man really confident of a Hampshire win was Vic Cannings. He produced his well known 'dab' on no less than three occasions and lunch-time arrived with Hampshire needing 15 runs for victory. The Kent and England leg-spinner, Doug Wright pronounced at lunch-time that it was such an exciting game that the result must be a tie. A few more 'dabs' from Cannings and a genuine driven four from Knott took Hampshire to within three runs of their target. Wright was bowling, Knott lashed out and the ball flew over gully's head, the batsmen ran two and despite their efforts to try for a third, Knott was caught next ball.

Vic Cannings made several useful runs at the end of an Hampshire innings and his top score for the county was an unbeaten 43 made off the Sussex attack, raising the Hampshire total from 147 for 8 to 236 all out in a game Hampshire went on to win.

Sussex were Hampshire's opponents in yet another match that Cannings was involved in at the death. During the 1955 season in a game of swaying fortunes, Hampshire were left with 140 to make for victory. On a wearing pitch, they were 84 for 8 when Cannings joined Sainsbury. At the tea interval, seventy-two minutes later, only 13 runs were needed and the two Hampshire batsmen were still together. The score crept up until the match was level before Sainsbury was bowled. In walked Burden to find that Cannings was on strike – the fourth ball of this over proving fatal to the Hampshire bowler – another tied match (the third in Hampshire's history) with Cannings yet again the last man to be dismissed!

In 1952, he shared in an outstanding victory over Kent at Southampton, as he and Derek Shackleton bowled unchanged throughout both completed Kent innings – the first time the feat had been recorded since 1935 – Cannings taking 8 for 55 as Kent were dismised for 32 and 91 on what was a very nasty and dangerous wicket – many batsmen were hurt and two suffered black eyes which lasted for some weeks! It was his best season with the ball, as he took 109 wickets at 21.67 runs apiece. The following summer, he was the only bowler in England to dismiss W A Johnston on the 1953 Australian tour.

In 1954, he took 100 wickets for the fourth consecutive season and bowled better in August than he had ever done before. The following year saw Hampshire's first victory at Canterbury since the war and was a result of Cannings taking the final Kent wicket, lbw with the last ball of the day! He went one better in 1956 when Hampshire defeated Oxford University at Oxford by one run. Cannings taking the last two Oxford wickets with the last two possible balls of the match.

Playing his final game for the County in 1959, he ended his career with Hampshire with 834 wickets at 21.69 runs each.

On retirement, he travelled the world as a cricket coach and was regarded as one of the best teachers of the art of bowling, coaching at Eton.

# CARDIGAN CONNOR

Born: 26 March 1961 Anguilla, West Indies
Played: 1984–1992

FIRST-CLASS HAMPSHIRE RECORD

| Matches | Innings | NO | Runs | HS | Ave | 100s |
|---|---|---|---|---|---|---|
| 160 | 129 | 38 | 889 | 51 | 9.76 | 0 |

| Runs | Wkts | Ave | Best |
|---|---|---|---|
| 13326 | 405 | 32.90 | 7-31 |

NOTABLE FEATS

- He took 7 for 37 v Kent in his first season with the county.
- His career best figures of 7 for 31 came in the match against Gloucestershire at Portsmouth in 1989.

The splendidly named Cardigan Adolphous Connor was pluck-ed from the relative obscurity of Minor Counties cricket to instant success in his first season for Hampshire.

Born on the little island of Anguilla in the Caribbean, Cardigan Connor came to England when he was fifteen to join his parents who had emigrated to Slough when he was a baby; the date of his arrival was important, because it meant that when Hampshire registered him, he was already qualified for England, so avoiding complications for a county that had Robin Smith and Reifer as overseas players in 1984 and Greenidge and Marshall returning in 1985.

His success in club cricket for Slough, was recognised by selection for Buckinghamshire, but five seasons of Minor County cricket brought him no definite offers until Hampshire suffering a mid-May crisis in 1984 offered him a chance. He was specially registered and showed promise in two Second Eleven matches. He joined Hampshire at a low ebb in the County's seam bowling fortunes. Malcolm Marshall was to miss the season because of the West Indies tour, as was his chosen replacement Milton Small and Elvis Reifer (the eventual replacement) had no first-class experi-ence and was already finding county cricket tough going, though the season was barely three weeks old!

He made his first-class debut at the end of May 1984 against Somerset at Southampton. One can imagine captain Nick Pocock's feelings as he threw the ball to Connor to open the Hampshire attack, because he had never seen him bowl! Connor's selection in

47

the Hampshire side proved to be an inspirational choice. The very first ball he bowled saw Somerset opener, Julian Wyatt, play and miss, whilst in the next over, he did the same to the experienced Peter Roebuck. Then, with his seventeenth delivery in first-class cricket, he clean bowled Wyatt. Answering his captain's congratulations with a polite 'Thank you, sir' his new colleagues quickly advised a much less reverential approach to the Hampshire skipper. A couple of balls later, he trapped Richard Ollis lbw for a 'duck' and would have had a third wicket inside five overs if Pocock had held a difficult chance at slip. His third wicket came when he clean bowled Roebuck to end his first spell with 3 for 15 in 10 overs. He returned to take another wicket to finish with 4 for 31 from 19 overs. In the second innings, Roebuck again fell to Connor before Brian Rose was bowled for a 'duck' to give Hampshire their first Championship victory of the season.

In the next match against Nottinghamshire at Bournemouth, he took six more wickets to give him figures of 12 for 195 in his two first-class games. Bournemouth was the scene of his best performance that summer, when he took 7 for 37 against Kent, on a wicket of variable bounce.

He impressed a number of shrewd judges in his first season with his easy economical action and great accuracy, bowling well within his five foot eight inch frame. A very fit cricketer, as befits one who considered becoming a PE teacher – he bowled many long spells, including 40 overs in a day at Portsmouth in 1984.

Cardigan Connor bowls commendably straight and is grateful for the experience of bowling on unsympathetic Australian pitches, initially as a member of a Club Cricket Conference tour and then when he took leave from his job as a mechanical engineer to pay his own way to go to Newcastle in New South Wales – later returning as a winner of an award from Hampshire's sponsors TNT Tristar.

Of course, Connor's first name aroused a great deal of curiosity, though he was quick to point out that cardigan was not an unusual Christian name in Anguilla. Inevitably, his colleagues nicknamed him 'Woolly' or 'Jumper' and even 'Buttons' – there were of course plenty of references to 'Cardigan taking his sweater'.

The following year, he opened the bowling with Malcolm Marshall, but his 49 Championship wickets cost him 32.97 runs each. The summer of 1987 was a difficult one for him, because he was under more pressure than ever before for a regular place from the other uncapped bowlers on the staff, notably Stephen Andrew. Yet, he still retained his cheerful zest for the game and in the Sunday League was the side's most economical bowler after Marshall, with 17 wickets at 23.70, as he missed just one game.

With Marshall absent in 1988, he grabbed the opportunity to take 55 wickets at 27.21 and win his county cap. The following year, he came seventeenth in the national averages with 59 wickets at 21.27 including a career best seven for 31 against Gloucestershire at Portsmouth. In 1990, his wickets were more expensive. A disappointing season in 1992, but it did see him make his top score for the County with the bat, 51 v Yorkshire at Headingley.

At the time of writing, he has taken 405 wickets for Hampshire, yet his first season of 1984 remains his most successful, with 62 at 31.43.

The first Anguillan to appear in County Cricket, he will be hoping to beat that record before he ends his playing days.

# BOB COTTAM

Born: 16 October 1944, Cleethorpes
Played: 1963–1971

### FIRST-CLASS HAMPSHIRE RECORD

| Matches | Innings | NO | Runs | HS | Ave | 100s |
|---|---|---|---|---|---|---|
| 188 | 178 | 65 | 615 | 35 | 5.44 | 0 |

| Runs | Wkts | Ave | Best |
|---|---|---|---|
| 14354 | 693 | 20.71 | 9-25 |

### NOTABLE FEATS

- He took 9 for 25 v Lancashire at Old Trafford in 1965. (County record).
- In 1968, he took 128 first-class wickets for Hampshire.

Bob Cottam might well have played for Middlesex, for he spent his early school days at Wembley, where he played for the Wembley Boys. If Lincoln had a first-class county side, then birth qualifications would have put him in line for that county, for he was born in Cleethorpes, but left at an early age. At Wembley, his first school was Lyon Park Junior, where sports master, Frank Edwards realised that the young Cottam had a natural aptitude for the game and gave him some early coaching.

When his family moved to Berkshire, he joined the Wargrave Piggott School, also playing weekend cricket with a Henley brewery side and representing Berkshire Bantams during the school vocation. The brewery ground was used by the Hampshire Second Eleven for their game against Oxfordshire and during their visit, the Hampshire coach, Arthur Holt glanced through the scorebook and noticed that the name of Cottam was always among the wickets. From this chance inspection of the scorebook, Bob Cottam was invited to play for the Hampshire club and Ground side at Basingstoke. He was sufficiently impressive to have an extended trial on the county ground.

Whilst he was playing for the Berkshire side, they travelled to Warwickshire for a match against the County's Second Eleven. Warwickshire were proving to be very strong opposition and the Bantam's attack made no headway. Coming on as the fifth bowler, Bob took six very inexpensive wickets to raise immediate interest in the Warwickshire camp. They were prepared to offer him a trial, but it came too late and he signed for Hampshire in the winter of 1961.

Making his first-class debut as an eighteen-year-old, he bowled at a lively pace off about fifteen yards, swinging the ball away from the batsman. The Lord's pitch helped him to take nine Middlesex wickets in only his second game as Hampshire won with ease. In August of his debut season, a rain affected wicket at Portsmouth made him almost unplayable and his six wickets cost only 10 runs in nine overs.

He didn't show much improvement in 1964, taking only 18 Championship wickets at over 30 runs each, though against Wiltshire at Chippenham in the Gillette Cup, he took four wickets for 9 runs as Wiltshire collapsed to 81 all out.

The following season saw him confirm his place with the county, for he claimed 73 Championship wickets at 16.53 and was rewarded with his county cap. He had a high action with plenty of pace and usually came on as a change bowler, and in this capacity, he was establishing himself in the county side. His 9 for 25 at Old Trafford on 9 and 10 June 1965 was his best performance and is the best ever performance by any Hampshire bowler. Batting first, Hampshire made slow progress and could only total 174. Lancashire started brightly, with Shackleton taking the overnight wicket of Knox, then as green and 'Noddy' Pullar began building a good score – Lancashire were 102 for 1 – Cottam produced an outstanding spell to run through the side. His figures were:

| O | M | R | W |
|------|---|----|---|
| 11.1 | 4 | 25 | 9 |

Dismissed for 136, Lancashire then ran through the Hampshire side to bowl them out for just 77. Though Cottam didn't take a wicket in the second innings, Shackleton and White bowled well to give Hampshire victory by 13 runs.

There was a strong feeling that these shock tactics revealed him in his most dangerous form, for in 1966, he took 61 Championship wickets and followed this with 102 wickets in all matches for the first time in 1967 – his progress was the most heartening feature of the season. He improved even further in 1968 when he topped the

50

Hampshire averages and claimed 128 wickets, gaining the recognition of the Cricket Writers Club, who nominated him the 'Best Young Cricketer of the Year'. He certainly had a successful season and no one was surprised when he was invited to tour Ceylon and Pakistan, where he played in two Tests, taking 4 for 50 on his debut at Lahore. The year of 1968 also saw the end of the Shackleton era and it was beginning to appear as though Bob Cottam would be asked to bowl more overs in the role of stock bowler, and thus lose some of his effectiveness as a quick seamer. After coaching at a couple of schools in South Africa during the Christmas holidays and three weeks spent in the nets with Middlesex's Mike Smith, he developed a variation on his style. Using the swinging delivery, varied with a ball that left the batsman off the wicket or moved into him at an alarming pace, he was a daunting prospect on responsive pitches when he could extract deep bounce.

At the end of the 1971 season, he decided that he needed a change, and was released to join Northamptonshire. Here he bowled his cutters effectively and at a reduced pace, cultivated a devastating breakback, to take 241 wickets at 20.24 in his five seasons.

After a spell as the NCA's chief coach in the West Country, he was appointed Warwickshire's cricket manager in 1987. His position at Edgbaston ended acrimoniously over a demarcation dispute with their captain, Andy Lloyd, but his talents in this area are widely acknowledged and so, his appointment at Somerset in a managerial capacity was a popular choice.

Bob Cottam always used his lean body to full effect in a rather slingy action and was always a capable and effective part of the Hampshire attack.

# NIGEL COWLEY

Born: 1 March 1953, Shaftesbury
Played: 1974–1989

FIRST-CLASS HAMPSHIRE RECORD

| Matches | Innings | NO | Runs | HS | Ave | 100s |
|---|---|---|---|---|---|---|
| 257 | 358 | 58 | 6773 | 109* | 22.57 | 2 |

| Runs | Wkts | Ave | Best |
|---|---|---|---|
| 13979 | 425 | 32.89 | 6-48 |

- In 1977, he added 109 with D R Turner for the fifth wicket v Gloucestershire at Southampton – Benson and Hedges Cup Record.
- In 1981, he added 120* with D R Turner for the fifth wicket v Northants at Southampton – Sunday League Record.
- In 1982, in the match v Leicestershire, he scored 104 and took 6 for 48, his best first-class bowling figures.

Nigel Cowley or 'Dougal' as he is universally known throughout the game, typified the yeomen who are the backbone of English cricket. He was raised in Mere, where his father was a well-known club cricketer and where his mother scored for the team while her husband played. The young Cowley's uncoached abilities marked him quickly as a cricketer of potential, earning him representative honours for both Dorset and Wiltshire Schools as a fourteen, fifteen and sixteen year-old. In these games he was a seamer rather than an off-spinner and it was not until Wiltshire Schools awarded him a scholarship to a course at Lilleshall that he was first coached and persuaded to turn from seam to spin. Arthur Holt received a letter from a Hampshire supporter in Salisbury, pointing Nigel in the club's direction and saying how much he had been impressed by the young off-spinner. When he showed up for his trial, the boy from Mere had hair down to his shoulders and certainly did not look a cricketer! It did not take Arthur Holt long to realise that Cowley was a valuable talent, for in one over, he bowled four different types of delivery.

The next step was to play in Holt's Colts, where it was seen that those favourable first few overs on trial were no flash in the pan – for he was soon on the way to making his first-class debut against Sussex at Bournemouth in 1974. It was perhaps fitting that the county should decide to 'blood' him at Dean Park, which boundary changes had decreed should then be in Dorset for government purposes, since Cowley is a son of Hardy's County. Unfortunately, he did not have much chance to make an impact in that debut match; being restricted to a single over and that a maiden, but he did make a useful 36 in a seventh wicket partnerhsip of 59 with Peter Sainsbury as Hampshire won their fourth successive innings victory to go top of the table.

However, his typically defiant innings was not enough to keep him in the Hampshire side and he had to wait another two weeks for his second chance against Leicestershire at Portsmouth. He was not required to bowl a single over, but again his batting ensured that he made his mark, as he scored a gutsy 43, despite hooking an early delivery into his face. He kept his place in the side, but did not get a chance to bowl – in fact, it was his ninth appearance before he could boast his first Championship wicket – Ellis of Glamorgan. He had his longest bowl in that match, finishing with 2 for 43 in 21.1 overs, but went one better in the return match at Southampton a week later, with 3 for 31, including the obdurate Alan Jones.

Though he made eleven appearances by the end of that summer, he only made five the following season and played in ten championship matches in 1976. In 1977, he bowled slightly quicker than in his previous matches and as a result, improved, though his batting was the main reason for his inclusion in the side. At Taunton, he hit his maiden championship century – 109 not out against a Somerset attack with Botham at his best. It was a remarkable effort, for Hampshire were 91 for 6 and though the county didn't win the match, it enabled them to lead on first innings.

Cowley's career coincided with a big change in the way spin bowlers were used in cricket at the top level. It says much for his talent that he not only conformed, but became a much respected cricketer all around the county circuit. Initially of course, he was an off-spiner employing flight, guile and a change of pace in an attempt to winkle out the batsman, but as the one-day game became a dominant factor in his life, he worked with Peter Sainsbury to develop a flatter and quicker delivery. Able to attack leg stump and contain, only Trevor Jesty, Tim Tremlett, Malcolm Marshall and Cardigan Connor have bettered his 143 Sunday League wickets for the County.

Promoted to No. 3 for most Sunday matches, he topped the County averages in 1981, with 48.30 from his fifteen innings. However, in the Championship he rarely found himself higher than seventh in the order and had to wait until 1982 before he scored his second century. It came in the opening Championship match of the season and was a typical Cowley innings – dogged in defence, but punishing any loose delivery. His innings of 104 contained two sixes, a five and 14 fours. Replying to Leicestershire's 281, Hampshire were 120 for 5 when Cowley came to the wicket, and the score slumped to 165 for 7, before he and Parks added 21 in 26 overs. It was a good match for 'Dougal' for he wrecked Leicestershire's batting in the second innings with 6 for 48, which remained his best Championship return. His career haul of 425 wickets for Hampshire is comparatively modest, but he tended to play in a team which like so many was dominated by pace or seam and in his later years when the County decided to play only one spinner, he often found himself giving way to Raj Maru.

A player who took his game seriously, he was brilliant in the outfield; a safe pair of hands and a throw to match anybody in the game. The 1983 Nat West semi-final saw him lunge forward to his right to claim Kent's Mark Benson only millimetres from the ground – it was a tremendous catch, for the Kent opener had threatened to take control.

His undoubted keeness and commitment to Hampshire County Cricket Club was rewarded with a Benfit Year in 1988. Of immense value to the County over the years, he moved to Glamorgan where he played in thirteen matches in the 1990 season.

Hampshire's main off-spinner and middle-order batsman for many seasons, his records show his reliability, but as Lancashire's Jack Simmons said: 'Nigel was the first with a friendly word and smile and ever-ready to share a pint in the bar at the end of a day's play.'

# LEN CREESE

Born: 28 December 1907 Parktown, South Africa
Died: 9 March 1974
Played: 1928–1939

## FIRST-CLASS HAMPSHIRE RECORD

| Matches | Innings | NO | Runs | HS | Ave | 100s |
|---|---|---|---|---|---|---|
| 278 | 453 | 41 | 9894 | 241 | 24.01 | 6 |

| Runs | Wkts | Ave | Best |
|---|---|---|---|
| 11141 | 401 | 27.78 | 8-37 |

## NOTABLE FEATS

- He scored 1,000 runs in a season for Hampshire on five occasions.
- In 1936, he scored 1,295 runs at 31.58 and took 92 wickets at 22.57.
- His highest score of 241 was made in the match v Northamptonshire at Northampton in 1939.

Born in South Africa, Len Creese was the son of W H (Bill) Creese, whose family were curators, caterers and even secretaries at the famous Newlands Ground, Cape Town, for nearly sixty years. His father did play once for Transvaal in 1897–98 and once for the MCC team in a minor engagement against Border at King Williamstown in 1913.

Len Creese came to England at his own expense, determined to make a career in county cricket.

At the end of the 1926 season, the Hampshire committee decided not to re-engage Hayward and Len Creese was taken on in his place.

A left-hand bat and left-arm bowler, he was sturdily built, strong, brave and a combative, but consistent cricketer. In those early days, he was brilliant in the field, especially close to the wicket, but below County standard as a batsman. From this rather undistinguished start, he took five years to establish himself in the county team, then in 1933, he scored 1,000 runs in a season for the first time, and remained a more than useful county all-rounder until the outbreak of the Second World War.

The following season, he began to improve as a bowler. He bowled with a low, busy action at almost medium pace, but on a responsive wicket – even if it was slow – he turned his breakaway sharply.

As a batsman, Creese was extremely strong off his back foot and a fine player against fast bowling. In his first county match against Sussex, Maurice Tate, the lion-hearted right-arm fast-medium bowler, had decimated the early Hampshire batting. Creese often left his stroke extremely late and was warned to play forward to one of such pace. Characteristically, Creese rocked back to the first ball he faced and hooked it for six! Creese was never at a loss against pace, in fact, the faster the bowling, the better he seemed to like it. His straight drive off the back foot was a stroke of remarkable, even impressive power. His cutting, and hooking too, was immensely powerful, but he could be completely baffled by spin, especially leg-breaks. Overall though, he batted with consistent power. In 1935, he topped the 1,000 run mark for the second time, a feat he was to achieve right up to the outbreak of war and captured 65 wickets to have a good all-round year.

Over his career, Creese's bowling probably deteriorated, but he did have phases, usually of several weeks duration, when his left-arm breakaways, delivered at nearer medium-pace were very successful, for he spun the ball considerably. In 1936, he topped the County batting averages with 1,331 runs in all matches at 30.92 and took 95 wickets at 22.93 – he was immensely effective.

The following year in the match that R H Moore scored 316, Creese bowled his left-arm slows so accurately, that the home county won inside two days. His second innings analysis was:

| O | M | R | W |
|------|------|------|------|
| 22.3 | 3 | 85 | 7 |

He had match figures of 10 for 159 – the only time he captured 10 wickets in a match in his career.

Creese was a safe catcher in the gully, at short leg or cover point, and took 191 catches in his 278 match career.

The hard-hitting batsman scored six centuries for Hampshire, with the highest being 241 against Northamptonshire – an innings that contained 37 boundaries.

After the Second World War, he became coach at Sherborne and later groundsman at the Central Ground at Hastings and then Hove. In the latter half of his life, a series of disasters – including him suffering the terrible experience of seeing his small grandson killed by a heavy roller in the interval between innings in a Festival match – threw him into inconsolable grief.

William Leonard Creese died in a Dover hospital on 9 March 1974 – a man who played his cricket hard, celebrated exuberantly and was deeply loyal to all his friends.

# DESMOND EAGAR

Born: 8 December 1917, Cheltenham
Died: 13 September 1977
Played: 1946–1957

## FIRST-CLASS HAMPSHIRE RECORD

| Matches | Innings | NO | Runs | HS | Ave | 100s |
|---|---|---|---|---|---|---|
| 311 | 514 | 34 | 10091 | 158* | 21.02 | 8 |

| Runs | Wkts | Ave | Best |
|---|---|---|---|
| 937 | 15 | 62.46 | 2-10 |

## NOTABLE FEATS

- He scored 1,000 runs in a season for Hampshire on five occasions.
- He captained the county from 1946 to 1957.
- He took 333 catches in his first-class Hampshire career.
- He is the only first-class cricketer to have taken part in three tied championship matches.

Desmond Eagar's successes were of character rather than of statistically impressive performance.

Even as a schoolboy at Cheltenham, he was a notable captain. Wisden of 1937 comments: 'Eagar kept his side always on their toes and their keeness in the field furnished a real tribute to his captaincy.' He achieved 878 runs at 54.87 in 1935 and achieved a good 'double' against Marlborough the following summer with scores of 13 and 68*, whilst his slow left-arm bowling brought him match figures of 11 for 79. His form was so outstanding that he played during the summer holidays for Gloucestershire along with Walter Hammond, Charles Barnett, Charlie Parker and Tom Goddard, after which he was in the Oxford side of 1939. He probably lost a considerable career as a hockey player to the Second World War. He was a major candidate for a place in the England side in the never-played season of 1939–40 – once remarking that he thought he was potentially a better hockey player than cricketer! Yet his services to cricket, especially Hampshire cricket, amounted to more than many Test caps.

Desmond Eagar had intended to become a regular soldier but, after a war-time illness, he decided to give up the Army. At the very moment that he reached this decision in 1945, he chanced to see an advertisement in *The Cricketer* for a secretary-captain of Hampshire. He applied for the job and was appointed.

He began Hampshire's first post-war season of 1946 in far more modest company than he'd encountered in his days with Gloucestershire. 'We were all so old' he would say 'and fielded terribly'. With his infectious enthusiasm he soon made Hampshire into one of the best fielding sides in the country. But good fielding, though a great help and much to be encouraged, is not everything and it took further 'accidents of cricket' as when Eagar joined the County, to produce batsmen and bowlers who by 1955, had taken Hampshire to third place in the Championship, after which the team was given a dinner at the House of Lords. In 1975, when the county also came third, the result was described as 'disappointing'. He used to relish this contrast, rightly seeing it as a reward for many years of hard labour.

Though a new era of Hampshire cricket began with the arrival of Desmond Eagar, be carried the confidence of some pre-war players and administrators. He had the guidance of Harry Altham, Cecil Paris and Ronnie Aird, all MCC Presidents in their time and Charlie Knott, his first vice-captain.

As a batsman, Desmond Eagar was elegant, but would always attack when possible and was successful against all but the highest class of bowlers. For Hampshire, he scored 10,091 runs at 21.02 and a top score of 158 not out against Oxford University in 1954. A slow left-arm spin bowler, he put himself on when everything else failed and sometimes surprised himself by taking a wicket!

He was one of the best old-style county captains and frequently gambled with the idea of putting his opponents in to bat, but there were times when his experiments failed.

The 1957 season was Desmond Eagar's last as captain of the County. There can be no doubt, that the work done under him had much to do with Hampshire winning the County Championship under Ingleby-Mackenzie for the first time in 1961.

As Secretary, he worked tirelessly to improve the club's public relations – attending countless dinners and meetings and persuading the other Hampshire players to do likewise. In doing so, he built up the membership of the County Club. His interest in the game never flagged; every young player for him was a fresh hope for the county. He was also Chairman of the Hampshire Cricket Association and this helped to encourage local cricket as well as county cricket.

Desmond Eagar was a considerable authority on cricket history and was one of the joint authors of the history of Hampshire County Cricket Club. He was absorbed by every aspect of cricket and a devoted collector of cricket literature and cricketania. He was editor of the Hampshire Cricket Year Book, creator of the County Club's library, picture gallery and museum, and proud president of the Hambledon Cricket Club.

His standards were very high. Once, as he walked into the ground, a bystander asked him: 'Why didn't you win that match yesterday, Des?' 'Because they were too good for us,' was the answer, 'and don't call me Des.' 'Well the Daily Sketch does,' was the silencing retort! Four days after the end of the 1977 season, Desmond Eagar died on holiday in Kingsbridge, Devon. He had had a serious operation the year before, but had been able to resume his secretarial duties and his death came as a shock to the cricket world.

By the time Desmond Eagar died, he had helped Hampshire to years of success inconceivable in 1946.

# RICHARD GILLIAT

Born: 20 May 1944, Ware
Played: 1966–1978

FIRST-CLASS HAMPSHIRE RECORD

| Matches | Innings | NO | Runs | HS | Ave | 100s |
|---|---|---|---|---|---|---|
| 220 | 351 | 40 | 9358 | 223* | 30.09 | 16 |

| Runs | Wkts | Ave | Best |
|---|---|---|---|
| 133 | 3 | 44.33 | 1-3 |

NOTABLE FEATS

- Awarded four Blues at Oxford University 1964–67.
- Scored 223* v Warwickshire at Southampton in 1965.

- Added 132* with D A Livingstone for third wicket in the John Player league match against Yorkshire at Southampton – a Hampshire record.
- Captain of Hampshire 1971–78.

As a youth, Richard Gilliat was an all-round games player. Until he was seventeen, his major enthusiasm was for lawn tennis; he was for three years a serious competitor at the junior Wimbledon.

Born in Hertfordshire – his father was Vicar of Chorley Wood – he was a brilliant left-hand bat at school captaining the Charterhouse XI. Brought up on good wickets, he crowned his school career by leading the Public Schools against the Combined Services at Lord's in 1963. At Charterhouse, he won his colours for cricket in four seasons; soccer and fives in three and hockey in one.

Going up to Christ Church, he immediately found a place in the Oxford side as a middle-order batsman. In 1965, his second year, he was appointed Hon. Secretary of the University Cricket Club and in 1966, he captained the University when they achieved a resounding innings victory against Cambridge – Gilliat playing a significant innings. His leadership qualities were recognised by the authorities, for he was invited to capain the MCC President's XI against the West Indies. He was specially registered for Hampshire and in the 1966 vacation, made his first-class debut, though he had played a few matches for Surrey Second Eleven while he was at school.

His background at Charterhouse and Oxford hints at privilege and a smooth passage to the top. In fact, neither cricket nor life went easily for him; and because of the kind of person he is, he has been stressed by both.

In 1967, he made his first Championship century – an uncharacteristic 122 in six and a half hours – but he by no means became a county cricketer overnight. Appointed Assistant Secretary to Desmond Eagar, he was essentially a free, long-hitting left-hander whose eye was sharp enough to compensate for the fact that his bat was not always straight. In those early days, the old pros often thought him out by playing on his strengths, or probing him with spin, for that was his weakness – Gilliat being unflinching against pace. The coming of Richards, Jesty and Turner made competition for first-team places stern and in 1968, he played in only half of Hampshire's matches, spending much of his time in the Second Eleven.

Appointed vice-captain under Roy Marshall for the summer of 1969, he made a poor start, with no more than 51 runs from seven innings. Then he scored 59 out of 101 against Leicestershire; but in the next match against Essex, he hit the fastest century of the championship season in 101 minutes - despite being forced to retire early in his innings after being hit on the head by Keith Boyce. He then embarked on a sequence of splendid innings – 114 against Glamorgan, 100 not out against Somerset, culminating in an unbeaten innings of 223 against Warwickshire at Southampton on the final day of the month of June. He scored at a run a minute, this innings winning him his county cap. An injury kept him out of a number of matches, but in August, he scored two more centuries and a 99 against the New Zealanders.

His luck was not in, for if there had been an overseas tour that winter, the selectors must have been interested in a twenty-five-year-old batsman who had scored so many runs quickly. In fact, he ended the season with 1,348 runs at an average of 40.84.

Richard Gilliat was undoubtedly in the minds of the selectors at the beginning of the 1970 season when a winter tour to Australia lay ahead. With ill fortune though, in the first match of the season, he fractured his thumb while fielding and was out of action until June. In his first match back, he broke the same thumb in a different place and that was the end of his season – the team went to Australia without him.

He was appointed Hampshire's captain in 1971, and quite early in the season moved himself down from his regular No. 3 spot in the batting order to No. 5 to accommodate the young Greenidge and Turner along with Richards and Marshall. As a captain, he had extremely high fielding standards, bringing the best out of his players and encouraging the younger members of his side to great effect.

In 1973, he led the County to its second Championship title after the bookmakers had quoted odds of sixty-six to one against them lifting the title. They won the Championship by tidy bowling and superb fielding. The side won ten matches, and, in all but one of them – against Gloucestershire, who declared their second innings with nine wickets down – they bowled out the other side twice. That year, Gilliat was fourth in the county averages, scoring two important centuries at the crucial August run-in phase of the season.

The following summer after beating Worcestershire by an innings, they were hampered by rain and did not win one of their five remaining matches, though they were set to take three of them by wide margins. So Worcestershire took the title, beating Hampshire by two points. At the start of the 1975 season, Gilliat was asked to captain MCC against the champion county; a local radio reporter asked him if this indicated that the selectors were considering him for the England captaincy. 'Oh no' he said, 'I am not a good enough player for that.' Richard Gilliat though must have been seriously considered, for he was a batsman of courage and a captain who ensured that the spectators enjoyed their cricket.

He continued to lead Hampshire until the end of the 1978 season, when he retired from first-class cricket to go into business. Though it cannot be said that he fulfilled the hopes which his admirers held out for him, there was certainly no more courteous or considerate captain in the first-class game. During his captaincy, Hampshire won the county Championship, failed narrowly to do so a second time – the John Player League and the Fenner Trophy.

# JIMMY GRAY

Born: 19 May 1926, Southampton
Played: 1948–1966

## FIRST-CLASS HAMPSHIRE RECORD

| Matches | Innings | NO | Runs | HS | Ave | 100s |
|---------|---------|-----|-------|------|-------|------|
| 453 | 809 | 81 | 22450 | 213* | 30.83 | 30 |

| Runs | Wkts | Ave | Best |
|-------|------|-------|------|
| 13543 | 451 | 30.02 | 7-52 |

## NOTABLE FEATS

- He scored 1,000 runs in a season for Hampshire on thirteen occasions.
- He took 350 catches during his career with the county.
- He scored over 2,000 runs in a season on 3 occasions, with a best of 2,224 runs in 1962.
- He carried his bat on two occasions: 118* out of 208 v Essex at Portsmouth in 1956 and 118* out of 214 v Somerset at Bournemouth in 1964.
- He made his highest score of 213* v Derbyshire at Portsmouth in 1962.

Jimmy Gray was one of six boys – educated in Southampton at St Deny's School and then King Edward VI School, he was evacuated to Poole Grammar School during the Second World War. While he was at Poole, he took up football and on his return to Southampton, began to play at right-back for Swaythling Youth Club and Southampton's Youth team. There then came a season with Salisbury Corinthians before he joined Arsenal.

Despite having four seasons with the Gunners, he never

appeared in the first team, for competition was fierce with Wally Barnes and Laurie Scott holding down the full-back spots. On leaving Highbury, Jimmy spent three seasons with Bedford in the Southern League before ending his footballing days with Salisbury in the Western league, where he also played for three seasons.

Yet, it was as a cricketer that Jimmy Gray was to make a name for himelf. He made his Hampshire debut at Aldershot in 1948, where he scored 46 batting at No. 6 as Hampshire recovered from 15 for 4 to beat the Combined Services by an innings. He had been playing for Deanery Colts and was recommended to Hampshire by Sam Pothecary who was with the county at the time. Jimmy Gray was one of many young players to be blooded in 1948. He showed much promise though little success in the ten matches he was given as experience.

He became a regular in 1951, completing 1,000 runs for the first time and being awarded his county cap.

The following season he settled down to earn the position of his side's opening batsman and improved noticeably as the season advanced. He also developed as a bowler – bowling in swingers, he made a great advance as an all-rounder during the year and took 48 wickets. His best performance came against Nottinghamshire at Bournemouth, when he had match figures of 11 for 158, including his best ever figures of seven for 56 – a mounted cricket ball at Jimmy Gray's house serves as a memento of his performance.

In 1953, he and Rogers added 160 against Leicestershire at Lougborough in Hampshire's second innings to give the county victory by nine wickets on an uncertain surface. Gray had his best season for the Club to date with the bat, but started with a bad patch at Worthing which lasted throughout his next fifteen innings, for during that time, he did not total 200 runs. In 1956, Gray was the ideal batsman for the slower pitches – his careful approach paid dividends, as both his aggregate and average increased.

In all matches in 1960, Jimmy Gray was one of three Hampshire batsmen to reach 2,000 runs – an event unique in the County's history. During the County's Championship-winning summer of 1961, he and Roy Marshall began Hampshire's opening innings of the season with a run a minute stand of 117 in very bad conditions. He continued to fine form, taking 136 off the Northants attack in four-and-a-half hours, followed by a quickfire 'knock' in the second, but Hampshire couldn't force a victory. Against Lancashire, Gray and Horton attacked the red-rose bowlers to such an extent that they put on 170 in 160 minutes with Gray making a hundred. In 1962, he scored more runs than ever to head the county's batting averages. He also hit the only double century of his career on a perfect pitch at Portsmouth – 213 not out against a Derbyshire side containing England paceman Les Jackson. He had been working up to this, for in the previous match, he had scored 123 off the Glamorgan attack. Both of these innings came at a most opportune time, for Roy Marshall was absent with measles !

Before the start of the 1964 season, Jimmy Gray announced that his duties as deputy headteacher would mean him missing the first eight matches, though to be honest, when he did re-appear, he was in much better form than the previous season! He played part-time for the last three years of his career while teaching at Stroud School in Romsey. In all, he taught there for six years, specialising in mathematics and running the cricket, before becoming deputy headteacher – a post he held for ten years.

Then he and Peter Sainsbury ran a leading firm of sports equipment specialists in Southampton, before selling the business in 1989. A real Hampshire man, steeped in Hampshire cricket, he scored 22,450 runs, took 451 wickets and held 350 catches in 453 first-class matches for the County. He is now in his fourth season as chairman of Hampshire's cricket committee.

# GORDON GREENIDGE

Born: 1 May 1951 St Peter, Barbados
Played: 1970–1987

FIRST-CLASS HAMPSHIRE RECORD

| Matches | Innings | NO | Runs | HS | Ave | 100s |
|---|---|---|---|---|---|---|
| 275 | 472 | 35 | 19840 | 259 | 45.40 | 48 |

| Runs | Wkts | Ave | Best |
|---|---|---|---|
| 387 | 16 | 24.18 | 5-49 |

NOTABLE FEATS

- He hit six double centuries for Hampshire, with a highest of 259 v Sussex at Southampton in 1975, scoring a championship record 13 sixes.
- He hit hundreds in each innings of a match on three occasions.
- He carried his bat on two occasions, with a best of 196* out of 341 v Yorkshire at Headingley.
- In 1986, he established a new record for Hampshire, scoring

four hundreds in successive innings, to end the season with 2,035 runs.

- He hit 11 centuries in the Sunday League with a highest of 172 v Surrey at Southampton in 1987.
- He hit 5 centuries in the Benson and Hedges cup, with a highest of 173* v minor Counties (South) at Amersham in 1973.
- He hit 4 centuries in the Gillette Cup/Nat West Trophy, with a highest of 177 v Glamorgan at Southampton in 1975.
- He took 315 catches in his career with Hampshire.

Gordon Greenidge joined the elite band who have made a century on their Test debuts, when he made 107 for West Indies in the second innings of the first Test against India at Bangalore in November 1974. But for being run out for 93 in the first innings, he might well have emulated the achievement of his fellow countryman, Lawrence Rowe, who is the only player to have hit a century in each innings on a Test debut. Yet, Greenidge had no particular ambitions to make cricket his career when as a fourteen-year-old he followed his parents to England in the August of 1965. His parents had come to England some years before and settled in Reading.

Like most West Indians, Gordon Greenidge took up cricket at an early age. When he was thirteen, he was playing regularly, as an opener, for St Peter's, a Barbadian school, and was the first Test player they have produced. On his arrival in England, young Greenidge was soon making his presence felt on the school cricket fields around Reading. It was while playing for Berkshire schools that Greenidge played an innings of 135 not out against Wiltshire Schools, that was to fashion his cricketing destiny. Greenidge played only one game for Hampshire Second Eleven in 1967, scoring just two, but was however, invited to join the County staff the following season, when he played on a regular basis for the Second Eleven, then led by Leo Harrison.

He made his Championship debut for Hampshire at Bournemouth in August 1970, when batting down the order, he scored 24 and 18 against a Sussex attack which included John Snow. He played in seven championship matches that summer, scoring 351 runs in his 11 innings. Even that though, was enough for Wisden to decide that he had 'made a major breakthrough'. His partnership with Barry Richards was established, when he shared in two three-figure partnerships, including one of 201 against Lancashire. Gordon Greenidge had a vintage season in 1973. He started it by sharing in a record Benson and Hedges Cup second-wicket stand of 280 with David Turner – Greenidge finishing up with an unbeaten 173. He went on to hit five Championship centuries, including a then career best of 196 not out against Yorkshire, as well as taking 100 off Kent in a Gillette Cup match which, despite

Harry Baldwin 1877–1905

Edward Sprot 1898–1914

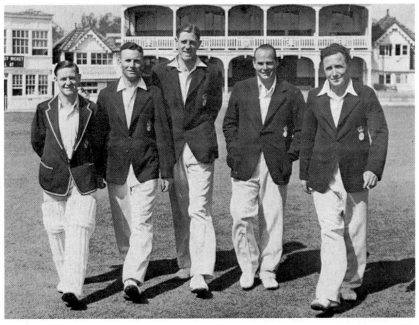

McCorkell, Arthur Hill (2nd from left) 1895–21 with Herman, Bailey and Arnold

Charles Llewellyn 1899–1910

James Stone 1900–14

Alec Bowell 1902–27

Philip Mead 1905–36

Jack Newman 1906–30

Alec Kennedy 1907–36

George Brown 1908–33

Walter Livsey 1913–29

Hon Lionel Tennyson 1913–35

Johnny Arnold 1919–50

Stuart Boyes 1921–39

Jim Bailey 1927–52

'Sam' Pothecary 1927–46

Len Creese 1928–39

'Lofty' Herman 1929–48

Richard Moore 1931–39

Neil McCorkell 1932–51

Arthur Holt 1935–48

Gerry Hill 1932–54

Charlie Knott 1938–54

Leo Harrison 1939–66

Neville Rogers 1946– 55

Desmond Eager 1946–57

Jimmy Gray 1948–66

Derek Shackleton 1948–69

Vic Canning 1950–59

Colin Ingleby–MacKenzie 1951–65

Mike Barnard 1952–66

his efforts, Hampshire lost. In the match at the end of the season againt Gloucestershire at Bournemouth, Greenidge decided to try to capture the Championship on his own, hitting 96 in 130 minutes – the home side collecting eight batting bonus points to take the championship title.

At the end of the season, he went 'home' where he won a place in the Barbados Shell Shield team. He averaged 38 in his first season and 41 in the second and was chosen for the tour of India, Sri Lanka and Pakistan – making that outstanding debut at Bangalore.

However, he did have a disappointing season for Hampshire in 1974, scoring 804 runs at 26.80 and managing only one Championship century, but he did achieve a new career best when, in a remarkable innings for Derrick Robins XI against the Pakistan touring side at Eastbourne, he hit 13 sixes in an unbeaten knock of 273.

In the second round of the 1974 Gillette Cup competition, Hampshire created an assortment of records at Glamorgan's expense. Richards and Greenidge put on 210 for the first wicket with Gordon Greenidge going on to make 177 out of Hampshire's 371 for four in 60 overs – the highest total ever recorded in a major limited-overs match anywhere in the world. On the West Indies 1975–76 tour to Australia, the pace of Lillee and Thomson fired him out for 0, 0, 3 and 8 – it cost him his Test place. With characteristic determination, he fought his way back, re-thought his technique and revised many of his attacking strokes.

One of his greatest achievements came in the Old Trafford Test the following summer when the West Indies chose to bat and found the pitch more awkward than they expected and quickly subsided to 26 for 4, three wickets falling to Mike Selvey on his England debut. Greenidge survived and took command, his 134 out of 211 forming 63.5% of the West Indies' total, the second highest proportion in Test hstory. After England had been shot out for 71, Greenidge then scored 101 in the second innings, only the second man to score a century in each innings of a Test between these countries. The West Indies won the game by 425 runs and Gordon Greenidge could hardly have done more towards it.

That was the first of many occasions when England have regretted missing out on Greenidge's services, for he could so easily have become an England player. Early in his career with Hampshire, Ray Illingworth, the then England captain recommended that the English authorities approach him, as he had been in the country from an early age, he could quickly have qualified. Greenidge, however, preferred to remain loyal to his native islands!

Greenidge learned a lot from Barry Richards, for early on, he was an impatient batsman, who wanted to hit the bowling to all parts. He learned the merits of building an innings from the elegant South African and to his impressive array of attacking strokes, Greenidge added a technically immaculate defence. His footwork was quick and positive, whether going back to cut or hook against the quick bowler, or dancing down the pitch to loft the spinner straight back over his head. Towards the end of his career, began to adopt a limp – fielding sides grew to dread that moment, for it was normally the prelude to a century!

On April 30th 1983, Gordon Greenidge scored his fiftieth first-class century, an unbeaten 154 for the West Indies against India at St John's Antigua. When play resumed on May 1, ironically, his 32nd birthday, Greenidge was in Barbados at the bedside of his young daughter, who was in a coma, a few days later she died.

After such a shattering personal blow, he could have been forgiven for spending time away from the game. Instead, he returned to duty for his thirteenth season with Hampshire his benefit year.

During the 1984 England-West Indies series, which the home side were to lose by a humiliating 5–0, Gower's side maintained a thread of control for the first four days of the Lord's Test. The England captain even dared to declare on the final morning, setting the visitors 342 in five-and-a-half hours. Greenidge hit no fewer than 29 fours in a ruthless exhibition of stroke-play. He ended up with 214 not out and the West Indies won by nine wickets with more than half-an-hour to spare. There are many who consider this to be his best-ever innings, but then, the candidates for that award are many and varied.

His exhausting cricket schedule accounted for some injury problems in the more recent years, but he often played for both county and country 'on one leg' and with much success!

Injury and convalescence for a knee operation forced him to miss more than half the fixtures in 1987, though he again showed his supreme quality in those he did play. He hit a spectacular 172 against Surrey (a new county record in Sunday league cricket) and 122 in the MCC Bicentenary Match.

In Tests, Greenidge walked out to open the innings with Desmond Haynes on 148 occasions, with sixteen of these producing century partnerships. It was unfortunate that Greenidge injured himself early on the last tour of England in 1991 and certainly, he was disappointed not to sign off in style. His absence was perhaps decisive against a revived England side. Earlier that year, faced with calls from the media for his replacement after a spate of low scores, be batted for eleven-and-a-half hours while registering his fourth double century and his highest in Tests, 226 v Australia. It was fitting that his last three-figure innings was played before the home crowd in the land of his birth.

On 28 November 1991, Greenidge informed the West Indies Cricket Board of Control that he had retired from participation in all first-class cricket matches organised under the aegis of the WICBC.

In many ways, his retirement marked the end of an era, for Gordon Greenidge was a great player and, at his best, for a very long time, the premier opening batsman in the world.

# LEO HARRISON

Born: 5 June 1922, Mudeford
Played: 1939–1966

FIRST-CLASS HAMPSHIRE RECORD

| Matches | Innings | NO | Runs | HS | Ave | 100s |
|---|---|---|---|---|---|---|
| 387 | 593 | 100 | 8708 | 153 | 17.66 | 6 |

| Runs | Wkts | Ave | Best |
|---|---|---|---|
| 166 | 0 | – | – |

*Number of dismissals:* 567 caught, 99 stumped.

NOTABLE FEATS
- In 1957, he added 154 with P J Sainsbury for the seventh wicket v Worcestershire at Worcester.
- In 1959, he set a new Hampshire record of 83 dismissals (76 caught 7 stumped) in twenty–nine matches.
- He helped dismiss 666 batsmen (567 caught 99 stumped) in his career with Hampshire.

Leo Harrison was one of the best wicket-keepers in England: playing innings soundly correct and admirable in style against the best bowling; he was also one of the best outfields in the country.

By the time he was twelve–years–old, Leo Harrison was already a successful batsman for Mudeford, his village team on the edge of the New Forest. During the winter of 1935–36, he went, as a left-handed batsman to the indoor cricket school at Bournemouth run by C C Brockway and Fenley. But, by the time he joined the county staff in 1937, still only fourteen, he had been converted into a right-hand batsman. It is highly probable that the switch from left to right was the first stage in the eye trouble later in his career.

The following year, he was opening the innings with Arthur Holt in the Club and Ground matches. He began the season with three successive 'ducks' yet within a month, the two put on 236 for the first wicket against Romsey. His innings in those matches ended not because bowlers beat him, but because in the main, he was so tired by an adult-length innings, that after an hour or so, he hadn't the strength to lift the bat.

Indeed, former Essex captain, Charles Bray, who was then cricket correspondent of the Daily Herald came down specially to see him and led his page on him with the headline: 'I Have Seen The New Bradman'. In 1939, he top scored for Hampshire Second Eleven against Sussex Second and though he was only seventeen years of age, his form was such, that he made his County Championship debut later that summer against Worcestershire. He played four innings as a batsman, the last against Yorkshire when Hampshire were put out for 116 and soundly beaten. Only Harrison and Pothecary made double figures – their partnership of 31 was easily the highest of the innings and showed that with experience, Harrison could become more than merely a good batsman. The war then intervened and for six years, he served in the RAF with few opportunities to play cricket. On two of the occasions when he did find time to play, he top scored for the County against Sussex and then played an innings of superb strokes against a very strong Civil Defence Eleven, twice putting James Langridge over extra cover for six.

In the meantime, a defect developed in his eyesight and during the summer of 1946, he was asked to keep wicket in an emergency and although he was forced to wear spectacles, he did the job so successfully, that he was chosen as wicket-keeper for the strong Combined Services side of that year. In 1947, he came back to the county staff, where with McCorkell available, there was no possibility of him keeping wicket. In 1948, Leo Harrison made his mark as a brilliant cover field, batsman and from June onwards, wicket-keeper, after McCorkell had injured his hand, with 38 catches and 11 stumpings. Over the next couple of seasons, with McCorkell fit once more, he struggled to keep his place in the side. In 1951, he reached a thousand runs in a season for the first time to finish third in the county averages and aggregates. His first century in county cricket – against Worcestershire – won him his county cap. Wisden said of that innings: 'Polished stroke-play and reliable defence removed any doubts as to his batting skill.' The following year, Prouton came back from the Lord's staff to keep wicket, but Harrison again scored a thousand runs and three centuries – more than anyone else in the side; though it must be said 632 of his runs came in seven innings, not as many coming in his other forty innings!

It wasn't until 1954 that Leo Harrison secured a regular place as

Hampshire wicket-keeper. The following summer, he was clearly among the best in the land, probably second only to Godfrey Evans – and was chosen for the players against the Gentlemen at Lord's. This was the season that lifted Harrison from the level of loyal county cricketer almost to the heights he had promised in those Club and Ground matches eighteen years before.

Leo Harrison was the least showy of wicket-keepers, having the high technical ability to leave his movement until the ball has 'done' everything and still get to it without hurry. He was highly rated by all the first-class players and was undoubtedly worth a Test place in the 1955 home series against South Africa when Godfrey Evans was injured.

Some of Harrison's stumpings were superb – from Shackleton and one from Gray's in swinger that he took one-handed down the leg-side, not to mention that time that he stumped a batsman and replaced the bail, before the victim could turn round! On the times the victim did turn round after being caught behind, he was met with: 'Hard luck, mate: It ain't half a bloody game, is it?' – one of first-class cricket's phrases of the time.

At the start of the 1963 season, Leo Harrison was replaced by Timms – though he continued to appear for the County up to 1966, having the previous year succeeded Arthur Holt as the County's coach. Coming to the ground at Southampton as the legendary era of Mead, Brown, Kennedy and Newman was ending, Leo Harrison was the last remaining player from the pre-war Hampshire staff.

# MALCOLM HEATH

Born: 9 March 1934, Bournemouth
Played: 1954–1962

FIRST-CLASS HAMPSHIRE RECORD

| Matches | Innings | NO | Runs | HS | Ave | 100s |
|---------|---------|------|------|------|------|------|
| 143 | 163 | 66 | 569 | 33 | 5.86 | 0 |

| Runs | Wkts | Ave | Best |
|-------|------|-------|------|
| 13237 | 527 | 25.11 | 8-43 |

NOTABLE FEATS

- In 1958, he took 126 wickets in all matches.
- Against Derbyshire at Buxton in 1958, he had match figures of 13 for 87, but still finished on the losing side.

Hailing from Bournemouth, the 6ft 5ins fast bowler made his first appearance for the County in 1954, picking up 17 wickets in the closing matches at a very reasonable cost to head the Hampshire bowling averages. His best performance was 7 for 64 in the match against Yorkshire, including the wicket of Len Hutton twice. He was Hampshire's first bowler since the war to make the opposing batsmen hurry their stroke and occasionally have to duck.

He was awarded his county cap in 1957 – a season which saw him take 67 Championship wickets at 26.37 runs each. He provided the County with some hostile pace and lift and this was never more evident than in the match against he West Indian tourists at Southampton. His final analysis in the tourists first innings as they were shot out for 110 was:

| O | M | R | W |
|---|---|---|---|
| 21 | 10 | 58 | 4 |

including the wickets of the West Indies two stroke-makers Ganteaume and Pairaudeau in his first two overs, though the latter made 163 in the second innings!

The summer of 1958 was Malcolm Heath's most successful, as he topped the 100 wicket mark for the only time in his career – 119 at 16.32 (126 in all matches). He took 6 for 53 against Gloucestershire at Bristol as Hampshire won by five wickets 13 for 86 v Sussex (Portsmouth) and 13 for 87 v Derby (Burton), but his most devastating performance came against Derbyshire, in the match played at Burton-on-Trent. He had match figures of 13 for 87 (six for 35 and seven of 52) though Hampshire lost by 103 runs as they were shot out for 23 and 55 by Jackson, Rhodes and Morgan. In 1959, he was having a dismal time with the ball and eventually gave way to a young bowler by the name of 'Butch' White. Heath returned the following summer to have a much better year and play in about two-thirds of the matches, taking 74 wickets at 26.82 runs apiece. In the match against Middlesex at Lord's, the home side only wanted 81 to win. Heath and Shackleton bowled so well, that at one stage, Middlesex were 35 for six. The two bowlers bowled unchanged through the innings, Heath finishing with the following figures:

| O | M | R | W |
|---|---|---|---|
| 19 | 3 | 47 | 4 |

as Middlesex scraped home by one wicket.

In Hampshire's Championship winning year of 1961, he took 54 wickets (63 in all matches at 26.73) providing good back-up to the county's two opening bowlers, Shackleton and White. He turned in some devastating spells, especially at Portsmouth, where he was brought in for the 'green' and hard wickets, when he bowled with steam to spare.

# 'LOFTY' HERMAN

Born: 18 September 1907, Cowley
Died: 24 June 1987
Played: 1929–1948

FIRST-CLASS HAMPSHIRE RECORD

| Matches | Innings | NO | Runs | HS | Ave | 100s |
|---|---|---|---|---|---|---|
| 321 | 495 | 105 | 4327 | 92 | 11.09 | 0 |

| Runs | Wkts | Ave | Best |
|---|---|---|---|
| 28137 | 1041 | 27.02 | 8-49 |

NOTABLE FEATS

● He took 100 wickets in a season for Hampshire on four occasions.
● He scored 41 in eighteen minutes v Glamorgan at Bournemouth in 1936.
● He took 142 wickets for the County in 1937 at 22.07 runs each.
● He performed the hat-trick v Glamorgan at Portsmouth in 1938.

Tall and known universally as 'Lofty' he was yet another player to come to Hampshire from the Oxfordshire district. Apart from the war years and the season of 1939 when he took a League engagement in Lancashire, this most popular of Hampshire players, played regularly for the county from 1929 to 1948, taking 1,041 wickets at 27.02. During his school days, he thought far more about soccer than cricket and played for Oxford Boys in the same side as Johnny Arnold, but his natural action with the cricket ball was recognised by a school master whose encouragement produced a county player. He joined the Morris car works where he painted wheels and bowled for the works team and it was here that he was seen by Alec Bowell, himself an Oxford man and 'Lofty' was invited to Southampton for a trial.

Like Brown, Arnold and Rogers, he had to serve a two-year qualification before making his first-class debut in 1929, a season in which he took 53 Championship wickets. The following year, he recorded a career best 8 for 49 in the match against Yorkshire at Bournemouth, but his misfortune was to play in a Hampshire side which only once (eighth in 1932) finished in the top half of the table in the 1930s. With the County often weak in bowling after the departure of Kennedy and Newman, 'Lofty' often had to bear the brunt of the attack and inevitably suffered from being over-bowled.

Necessity made 'Lofty' a defensive bowler, for although his stamina was suspect in the early days of his county career, he soon learned to bowl well within himsef and to control both length and swing.

He bowled mainly the inswinging ball, but his greatest quality lay less in the swing than in his pace from the pitch.

He had a high, smooth action in which his arm seemed to come over quite abnormally freely and until as I said earlier he was sadly overbowled like Kennedy and Newman, solely because there was no one else to contain the opposing batting late in the day, he could be extremely penetrative – he was always difficult to play on a green wicket because his arm was so high.

In 1932, he took 96 wickets at less than 24 runs each and represented the Players against the Gentlemen at the Oval.

As a batsman, he scored his runs very quickly to general delight, including 41 in eighteen minutes against Glamorgan at Dean Park in 1936. That season, he took 113 wickets, the first of three successive seasons in which he achieved that feat – his best performance being seven for 71 v Lancashire and first seven for 59 v Kent.

The following year, he made 67 against the New Zealanders at Bournemouth out of 77 in twenty-two scoring strokes, with two sixes and 10 fours – in fact, his uncomplicated and entertaining batting, brought him 801 runs that summer. In the match against Warwickshire, he took 5 for 42 in the first innings – it was the match in which Moore broke the Hampshire record for the highest individual innings. He had a very successful summer in 1937, making the ball rise sharply off the wicket, he took 133 Championship wickets and 142 at 22.07 in all matches. In 1938, he took 101 wickets at 32.30, before he left to play Lancashire League cricket for Rochdale.

He returned to the County after the war to give more valuable service and took over 100 wickets again in 1946, as he had in his last full season in 1938; he still shared the new ball, but his main successes only came when he took to bowling off-spinners seriously.

Always saving something special for the tourists, he was Hampshire's best bowler in 1947 in the rain-affected match with the South Africans. He took four for 46 in 15 overs, with three of his wickets being obtained in four balls. In his final season, he still turned in the odd good performance and took four for 62 against Kent, being chiefly responsible for bowling the top county out for a reasonable score. He did score 719 runs that summer and was a constant source of delight to schoolboys wherever he played, coming within eight runs of a century in the match against

Leicestershire, only to be caught and bowled off a carelessly lofted shot.

After his retirement in 1948, he had a further couple of seasons with Wiltshire, then coached for four years at Oxford University, during the time of Colin Cowdrey and Mike Smith, followed by four years at Harrow before going to South Africa to continue as a coach at several schools in East London.

In 1963, he was appointed to the first-class umpires list and continued to enjoy a life that was devoted to cricket. For a brief period he was landlord of the Anchor Inn in the Hampshire village of Bishopstoke but one rarely makes a fortune in a small village pub and he needed little persuasion to return to cricket.

John Arlott desribed 'Lofty' as 'very much an Oxfordshires countryman, with a dry humour and occasionally, a wryly acid wit.' Kindly and genial, 'Lofty' Herman was a popular figure as a player (the seventh highest wicket taker in the County's history) coach, umpire and frequent spectator at Hampshire matches in his later years.

# ARTHUR HILL

Born: 26 July 1871, Bassett
Died: 6 September 1950
Played: 1895–1921

### FIRST-CLASS HAMPSHIRE RECORD

| Matches | Innings | NO | Runs | HS | Ave | 100s |
|---|---|---|---|---|---|---|
| 161 | 291 | 17 | 8381 | 199 | 30.58 | 17 |

| Runs | Wkts | Ave | Best |
|---|---|---|---|
| 6213 | 199 | 31.22 | 7-36 |

### NOTABLE FEATS

- He was awarded four Blues at Cambridge from 1890 to 1893.
- He took 31 wickets at 19.16 in 1897 to finish eighth in the national averages.
- In 1905, he scored 124 and 118* v Somerset at Southampton
- In 1907, he scored 705 runs at 44.06 to finish fifth in the national averages.
- In 1898, he hit the highest score of his career, 199 v Surrey at the Oval.

Tall and stylish and recognised as one of the finest amateur batsmen in England, Arthur James Ledger Hill, combined a sound defence with an array of attacking strokes, dominated by the drive, both on the left and off side. He was also a useful fast bowler before taking to lobs and in addition, he was a reliable field, notably at short slip.

He made his first appearance as a player at Lord's in 1887, a day after completing his sixteenth birthday, for he was in the Marlborough XI three seasons, during which time he played for Wiltshire in 1888. Going to Cambridge, he played four times against Oxford from 1890–1893. In 1891, he performed the 'hat-trick' for the university against Next Sixteen – a feat he also achieved the following year for Lord Hawke's team against Madras Presidency at Madras.

A banker by profession, Hill excelled at most games and captained Hampshire teams at rugby football and hockey and he was also good at boxing, fishing, hunting and racquets.

He came into the Hampshire side at the end of his third year at Cambridge and played some attractive innings. In 1894, Hampshire's last season as a minor County, he scored 114 in the county's second innings when they beat Essex at Leyton – Essex were one of the new first-class counties. Playing in Hampshire's first game in the County Championship of 1895, he turned in some useful performances throughout their first season of first-class cricket. Againt Yorkshire at Sheffield, he batted well for 46 in the first innings and then combined brave hitting with the most admirable defence in a splendid innings of 49 as Hampshire won by two wickets.

Touring South Africa in 1895–96, he played in three Tests, scoring 251 runs at an average of 62.75. He saved England in the game at Cape Town by scoring 124 out of an all out total of 265. In the last match he also took four wickets for 8 runs - there can't have been too many players who scored a hundred and had bowling figures like that who didn't represent their country again. His appearance at Cape Town was the last for England by a Hampshire-born cricketer. At the end of the tour, he informed the Hampshire committee that he had decided to spend the summer of 1896 in South Africa – it was a season in which Hampshire not only missed his batting, but also his slip fielding.

Returning to the Hampshire side in 1897, he strengthened the batting and against Leicestershire in August, he not only top scored in his side's first innings, but had match figures of ten for 63. The following season, he hit his highest score for the County, 199 against Surrey at the Oval. It was a good summer for him, as he averaged over 30 with the bat, took 40 wickets at just over 20 runs each, whilst his slip catches and fighting spirit were constant assets to the side.

Playing for the Hampshire Hogs in 1901, Hill hit 50 off two consecutive overs from E R Kinnersley – 28 and 22.

Though the summer of 1903 was about the wettest in the County's history, Hill hit an unbeaten 150 in a fine win over Derbyshire at Southampton. Againt Worcestershire the following season, he scored 98 not out and 117.

In 1905 in the match between Hampshire and Somerset at Southampton, he hit 124 and 118 not out. In the second innings, he was involved in a remarkable stand of 150 with E G Wynyard. Hill was lame and Wynyard could only bat with one hand owing to a damaged thumb. Yet Hill made his runs in two hours, hitting one six, one five and 22 fours. He scored 80 while his partner made 7 – in fact, Wynyard spent over an hour getting his first two runs. He scored another century, 113 against Surrey in a match played on the Officers' Ground at Aldershot, a successful innovation, but Surrey got home by seven wickets. It was sad indeed that this fine batsman could play in fewer than half the matches.

He averaged 44.06 for the nine matches which he could manage in 1907 and had never played better, being honoured with a place in the Gentlemen's side at Lord's.

Once again, playing his usual quota of matches the following season, Hill headed the batting averages for the fifth time and was seen at his best with a century againt Middlesex at Lord's. Middlesex were the county to suffer at Hill's hands in 1920, when at the age of forty-eight, he hit 74 in ninety minutes off their attack - Middlesex were the County Champions that season – but unfortunately, Hill only played twice.

He later served on the County committee, held the office of chairman from 1935 to 1938 and was elected president of the Club in 1939. Altogether, his cricket career covered thirty years and finished with him appearing with his son, Anthony in the Hampshire side.

# GERRY HILL

Born: 15 April 1913 Brook, Hants
Played: 1932–1954

FIRST-CLASS HAMPSHIRE RECORD

| Matches | Innings | NO | Runs | HS | Ave | 100s |
|---|---|---|---|---|---|---|
| 371 | 595 | 94 | 9085 | 161 | 18.13 | 4 |

| Runs | Wkts | Ave | Best |
|---|---|---|---|
| 18464 | 617 | 29.92 | 8-62 |

NOTABLE FEATS

- He took 8 for 62 (14 for 146 in the match) against Kent at Tonbridge in 1935.
- He added 235 with D F Walker for the fifth wicket v Sussex at Portsmouth in 1937 – a Hampshire record.
- He added 202 with J R Gray for the sixth wicket v Essex at Southampton in 1952.

During his time with Hampshire, Gerry Hill did more or less whatever was demanded of him. Really an off-break bowler and at his best, a very good one, he often bowled at medium-pace with the new ball, changing when told, to his off-breaks.

Hailing from Brook in the New Forest, he was for some twenty years, a good hard-working, conscientious professional for Hampshire. He bowled off-breaks as dangerous by virtue of their flight as their spin, though in his early days, he appeared to bowl them off the wrong foot.

By 1935, he had improved his action to take 93 wickets, including his best every figures of 8 for 62 (14 for 146 in the match) against Kent at Tonbridge. It was a season when he also scored 549 runs – he and Boyes were involved in two last wicket partnership of over fifty in the match against Middlesex at Lord's. The summer also saw him rejoice in the fact that at that time he shared in a world record – entering the record books, but for a wrong reason, as he was hit for 32 run (6,6,4,6,6,4) off one over by Cyril Smart of Glamorgan in the match at Cardiff. It was an event about which Gerry Hill has exhibited a humorous pride ever since!

As a spinner, the presence of Charlie Knott in the side denied him a certain amount of opportunity. He tended to do most of his bowling on plumb wickets. It was on a dead wicket at Southampton, that he bowled a long and accurate spell to Don Bradman and kept the great man extremely quiet after he had shown clearly that he intended to go 'on the kill.' Hill's best bowling ususally came on hard wickets, when his patient length was a major asset.

A fair field at either mid-off or mid-on, he took 172 catches in his career with Hampshire.

As a batsman, Gerry Hill often revealed his golfing powers in his lofted drives – a shot with which he accummulated most of his runs. He could be a dangerous forcing batsman, but on the other hand, when the situation demanded it, he was content to put his head down and battle with, however, a heavy bat always ready for the bad ball. His highest score of 161 came in the 1937 match against Sussex at Portsmouth as he and "Hooky" Walker, who also hit a century, added 235 for the fifth wicket to set a new county record after Hampshire had seemed to be heading for defeat. The summer also saw him enjoy the remarkable innings bowling analysis of:

| O | M | R | W |
|----|----|---|---|
| 17 | 11 | 8 | 5 |

in the match against Lancashire at Portsmouth.

In the first season of county cricket after the war, he was second to Knott in the County's bowling averages, whilst in 1947, he got through a tremendous amount of work and topped 1,000 runs with the bat.

A loyal servant of Hampshire, Gerry Hill was one of five senior professionals in 1948, granted a joint benefit – owing to the war years, those deserving a benefit outnumbered the seasons available and the Hampshire committee thought this to be the most equitable way of dealing with the situation. That summer, he bowled well on occasions, but an injury to his finger, prevented him doing full justice to himself, for he appeared not to recover his confidence or form.

As a man, Gerry Hill was a magnificent example of the professional cricketer at his best. As a player, he was pessimistic in outlook, always anticipating a bad wicket to bat on and a plumb wicket on which to bowl.

By 1952, he was the only pre-war Hampshire player to represent the County on a regular basis.

Though he was pessimistic, Gerry Hill always had a good-natured word, was extremely fit and always interested in both the game and other people's successes.

# ARTHUR HOLT

Born: 8 April 1911, Southampton
Played: 1935–1948

FIRST-CLASS HAMPSHIRE RECORD

| Matches | Innings | NO | Runs | HS | Ave | 100s |
|---|---|---|---|---|---|---|
| 79 | 140 | 13 | 2853 | 116 | 22.46 | 2 |

| Runs | Wkts | Ave | Best |
|---|---|---|---|
| 47 | 1 | 47.00 | 1-24 |

NOTABLE FEATS

● He hit his highest score of 116 v Leicestershire in 1938.
● He coached many cricketers who went into the first-class game and is held in high esteem throughout the county of Hampshire.

A major figure in the development of Hampshire cricket, Arthur Holt had been on the staff of Southampton FC since 1932 and in the summer played club cricket with Deanery and various other local sides. After he had scored two or three hundreds in the Wednesday League, he was offered a job at the County Ground at £2 a week plus ten bob for each Club and Ground or Second Eleven match.

Arthur Holt joined the county staff in 1934 and made his debut the following season against Somerset at Taunton. Batting at No.9, he scored his first run off the bowling of J C White, whilst his next match was a couple of weeks later at the County Ground in a side captained by Lord Tennyson – one of the few occasions he played under him.

In those days, there was no coach on the County Staff and the players had to organise their own practice. In 1938, the County decided to appoint Sam Staples, the ex-Notts and England player, but by then, Arthur Holt had already developed his bad habits! It didn't stop him hitting the highest score of his first-class career that season, 116 against Leicestershire. Though he played some good innings, he was never able to command a regular place in the Hampshire side. A solid and patient defensive batsman, his expected development was held back by the outbreak of war.

During the hostilities, he spent most of the time as war reserve police. He did however, find time to play for the Players v

Gentlemen – a charity match arranged by Lord Tennyson on the College Ground at Winchester – opening the batting, he was bowled by Charlie Knott for 27. He also played in another notable war-time cricket match for Southampton and District against an RAF side in the Parks. A couple of Australians in khaki shorts from a unit recently arrived at Bournemouth played – they played in borrowed flannels and pullovers. One of them bowled to Arthur, as he tried to hook, the ball hit him on the temple and he spent the next two days in bed – the bowler's name was Keith Miller!

In the first season after the war, he was promoted to partner Johnny Arnold in opening the innings and against Essex, he missed his hundred by just six runs in his side's nine wicket victory. He continued to play until 1948, whereafter he was appointed County Coach as successor to Sam Staples. His appointment was a very happy one, though as Desmond Eagar wrote in the Official History of Hampshire County Cricket Club, he would have scored many runs for the County if his best years hadn't been lost to the war. As it was, he scored 2,853 runs at 22.46.

Arthur Holt had that wonderful gift of imparting confidence to the younger players on the staff. He was specially interested in coaching, because he had missed out himself.

His first years in the job coincided with the development of coaching in an organised way by the MCC and in 1951, he went on the cricket coaching conference at Lilleshall. From then on, he went every year for twenty-one years – he must have known Harry Altham's introduction word for word! One of the first to be awarded the MCC's Advanced Coaching Certificate he began by going to the local schools and teaching the teachers.

Building up a network of contacts in the County and further afield, he would arrange to go and watch any promising youngsters play. Arthur Holt coached may cricketers who eventually went into the first-class game, players like Gordon Greenidge, Trevor Jesty, David Turner, Bob Cottam, Peter Sainsbury and Henry Horton.

In 1954, his great services to the club were recognised and his Testimonial Fund was closed in November with a sum of almost £1,700. Considering the terrible weather of the day, the Testimonial bore full tribute to the high esteem in which Arthur was and still is held throughout the county of Hampshire.There were few people other than those connected with the club who realised the amount of work he put in during the winter months as well as summer. Hundreds of schoolboys will have appreciated all they learned from him, both on and off the field.

When he retired as County coach, he carried on with the colts team – Holt's Colts as they were known. It kept Arthur in contact with the part of the job which gave him most satisfaction.

He had two rules for all young cricketers – never tuck your trousers inside your socks and always walk if you get an edge.

In 1981, Arthur Holt retired from running the Colts and was elected a Vice President of Hampshire. His work and enthusiasm have been immeasurable over the years – long may he enjoy watching all Hampshire elevens.

# HENRY HORTON

Born: 18 April 1923, Hereford
Played: 1953–1967

FIRST-CLASS HAMPSHIRE RECORD

| Matches | Innings | NO | Runs | HS | Ave | 100s |
|---|---|---|---|---|---|---|
| 405 | 723 | 80 | 21536 | 160* | 33.49 | 32 |

| Runs | Wkts | Ave | Best |
|---|---|---|---|
| 162 | 3 | 54.00 | 2-0 |

NOTABLE FEATS

- He scored over 2,000 runs in a season for Hampshire on three occasions with a best of 2,428 in 1959.
- He hit his highest score, 160 not out v Yorkshire at Bournemouth in 1961.
- In 1966, he added 272 with D A Livingstone for the third wicket v Middlesex at Bournemouth.

Henry Horton's stance - bottom jutting out, knees bent, bat at an angle of forty-five degrees - caused much amusement to crowds around the county circuit for more than twenty years.

In his youth, he was overshadowed by his elder brother, Joe, who played for Worcestershire for several seasons prior to the second World War, and when county cricket resumed in 1946, Henry Horton was far more interested in bowling left-arm spin than in his batting. A Hereford man, he had a trial with Worcestershire in 1946 and went on the staff at New Road the following year, but had little opportunity to bowl and was unable to gain a regular place as a batsman. At this stage, his cricket career was unsuccessful, but he began to become noted on the soccer field. After ninety-eight games for Blackburn Rovers at full-back and wing-half, he was transferred during the 1951–52 season to Southampton.

He found when he reported for pre-season training that the Club encouraged the players to participate in a few cricket matches as part of the training and public relations exercises – it used to wind up with a match against Portsmouth FC.

Henry made a few runs in the matches and was approached by Arthur Holt who was then Hampshire coach, who asked if he was interested in playing a few Club and Ground matches. He duly accepted and again made a few runs. He did this again in the following pre-season training and it was then that Arthur asked him if he had thought about having another bash at playing County Cricket. Henry's answer to Arthur was thank you, but no not interested. He felt another couple of seasons in League football, a few seasons in Non-League football and then call it a day. However, that wasn't the end of it because Arthur refused to let it be. He had another go at Horton in the spring of 1953, painting a nice picture of playing with the Club and Ground in the Hampshire countryside. Being paid for it certainly made him think again – Arthur adding that he might even get a game in the First Eleven for which he would be paid extra. Henry Horton dismissed the first team as just myth, but the money he would get playing for the Club and Ground plus his retainer from the Football Club gave him a great thrill.

He started playing for the Club and Ground in 1953, the same time as Roy Marshall, though the West Indian could only play friendly matches because of qualification.

He was forced into first team action against Leicestershire at Portsmouth because of injuries to first team players. Leicestershire were put into bat on a greenish wicket and were bowled out by Shackleton, Cannings, and Gray for 91. Hampshire started to bat late afternoon and lost three wickets quite quickly. In walked Horton – Geoff Goodwin was the bowler for Leicestershire, left-arm round the wicket with an attacking field, he pitched the first ball up and Horton pushed it away for 3 runs. He went on to make 49 – an innings he has never forgotten.

That season went on and he was in and out of the team, with the following season the same. When the 1955 season started, he was included in the team almost at the start. He went on the first tour to Lord's, Middlesex, Worcester and Lancashire, but could only muster 15 runs in five knocks. On his reurn he was dropped and continued to make nothing in Club and Ground and Second Eleven matches – he really felt that it was the end of yet another try at playing County Cricket. It was then mid-summer and the Varsities were on tour. He was picked to play against Oxford at Bournemouth, scoring 22 and 5 and keeping his place for the match against Gloucestershire at Bristol, where he made 12 and 12 not out. Going on to Swansea to play Glamorgan, he scored 89 and a first ball 0. He was retained for the next match, Leicestershire at Bournemouth, where he made a hundred and was presented with his County Cap. He finished the season with 1,231 runs at an average of 56.

Henry Horton wielded one of the straightest bats in England, with an unflagging hunger for runs and a steady devotion. He never failed to work out the reason for his dismissal and to ponder it while he faithfully scraped his bat: only run-outs – to which he was sadly prone – left him with no philisophic answer to his self-questioning.

Despite his ugly stance at the wicket, he offered immense promise and there are qualities besides elegance which win matches – Henry Horton had the others – his defence was sound and his temperment superb. His defensive batting saved many matches for the County, but he could if he so desired, also attack the bowling, scoring most of his runs in front of the wicket by putting a great deal of power behind his 'pushes' to the off-side.

His best season was 1959, when he was one of three Hampshire batsmen to top the 2,000 runmark – Horton scoring 2,428 runs at 47.60. He did so again the following season and in 1961 when the county won the championship. During that successful summer, he played many important innings. Against Surrey at the Oval, he made an unbeaten 85 in 230 minutes and was the only Hampshire batsman in control. In the second innings he hit 84 as Hampshire won by five wickets. Also that season, he hit 141, the highest score of his career to date. The opponents were Derbyshire, Horton occupying the crease for five hours at the Racecourse Ground, Derby. He went one better in the match against Yorkshire at Bournemouth, as he hit 160 not out in Hampshire's first innings total of 340 for 6. He had his benefit season in 1964 and was as reliable as ever. In the game against his former county, Worcestershire, at New Road, it was his resolute batting in an innings of 280 that gave Hampshire a commanding first innings lead of 171 runs. He retired at the end of the 1967 season, despite his average of 25.95 as he had lost his place through injury. A football coach at Colwall School, he also holds the MCC advanced coaching certificate and on being released by Hampshire at the age of forty–three, became coach to Worcestershire, whom he was originally associated with in 1946.

# COLIN INGLEBY-MACKENZIE

Born: 15 September 1933, Darmouth
Played: 1951–1965

FIRST-CLASS HAMPSHIRE RECORD

| Matches | Innings | NO | Runs | HS | Ave | 100s |
|---------|---------|-----|-------|------|-------|------|
| 309 | 513 | 60 | 11140 | 132* | 24.59 | 10 |

| Runs | Wkts | Ave | Best |
|------|------|-----|------|
| 22 | 0 | – | – |

NOTABLE FEATS

- He captained Hampshire from 1958–65, including leading the County to its first County Championship title in 1961.

Colin Ingleby-Mackenzie began his county cricket career with a 'duck' in a match restricted by rain to a bare three hours play. He became captain of Hampshire in 1958, leading the county to the highest position they had known – second – and they might even have taken the title if they hadn't fallen away in August. The plan to make him captain of Hampshire was the joint idea of Harry Altham and Desmond Eagar. Both of them took their cricket much more gravely than 'the young man' who more than once made their hair stand on end. They first knew Ingleby-Mackenzie as an Etonian whose natural eye and ball sense gave him pleasure and success without undue worry about technique. He could have been equally successful as a tennis-player: there is little doubt that he took to cricket because he found the atmosphere much more congenial.

Against Somerset in his first season as captain, he hit a hundred in sixty-one minutes and only rain prevented Hampshire from an innings victory. In the match against Kent at Southampton, Hampshire set 305 in 270 minutes, won with thirty minutes to spare as Ingleby-Mackenzie hit his hundred in ninety-eight minutes.

That innings against Somerset was the fastest hundred of the season – he was also voted 'Best Young Cricketer of the Year.'

Ingleby-Mackenzie's attitude was, that if the slimmest chance of winning existed, then he would flirt with defeat to attain it. His willingness to gamble with declarations was never more clear than in 1959 when four of Hampshire's eleven wins were achieved in the last over.

As a batsman, he was not above hurling a crooked bat at his first ball; But apart from scoring the fastest century of the season, he was able to put his head down and play a long handle to save a match that could not be won, and notably in Hampshire's Championship winning summer of 1961, turned a losing game against Essex into a remarkable win. The dropped catches that cost Hampshire the championship in 1958 made a deeper impression on him than he ever voiced. He set to work, within his limitations, to improve his down fielding. In 1961, he brought off at least four run-outs by hitting the stumps direct with long throws; apart from their immediate effect, those efforts made an impact on the rest of the team.

He was no deep strategist; at times, it seemed he would let a match drift to the point of disaster. That may have been because of the problem of what would win the 3.30 race was on his mind; certainly he seemed to concentrate more on the game in hand by about six o'clock, when all the racing results were through! Final day declarations are tricky affairs and in recent years have occasionally degenerated into something between the pointless and the downright silly. But Ingleby-Mackenzie's uncanny blend of luck and judgement was not unconnected with his service in the Royal Navy, where they set some store by such phrases as the 'Nelson Touch' and 'By Guess and By God'.

In 1961, an experimental law had disallowed the follow-on and so a skilled assessment of the alternatives was needed. Ingleby-Mackenzie's perceptions became so good that more than half of the County's wins were as the result of clever declarations.

As captain, Ingleby-Mackenzie had four considerable assets. He was a good enough gambler not to be afraid of losing, possessing a sense of humour that was greater than even his most righteous indignation. He never made the mistake of thinking that cricket was all-important and always saw cricketers first as human beings and only afterwards as batsmen, bowlers or fielders.

Among his friends, he did not answer to – and was not addressed by – any of the sobriquets found for him in some newspapers. He was simply 'Colin,' 'Ingleby,' 'Skipper' or at most, 'the young man'. He had a tongue-in-cheek claim that his policy was one of rigid team/discipline: When asked 'Is it true that you insist on all your men being in bed before eleven?' he replied 'Certainly. After all, play begins at eleven thirty.' At the end of August 1961, he found himself captain of the County Champions. He went out on the Dean Park pavilion balcony to tell the Hampshire supporters: 'I would like to toast the luckiest captain and the great men who have made this possible.I am too excited to say much more. I just hope I won't wake up tomorrow morning and find that we are twelfth in the table.'

It was a situation which he had never really expected, even

though he had put money on it – 'The odds were so good it would have been ridiculous not to have a go.'

Ingleby-Mackenzie was utterly likeable – the national Press loved him and gave him the title 'the gay cavalier of cricket'. His affability made him essential to any 'friendly' touring team and he went with E W Swanton's side to the West Indies and India, with the Duke of Norfolk's to Jamaica and with the cavaliers to South Africa and the West Indies.

At the end of the 1965 season, he retired. He had led the side with a sense humour, immense spirit and with great shrewdness. Still remembered with affection, he was a successful captain of Hampshire not through any profound knowledge or study of cricket, but because he is, essentially, a kind person.

# TREVOR JESTY

Born: 2 June 1948, Gosport
Played: 1966–1984

### FIRST-CLASS HAMPSHIRE RECORD

| Matches | Innings | NO | Runs | HS | Ave | 100s |
|---|---|---|---|---|---|---|
| 340 | 538 | 74 | 14753 | 248 | 31.79 | 26 |

| Runs | Wkts | Ave | Best |
|---|---|---|---|
| 13596 | 475 | 28.62 | 7-75 |

### NOTABLE FEATS

- He hit 105 v Glamorgan in the Benson and Hedges Cup at Swansea in 1977.
- In 1980, he scored 118 v Derbyshire in the Gillette Cup at Derby.
- He hit four Sunday League centuries, with a best of 166* v Surrey at Portsmouth in 1983.
- In 1983, he added 321 wih C L Smith for the third wicket v Derbyshire at Derby.
- In 1984, he added 302 for the second wicket with V P Terry v Cambridge University, scoring 248.
- During the same season, he scored 143* and 141 v Worcestershire at Worcester.

Trevor Jesty will probably always remain the subject of contention and argument for Hampshire cricket lovers – is he the best uncapped, Hampshire – born, first-class cricketer?

Although he played very little cricket at his secondary school, Trevor Jesty attracted enough attention in local games to win a place in the Hampshire Schools side and later the English Schools XI. Playing for Gosport CC, he was heading for a career as a yacht-building shipwright when Hampshire offered him his chance.

He made his Championship debut against Essex in 1966 – a debut in which he scored only two and took no wickets for 52 runs. This was a transitional time for the county: Colin Ingleby-Mackenzie had gone and the side that had won the Championship in 1961 was beginning to break up. He didn't play at all in 1967 and a little in 1968, although that was an important year for Hampshire and for Jesty with the arrival of the brilliant South African, Barry Richards. The following year, be began to establish himself as part of the gradually improving Hampshire side, though his figures – 596 runs (22.92) and 33 wickets (27.96) were not particularly exciting. For the next few seasons, his career did not run smoothly, perhaps because he was at times not in accord with Richard Gilliat, the Hampshire captain. He was capped in 1971 and along with fellow all-rounder, Peter Sainsbury and former Notts bowler, Mike Taylor, he played a crucial role in Hampshire's Championship-winning season of 1973. In this season, his bowling was more successful than his batting; his controlled medium-pace swing accounting for thirty-six batsmen, including 5 for 24 against Lancashire at Southport. But the suspicion remained that there was potential unfulfilled here, and that it was in his batting rather than his bowling.

Though he still hadn't reached the magical three figures, he certainly answered the doubters of his application and stamina, who maintained that he lacked the steel to play a long, disciplined innings,in the match against Kent at Basingstoke in 1974. It has gone down in Hampshire history as Andy Roberts' match, but it was so very nearly Jesty's. Roberts of course finished with nine wickets, his pace and hostility giving Hampshire victory by an innings and 71 runs. However, it was Jesty who provided the base for him to attack. Hampshire too found batting difficult, all that is except Jesty, who had produced an innings of total mastery and was 90 not out at tea. The Basingstoke crowd spent the interval preparing the ovation for his maiden first-class century, but it wasn't to be, for the break had disrupted his concentration and he was leg-before immediately afterwards.

By 1975, he was being spoken of as a potential Test player, but as Wisden noted: '762 runs from 28 innings hardly bore this out; yet he possessed a fine range of attacking shots . . and certainly should be capable of scoring 1,000 runs in a season and of scoring a Championship hundred.' In the close of season of 1975–76, he broke through, scoring his first first-class century whilst playing for Griqualand West against Natal 'B'. Now he had to do it for

Hampshire – it looked like coming in the early weeks of the season, when he had reached ninety-one against Essex at Chelmsford, but he ran out of partners. In the next match, at Portsmouth, he was 83 when run out against Yorkshire. The day arrived against Gloucestershire at Southampton – Jesty scoring 134 as he and Gilliat shared a magnificent 237 run partnership in 147 minutes. By the end of that season, he had lifted his personal best to 159 not out against Somerset – a brilliant innings launched from 47 for 2, which had rapidly deteriorated to 52 for 6, before Peter Sainsbury steadied things down with him. He finished the season with 1,288 runs at 35.77, and came second in the bowling with 42 wickets, including seven for 75 against Worcestershire.

He never looked back, for in the summer of 1977, he topped 1,200 runs for the second season running. There were four more centuries and a place on the back-up list of players for England's tour of Pakistan and New Zealand. But, he was never called up, for when injuries and sickness produced an emergency, the authorities turned to Clive Radley who was coaching for Kerry Packer in Australia.

To show them what they had missed, he hit five more centuries in 1978, but in only two of his 37 other innings did be score 50 !

Yet, on his day, there were few English batsmen playing who were better to watch. Many was the time when the casual observer found Jesty and the great Barry Richards near-impossible to distinguish. He was a right-handed batsman with an essentially classical approach – broad shouldered, upright and aggressive, his driving, particularly in the arc from square to mid-off was as fluent as any who have represented the county.

The forty minute whirlwind in which he hit the Somerset attack for 96 incredible runs (6 sixes and 11 fours) on Sunday 20th July 1980, may not have been first-class, but it was certainly England class!

His 52 Championship wickets at 19.86 in 1981, was welcome evidence of complete recovery from a shoulder injury that had reduced the effectiveness of his medium-pace outswing in recent years.

His greatest year was 1982, when he scored 1,645 runs at 58.75, with eight centuries – his Benefit year! He was seventh in the national averages and for good measure topped the county's bowling with 35 wickets at 21.42. He was selected as one of Wisden's 'Five Cricketers of the Year' but did not amazingly, attract the attention of the Test selectors. The team to tour Australia that winter was announced on the first day of the Warwickshire v Hampshire match – Jesty's response was to score a century in sixty–four minutes, finishing with 134, including two sixes and 20 fours. He did in fact fly out to Australia as a replacement and played in ten limited-overs internationals in the

World Series cup between Australia, England and New Zealand.

Trevor Jesty was one of the great one-day players of his generation – in 1983, he hit 166 not out in the John Player League match against Surrey at the United Services Ground, Portsmouth, as he and Gordon Greenidge added an undefeated 269 for the second wicket, which was a record for any partnership by the county in the Sunday League.

At the end of the 1984 season, he left Hampshire after being passed over for the captaincy, and joined Surrey. Ironically, he immediately took on the role as acting captain in the absence of Geoff Howarth. In 1986 at the Oval, he almost defeated Lancashire single-handed in the Nat West semi-final, scoring 112 out of 225, the last third of it with a pulled hamstring, before being last out with Surrey five runs short of victory. At the end of 1987, he was released to make way for youth and joined Lancashire. After a disappointing season in 1988, he seemed to have established himself the following summer, when he scored over a thousand runs, without scoring a century. In 1990, in spite of scoring 786 runs at 43.61, pressure grew for him to make way for Lancashire's wealth of young talent. In 1991, he appeared only once, scoring a century, as he guided an inexperienced team to victory over Oxford University in The Parks. Trevor Jesty had a rare talent, though he did not accumulate the runs he might have scored with a more cautious outlook – but then again, he would have entertained much less had he opted for caution !

# ALEC KENNEDY

Born: 24 January 1891, Edinburgh
Died: 15 November 1959
Played: 1907–1936

FIRST-CLASS HAMPSHIRE RECORD

| Matches | Innings | NO | Runs | HS | Ave | 100s |
|---------|---------|-----|-------|------|-------|------|
| 596 | 916 | 110 | 14925 | 163* | 18.51 | 10 |

| Runs | Wkts | Ave | Best |
|-------|------|-------|------|
| 53950 | 2549 | 21.16 | 9-33 |

NOTABLE FEATS

- He took 100 wickets in a season for Hampshire on twelve occasions with a best of 190 at 15.61 in 1922.

- He performed the 'double' on three occasions – 1921, 1922 and 1923.
- He performed the hat-trick on three occasions: v Gloucestershire at Southampton in 1920, v Somerset at Bournemouth in the same season and v Gloucestershire again at Southampton in 1924.
- He carried his bat for 152* out of 344 v Nottinghamshire at Trent Bridge in 1921.
- He took nine for 33 v Lancashire at Liverpool in 1920 and nine for 46 v Derbyshire at Portsmouth in 1929.
- In 1921, he had figures of:

| O | M | R | W |
|----|----|----|----|
| 13 | 7 | 11 | 8 |

v Glamorgan at Cardiff.

- In 1922, he had match figures of 15 for 116 v Somerset at Bath.
- In 1927, he took all ten wickets in the first innings of the Gentlemen v Players match at the Oval.
- He took 482 catches in his career with Hampshire.

Although born in Edinburgh, Alexander Stuart Kennedy moved with his parents to Southampton in 1896, whilst a child and would spend hours at the County Ground willing to bowl to anyone and everyone. When he left school at fourteen, he joined the Hampshire groundstaff. There was no coach at the county ground in those days, but C B Llewellyn helped him with advice in those early years when he was founding his subsequent control by long hours of solitary bowling in the nets.

He was only sixteen-and-a-half when in 1907, he made his first-class debut against Leicestershire taking 4 for 33 in their only innings. He ended the season with seven wickets for 83 runs to put him theoretically top of the bowling table.

He did not become a regular in the Hampshire side until 1909 and in 1912, now physically matured, could and often did, bowl all day without losing his line and control. He was able to 'straighten' the ball from both off and leg without any apparent change in his rhythmical action to take 112 Championship wickets at 17 runs each. The side's best win of the season came against the Australians, Kennedy taking 11 wickets. After a serious operation at the beginning of the following season, he returned to the game in July to take 82 wickets at 22 runs each to head the Hampshire bowling averages. Now restored to full health, he took 148 Championship wickets in 1914 and bowled more overs than anyone else in England.

After the war, he settled into eighteen remarkable seasons of bowling. A fast-medium bowler, 'Alec' Kennedy was a Hampshire forerunner of Derek Shackleton. Though he could swing the ball both ways, his main ball was the inswinger while the seam was sharp. But, this most consistently effective ball was the leg-cutter. One of the first to bowl it, he did so with remarkable accuracy, employing many subtly concealed variations of length and pace.

While he hardly bowled a bad ball, his bowling was never merely mechanical, for he studied the opposing batsmen and plied them with every possible variation of swing, cut and finger spin. He never 'used the crease' in case he 'telegraphed' his intentions to the batsman.

His run-up was so unvarying, that bowling for half a day on wet ground, he stamped out his footmarks precisely to a fraction of an inch!

He walked back to his mark (five measured walking paces and then eight unhurried running strides) as erect as a guardsman. His right arm was high as he bowled and in fact, brushed his right ear as it came over.

He delivered the ball with a full whip of the wrist, which I suppose was, perhaps, the cause of the doubts at one time entertained, as to the legality of his action.

In 1919, he had the remarkable figures of:

| O | M | R | W |
|---|---|---|---|
| 55 | 5 | 202 | 7 |

in an innings total of 607 for 7 declared at Lord's. The following season, Kennedy took 164 wickets at 17.62, including two hat-tricks against Gloucestershire at Southampton and Somerset at Bournemouth. In the match against Lancashire at Liverpool, he took 9 for 33 in Lancashire's second innings and was almost unplayable. It was a remarkable match in that Hampshire set 66 to win, had scored 54 for 5 but the last five wickets went down for ten runs and Lancashire won by one run. He bowled 1,107 overs in the season, taking ten for 135 against Yorkshire and twelve for 147 against Warwickshire as Hampshire won both matches with ease.

Alec Kennedy was inseparable from his bowling partner, Jack Newman, as they formed Hampshire's attack for most of the inter-war period. In fact, in 1920 each of them bowled five times – in 1921 and 1923 four times – as many overs as any other Hampshire bowler. Often they bowled unchanged throughout an innings and twice through a complete match, against Sussex in 1921 and Somerset in 1923.

As a batsman, he was not an outstanding stroke player, but his strength against swing bowling made him often a useful bat and he scored steadily on the leg-side. In the summer of 1921, he carried his bat for 152 out of 344 in the match against Nottinghamshire at Trent Bridge – a match in which he bowled 31 overs in the Notts first innings and 24 in the second! His highest score of 163 not out came against Warwickshire at Portsmouth in 1923.

His bowling achievements were outstanding. Only four men in the history of cricket – Rhodes, Freeman, Parker and J T Hearne – have taken more than his 2,874 wickets. Yet, he never played for England against Australia, nor in fact, did he play for England in England. He went to South Africa with F T Mann's team in 1922–23 and was top of the Test bowling averages with 31 wickets at 19.32 runs each.

In 1922, he scored 1,129 runs and captured 205 wickets in all first-class cricket. A E Trott and M W Tate are the only other players to achieve the 'double' of 1,000 runs and 200 wickets. Against Warwickshire at Portsmouth in 1927, he had a spell of six wickets in 14 balls, his final analysis being:

| O | M | R | W |
|---|---|---|---|
| 10 | 7 | 8 | 7 |

He played fairly frequently in Gentlemen v Players matches and in that summer of 1927, he took all ten wickets for 37 runs in the match at the Oval. For Hampshire, he probably produced his most impressive figures in the match against Glamorgan at Cardiff in 1921 when he returned the following analysis:

| O | M | R | W |
|---|---|---|---|
| 13 | 7 | 11 | 8 |

He cut down his run and grew more subtle with age, taking 140 Championship wickets at 17.27 in 1929. In 1931, as though the loss of Newman was a challenge, be bowled at his best to again capture most wickets, 126 at 17.07, including 7 for 29 as the New Zealand tourists were shot out for 79, their lowest total of the tour. Wisden included him in its Five Cricketers of the Year in 1933, when it closed its biographical note on him with the words 'A great but unlucky bowler.'

During his playing career, he spent several winters coaching in South Africa – at Johannesburg and Kimberley – and when he retired from county cricket in 1936, he became coach at Cheltenham College for several seasons before he again went to South Africa as the resident coach at King Edward's School, Johannesburg until 1952.

He returned to Southampton to run a tobacconist's and stationer's business with characteristic attention. Though his happiest moments were spent at the county ground, sitting on the professional's balcony, talking about cricket – preferably bowling!

In 1956, at the age of sixty-five, he was asked to play in a charity match against a strong touring club eleven at Portsmouth. He top-scored for his side with a well-made serious innings of 36. His captain suggested that he bowl a couple of overs. Typical of the man – his eagerness shone through – he bowled six overs of slow-medium leg-cutters to a perfect length, took several of the best wickets and then, out of politeness, went off. Towards the end of that innings, two tail-end batsmen became quite set. Alec Kenney peeled off his sweater and came on to immediately break the partnership!

On learning of his death in 1959, H L V Day expressed the opinion that there was never a greater hearted trier than Alec Kennedy, nor was there a fairer bowler.

# CHARLIE KNOTT

Born: 26 November 1914, Southampton
Played: 1938–1954

FIRST-CLASS HAMPSHIRE RECORD

| Matches | Innings | NO | Runs | HS | Ave | 100s |
|---|---|---|---|---|---|---|
| 166 | 235 | 94 | 1003 | 27 | 7.11 | 0 |

| Runs | Wkts | Ave | Best |
|---|---|---|---|
| 15224 | 647 | 23.53 | 8-26 |

NOTABLE FEATS

- He took 100 wickets in a season for Hampshire on four occasions.
- He took 7 for 26 v Gloucestershire at Bristol in 1950.
- He had figures of:

| O | M | R | W |
|---|---|---|---|
| 7 | 4 | 5 | 5 |

  v Sussex at Eastbourne in 1950.
- He achieved the 'hat-trick' for Gentlemen v Players at Lord's in 1950.
- He produced his best figures of 8 for 26 v Cambridge University in 1951.

Charlie Knott's first involvement with Hampshire was to operate the scoreboard with Phil Mead's son. But, he played a few games in 1938 and 1939 and though his great succeses were to come after the war, his quality as an off-spinner was already apparent.

He had a fine, flowing, sideways-on action and was deadly on turning wickets. In 1946, his cleverly flighted off-breaks took more wickets in the season than any amateur had ever done before, 121 in all first-class matches at 18.13 runs each. He achieved selection for the Gentlemen v Players at Lord's and in the second Test trial of the season at Canterbury. Against India at Southampton, Charlie Knott proved almost unplayable, taking seven wickets for 36 runs in 16 overs as the tourists were dismissed for 130, though they recovered to win by 6 wickets.

In 1947, he struggled to make his off-breaks turn and in despair, tried medium-pace instead, but unfortunately with equal lack of success. Having developed the ability to bowl accurately and tightly for long spells, he bowled really well on all types of wickets in 1948, including the batsman's paradise that the side encountered early season. He again topped the 100 wicket mark, including taking 5 for 57 in one of the best pieces of cricket seen that summer, as the all-conquering Australians were dismissed for 117.

During the summer of 1949, the Hampshire team had the proud privilege of being presented to the Duke of Edinburgh for the first time in the match against Kent at Canterbury. As soon as His Royal Highness had finished shaking the hands of the Hampshire side, the players resumed their positions on the field of play. Hampshire had lost eight wickets and Charlie Knott was last man in. He ran to the dressing-room to put on his batting trousers, but before he could even get one pad on, in walked Tom Dean, bowled Davies for nought!

Charlie Knott claimed five wickets in an innings no less than 47 times and enjoyed eight ten-wicket matches. Against Gloucestershire at Bristol in 1950, Hampshire's opponents needed 130 to win in 137 minutes, but were bowled out for 53 runs with Charlie Knott producing his best career figures at that time.

| O | M | R | W |
|---|---|---|---|
| 12 | 2 | 26 | 7 |

It was the result of some really clever bowling and magnificent close-to-the-wicket catching, for the wicket was by no means difficult. One of his best matches came against Sussex at Eastbourne. Hampshire scored 229, Sussex replaying with 247 for 9 declared, before bowling Hampshire out for 115 in their second innings. Requiring only 98 to win, they were bowled out for 38 and Knott's analysis reads:

| O | M | R | W |
|---|---|---|---|
| 7 | 4 | 5 | 5 |

It was an astonishing performance and one that must have brought him particular pleasure, for he was leading the side in

Eagar's absence. This was also the summer that Knott performed the 'hat-trick' when playing for the Gentlemen v Players at Lord's and was presented with the ball.

But the one thing that eluded him was an England cap, although he was measured for the suit that went with it. Charlie was asked if he was available for the 1950–51 tour to Australia, but despite being measured for his clothes, he was left out of the tour party. He was obviously disappointed, but considered himself not good enough at the time! However, when he really should have had a second chance, a man by the name of Laker was around.

As I said earlier, he was an accurate bowler and in 1951 when he was bowling to Sir Derrick Bailey in the match against Gloucestershire at Portsmouth, the ball in flight struck a butterfly and killed it! It was the summer that he produced his best-ever figures for the county, 8 for 26 against Cambridge University, whilst two years later, he produced another eight wicket haul, taking 8 for 36 against Nottinghamshire at Bournemouth.

His appearances were limited by business claims in 1952 and 1953, and though he only appeared in seven championship matches in that latter season, he topped the county averages with 38 wickets at 13.71 runs each – it was a great loss to Hampshire that he was not available more often.

Besides cricket, Knott's sporting interests were varied. He owned Chatham, a Mackeson Gold Cup winner, he promoted Poole Speedway and was a leading light in the operation of Southampton ice rink and for the Vikings who made it their home.

When his playing days were over, Charlie turned to the administration side and his influence off the pitch was as big as it had been on it. It was under his influential chairmanship of the cricket committee that Hampshire won a County championship, two Sunday League titles and the Benson and Hedges Cup. He always made sure Hampshire were in the forefront when it came to signing overseas players. His judgement of a player was spot on and synonymous with that period of success was the calibre of cricket played and the men whom Knott was instrumental in bringing to the County. Great names like Barry Richards and Andy Roberts, Malcolm Marshall and the Smith brothers

One of the finest amateur bowlers in Hampshire's history, his figures show a total of 676 first-class wickets, 647 of them for Hampshire – and he took 100 wickets in a season four times.

In March 1992, he resigned as vice-chairman after fifty–four years of active involvement with the club as a player, administrator and chairman of the cricket committee. As former Hampshire president Cecil Paris said: 'That he was never Hampshire captain was down to his own modesty. That he never played for England was down to bad luck.'

# DANNY LIVINGSTONE

Born: 21 September 1933 St John's, Antigua
Died: 8 September 1988
Played: 1959–1972

FIRST-CLASS HAMPSHIRE RECORD

| Matches | Innings | NO | Runs | HS | Ave | 100s |
|---|---|---|---|---|---|---|
| 299 | 516 | 63 | 12660 | 200 | 27.94 | 16 |

| Runs | Wkts | Ave | Best |
|---|---|---|---|
| 68 | 1 | 68.00 | 1-31 |

NOTABLE FEATS

- In 1962, he scored 200 v Surrey at Southampton, as he and A T Castell added 230 for the ninth wicket – a Hampshire record.
- In 1964, he scored 117 and 105* v Kent at Canterbury
- In 1970, he added 263 with R E Marshall for the fourth wicket in the match against Middlesex at Lord's – a Hampshire record.

Daintes Abbia Livingstone had averaged over 100 in Club and Ground matches in 1959 and qualified for Championship games the following season, but despite looking a promising batsman, he couldn't command a regular place in the eleven.

He quietly learned that the exotic strokes of second eleven play were uneconomic in county cricket. He made his mark in the 1961 Championship winning year, when he was capped, and provided with Sainsbury, much of the prviously missing stiffening in the middle-order. During that summer, he was one of six batsmen to score over a thousand runs for the county. He accumulated his runs very patiently that year, but made them much more readily once he had settled into the first-class game. A stocky hard-hitting left-hand batsman, he made his maiden first-class hundred that summer in the match against Northamptonshire at Southampton, enabling Ingleby-Mackenzie to declare just before the close of play on the first day. Of course, it was Danny Livingstone who was guarding the mid-wicket boundary at Dean Park, Bournemouth on the evening of September 1st when Hampshire were playing Derbyshire. The County were desperately trying to break the last wicket partnership. Suddenly, Derbyshire wicket-keeper Bob Taylor struck a mighty blow into the skies off Peter Sainsbury and Danny stood calm to take the towering skier in his safe pair of hands – Hampshire had won the Championship and Danny had certainly played his part.

He had his best year the following season, when his 1,817 runs included 200 against Surrey at Southampton. He was dropped before he had scored; his innings which was his highest first-class score, contained three sixes and 22 fours. He set a ninth wicket record for Hampshire of 230 in the innings with Alan Castell and later in 1970, also set a the Hampshire fourth wicket record, when he and Roy Marshall added 263 in the match against Middlesex at Lord's.

After that, he was a reliable provider of runs in a side which despite the arrival of Barry Richards, was still short of batsmen.

A batsman of application and occasional brilliance, he played in every championship match of 1964, and had his best season so far, topping the County's batting averages. His performances included 117 and 105 not out against Kent at Canterbury.

Like his captain, Colin Ingleby-Mackenzie, Danny Livingstone enjoyed investing his ill-gotten gains on the Sport of Kings and rumour had it, that some of his gains from his benefit season in 1962, ended up with the bookmakers!

A useful one-day cricketer, he made his presence felt in the Gillette Cup competition of 1966 when Lincolnshire came a little close to victory. Hampshire eventually won by 31 runs with Danny Livingtone hitting 92 to win the Man of the Match award.

Playing his last game for the County in 1972, his talents were deserving of more success, but he still scored 12,722 runs in all matches at 27.89 with 16 hundreds.

Livingstone was not as a rule, a cricketer sporting the customary exuberance of a Sobers or Kanhai, but of something more native and natural to Hampshire, of the unforgiving, immovable Mead!

On leaving Hampshire, he returned to the land of his birth, Antigua, to take up an appointment with the Antigua Government as Director of Sport in the newly-created Sports Division. In that capacity, Danny quickly set about organising and structuring sporting leagues in the schools cricket and football in particular – a move which was largely responsible the healthy state of the sports in Antigua today. Upon his return, he captained the Antigua cricket team and later was manager, on several occasions, not only of the Antigua cricket team, but also the Leeward Islands and the Combined Leeward and Windward Islands team.

He was also involved in coaching cricket and football at national level and in fact, continued playing cricket with the village cricket Club right up to his early death on 8 September 1988. He was only fifty–five and died after suffering a stroke and being in hospital for four days. At the time of his death, he was a national cricket selector and chairman of the Sports Council.

Danny's contribution to the development of sport in Antigua

was immeasurable. His death was a tragic loss to that country and met with much sorrow by all his friends and many supporters in Hampshire.

# WALTER LIVSEY

Born: 23 September 1893, Todmorden
Died: 12 September 1978
Played: 1913–1929

FIRST-CLASS HAMPSHIRE RECORD

| Matches | Innings | NO | Runs | HS | Ave | 100s |
|---|---|---|---|---|---|---|
| 309 | 443 | 131 | 4818 | 110* | 15.44 | 2 |

*Number of Dismissals:* 375 caught; 254 stumped.

NOTABLE FEATS

- In 1914, he helped to dismiss nine Warwickshire batsmen in the match at Portsmouth.
- His best season behind the stumps was 1921 when he had 80 dismissals in 29 matches.
- In 1921, he added 192 with Alec Bowell for the tenth wicket in the match v Worcestershire at Bournemouth – a Hampshire record.

Walter Livsey was born at Todmorden on the Lancashire-Yorkshire border. His family came to London and, like Philip Mead, after playing for West of London schoolboys against East, he became a junior member of the professional staff at the Oval. But, with Herbert Strudwick in his prime, there was no opening for him and he was persuaded to move to Hampshire by Francis Bacon.

He gave an immediate sign of his class in 1913 when he was qualifying for the County, in the match against Oxford, only allowing three byes in an innings of 554. As soon as he became qualified for the county by residence, he was given a first-team place. In his first full season, he dismissed 62 batsmen – including a sensational stumping of Jack Hobbs off a sharply lifting ball from Alec Kennedy which swung wide outside the leg stump.

He wasn't demobbed in time for the summer of 1919, but returned the following seson as the county's regular wicket-keeper until ill-health caused his retirement at the end of the 1929 season. It is certainly arguable that he, and not George Brown, was second to Herbert Strudwick among English wicket-keepers of the twenties, but he was an extremely unlucky player.

In 1921, his 48 catches and 32 stumpings, comprised the best wicket-keeping record in the country and in 1922, he was in the Players side against the Gentlemen at Lord's and Scarborough.

In the same year he went to South Africa in the MCC team under F T Mann. This seemed to put him in the direct line of succession to Herbert Strudwick. Then, after his selection, but before the end of the season, he broke the index finger of his left hand: he made the trip nevertheless, but had the misfortune in only the sixth match of the tour at Queenstown of breaking the third finger of his right hand while batting, and so missed the major part of the tour, the wicket-keeping was taken over by George Brown.

Walter Livsey was a very fast and neat wicket-keeper; he played once for South v North and twice for England v The Rest in trial matches, but was never chosen for England. He was unlucky with injuries, though of course, he was never a first Test choice – though George Brown had the rather odd experience of keeping for England in three tests, though Livsey was Hampshire's regular wicket-keeper.

Though he was an outstanding wicket-keeper, Walter Livsey was perhaps better remembered for the part his batting played in some memorable Hampshire matches.

For most of his early seasons, he batted at No 10. In 1921 against Worcestershire, he and Bowell put on 192 for the tenth wicket in 110 minutes – only rarely exceeded as a last-wicket partnership in English first-class cricket. His own contribution was 70 not out as the pair established a Hampshire tenth wicket record.

Against Warwickshire in the following season in one of the most remarkable matches ever played, he scored his first century. The match was played at Edgbaton, Warwickshire batting first and scoring 223 and then on a perfectly good wicket, bowling Hampshire out for 15. Following-on, Hampshire's sixth wicket fell at 186, when they still wanted 22 to avoid an innings defeat. Brown and Shirley put on 85 for the seventh wicket, but after Shirley was out, McIntyre scored only five and Hampshire were only 66 ahead. Then Livsey and George Brown put on 177 for the ninth wicket and then Boyes helped him to add 70 for the last wicket after Brown's departure. Livsey had scored his first hundred in county cricket without giving a chance and in almost unbelievable circumstances, Warwickshire were dismissed for 158, Hampshire winning by 155 runs!

He had never made a century in his life, but subsequently he often opened the innings steadily; but he was always a wicket-keeper – and a very fine one – rather than a wicket-keeper – batsman.

In 1924, he more than played his part in Newman's benefit match against Surrey at Southampton. Set 235 to win, Hampshire lost their ninth wicket at 192. Then Livsey (35) and Boyes (8) made 43 runs for the last wicket to win the match and be carried off the ground shoulder high. His only other century was an unbeaten 109 in eighty-five minutes against Kent at Dover in 1928.

Livsey opted for the match against Surrey at Southampton in 1929 as his Benefit, but the game was over inside two days and though he received £750, it was something which he was obviously not too happy about!

Walter Livsey took his cricket very seriously and at times, even anxiously. Characteristically, his batting mannerism was to gnaw his glove before every ball, and part of his speed as a wicket-keeper derived from sheer nervous tension. Off the field, he was Lord Tennyson's valet and the combined strain of his two jobs, sometimes left him completely exhausted.

Still a good wicket-keeper, he retired from county cricket due to nervous ill-health in 1929, but his death at his home in Merton Park, London on 12 September 1978, did not occur until he was eleven days short of his eighty-fifth birthday.

# CHARLES LLEWELLYN

Born: 26 September 1876, Pietermaritzburg
Died: 7 June 1964
Played: 1899–1910

## FIRST-CLASS HAMPSHIRE RECORD

| Matches | Innings | NO | Runs | HS | Ave | 100 |
|---|---|---|---|---|---|---|
| 196 | 341 | 23 | 8772 | 216 | 27.58 | 15 |

| Runs | Wkts | Ave | Best |
|---|---|---|---|
| 17538 | 711 | 24.66 | 8-72 |

## NOTABLE FEATS

- He scored 1,000 runs in a season for Hampshire on five occasions.

- In 1901, he scored 153 and took 10 for 183 v Somerset at Taunton, and 14 for 171 v Worcestershire at Southampton.
- In 1905, he scored 102 and 100 v Derbyshire at Derby.
- Against Sussex at Hove in 1909, he scored 130 and 101*.
- He performed the 'double' on two occasions, 1901 and 1910, with his best performance coming in the latter year, when he scored 1,110 runs at 29.21 and captured 133 wickets at 20.45.

Charles Bennett Llewellyn was discovered by Major Poore while he was serving in South Africa and persuaded to come to England and qualify for Hampshire by residence. Poore was impressed by Llewellyn's orthodox slow left-arm bowling, but the South African, born at Pietermaritzburg of a mother born in Essex and a father born in Bootle, Lancashire of Welsh descent, not only learnt the art of the 'chinaman' but developed into one of Hampshire's major run-getters. Indeed, Llewellyn was destined to become the county's best all-round player in its history until the days of Kennedy, Newman and Brown. He created quite a stir when making his debut for Hampshire against the 1899 Australians at Southampton, scoring 72 and 21 and in addition, taking 8 for 132. As a result of this fine performance, Ranjitsinhji invited him to tour America and, although his team proved too powerful for the local opposition, the company of the calibre of Jessop, Sammy Woods, Ranji, Archie MacLaren, Stoddart and Bosanquet, must have broadened the cricketing horizons of the young Llewellyn.

Llewellyn was basically a forcing left-hand bat who excelled in the drive and cut, while his bowling was of the orthodox slow to medium left-arm with a high arm action. He was one of the first bowlers in English cricket to bowl the 'chinaman' regularly, an art that took several years to master, based on the advice of his fellow South African, the googly bowler Reggie Schwarz. These abilities were backed up by his outstanding fielding, particularly at mid-off. In 1900, though still not qualified, he gave proof of his potential reinforcement of the Hampshire side in the match against the first West Indian side to visit this country, when in addition to taking 13 wickets, he scored 93 in the first innings – though Hampshire lost the game by 88 runs.

On becoming eligible for the County Championship in 1901, Llewellyn came into a weak Hampshire side. Lacking bowling support in particular, he carried the attack with the only real assistance coming from Victor Barton, and as a result bowled four times as many overs as any other bowler. In dismissing 115 batsmen in the Championship his figures were only surpassed in the entire country by George Hirst and J R Mason and were up to that time, the best performance by a Hampshire bowler since they entered the championship.

This same season saw two highlights of his career – his best bowling performance, 14 for 171 v Worcestershire at Southampton and a scintillating innings of 215 against the second South African tourists. This was to prove the highest of his 18 centuries in all matches, scored in three hours and studded with 30 boundaries. As a result, he was asked to assist the touring side in two matches v London County, where he scored 88 and took 13 for 241 and Liverpool and Distict, where he again featured with 12 for 130 and in an innings of 51, enough to enable him to head the touring team's averages for both batting and bowling in all matches. His only other three figure score in 1901 was 153 v Somerset at Taunton, scored in 100 minutes and supplemented by 10 for 183.

Great things were expected of him in 1902 and although scoring only one century, he took 170 wickets (98 for Hampshire) and received recognition from the England selectors by his inclusion in the England XIV for the Edgbaston Test against Australia; it was a time when England fielded one of the greatest teams in her history, but on the morning of the match he was omitted along with Tom Hayward and J R Mason.

The 1903 season began most encouragingly for Llewellyn as he hit 148 in a good win over Derbyshire, but he fell away tragically from his fine form of the previous year. After a winter's cricket in his native South Africa, he seemed a little stale and his total haul of wickets dropped to 45 with each costing him the same figure.

Success in the following season proved sporadic, although 1905 showed something of a renaissance with two centuries in the match against Derbyshire and a brilliant 186 for Players of South v Gentlemen of South at Bournemouth, but his bowling suffered a reaction to the tremendous burden he had shouldered. In 1908, he had his best all-round season for quite a few years, scoring 1,131 runs and taking 83 wickets. It was his benefit year and a sum of over £500, the largest figure in Hampshire history to that date.The following year brought increased consistency as a batsman with four centuries, including two in a match against Sussex.

Further recognition came with his selection in 1910 as one of Wisden's Five Cricketers of the Year, ironically in what was to prove the final year of his association with Hampshire. This was in many ways to be his most rewarding season, for it saw his association with the rising star Jack Newman and between them they took 289 of the 424 wickets that fell in county matches. Llewellyn's contribution being 133 backed by over a thousand runs. During one period in 1910 in the course of nine consecutive innings, Llewellyn and Newman took all but one of their opponents' wickets. With two centuries during the season came another innings of 91 against Kent at Dover, termed by Wisden one of the most dazzling innings of the year, scored in an hour and including six tremendous drives for six, five of which were scored off Colin Blythe.

So it came as a great blow at the end of the season when he decided in spite of every effort by the committee to retain him, to end his engagement with Hampshire to go to Australia with the South African side that toured there that winter.

In 1911, he returned to England to take up a professional engagement with Accrington and in so doing became the first Test player to sign for a Lancashire League club. While playing for Accrington in 1912, he was called on to represent South Africa in the Triangular Tournament, playing in the first Test against England at Lord's, an innings of 75, having been given not out of his first ball when caught at the wicket on the leg side. He followed this with a further half-century against Australia at Lord's.

In 1913 while stll with Accrington, he scored 188 not out against Bacup, which remained the highest score in the Lancashire League until beaten by Learie Constantine's 192 not out for Nelson v East Lancashire in 1939. He later played in the Bradford League for Undercliffe and even at the age of fifty-five, he topped the bowling averages, in addition to being the only man to take 100 wickets in the Bolton League.

Living to see the County win the Championship in 1961, his aggregate figures in all matches of 11,425 runs and 1,013 wickets represented by far the best all-round cricket so far played by any Hampshire man.

# NEIL McCORKELL

Born: 23 March 1912, Portsmouth
Played: 1932–1951

FIRST-CLASS HAMPSHIRE RECORD

| Matches | Innings | NO | Runs | HS | Ave | 100s |
|---------|---------|-----|-------|-----|-------|------|
| 383 | 675 | 63 | 15834 | 203 | 25.87 | 17 |

| Runs | Wkts | Ave | Best |
|------|------|--------|------|
| 117 | 1 | 117.00 | 1-73 |

*Dismissals:* 512 caught; 176 stumped.

NOTABLE FEATS

- He scored 1,000 runs in a season for Hampshire on nine occasions.
- He dismissed 688 batsmen (512 caught 176 stumped) in his career with Hampshire.
- He did not concede a single bye in Leicestershire's innings of 535 for 8 declared in 1938.
- In 1951, he scored 203 v Gloucestershire at Gloucester.

One of Hampshire's oldest surviving players, Neil McCorkell was a talented wicket-keeper/batsman and was considered unlucky not to be selected for England.

It was Robert Relf, the former Sussex all-rounder who recommended the young wicket-keeper to be placed on the Hampshire groundstaff. It needed a strong recommendation to persuade the committee to spend more money on wages, for the Club's overdraft at that time had grown to £3,000. It was a wise decision, for after making his first-class debut in the second match of the 1932 season, he appeared in every match afterwards. Strong in defence, he batted well on occasions and was the discovery of the season, dismissing seven batsmen in the match againt Glamorgan at Bournemouth.

In those early years, he was a defensive batsman, his most effective stroke being the square-cut, though he also made many runs through drives on both sides of the wicket. Not the most elegant of batsmen, he was at his best in a crisis, thwarting the best of bowlers.

In 1935, he was asked to open the Hampshire innings due to R H Moore's absence through illness and for the first of what was to be nine occasions, he scored 1,000 runs. He had now developed the hook, but the hallmark of his play was the lateness with which he could play his strokes. A small, neat man, Neil McCorkell fell only slightly short of test selection – unlucky not to be selected for England, he was in competition with Ames and then Gibb. He represented the Players against the Gentlemen at Lord's in 1936, then just missed out on the MCC team to Australia the following winter.

He kept equally well to fast and slow bowling and season in, season out, missed very few chances. His best season was 1937 when he helped dismiss sixty-eight victims (50 caught 18 stumped), it earning him selection for the 1937–38 tour of India, in Lord Tennyson's team.

Of compact build, Neil McCorkell carried out his duties behind the stumps with the minimum of fuss. In 1938 when Leicestershire scored 535 for 8 declared, he did not concede a single bye! a county record. As a batsman, he was going from strength to strength –

against Kent, he and Johnny Arnold put on 102 in the first innings and 100 in the second. Also in 1938 in the first Championship game to be played on the Isle of Wight against Northamptonshire at Newport, he hit a six with just five minutes remaining to produce a seven-wicket win.

Owing to the war years, those deserving a benefit outnumbered the seasons available and so the Hampshire committee decided that the five senior professionals should share a joint benefit. This was thought the most equitable way of dealing with a very difficult situation, though a £1,000 reward for each of them seems a meagre amount when compared with today's figures. In 1947, he topped 1,500 runs and kept wicket consistently well throughout the summer – allowing no byes in a Yorkshire score of 464 for five at Bournemouth.

Against Kent in 1948, Hampshire scored 443 for six, McCorkell scoring an unbeaten 153. In 1949, he lost his place as wicket-keeper to Leo Harrison, for he wasn't at his best behind the wickets. However, he was in splendid form with the bat, topping the county averages by a margin of six runs. The following season, McCorkell and Rogers were an admirable opening pair, putting on 199 against Nottinghamshire at Trent Bridge and 193 in the corresponding fixture in 1951.

In this his last season, he made the highest score of his first-class career, 203 against Gloucestershire at Gloucester, and as befitted this conscientious cricketer, he was given the Hampshire captaincy for the last match of the season against Sussex.

At the close of the season, he decided to retire and take a coaching post in South Africa, at Parktown Boys High School in Johannesburg.

After nearly thirty years at the school, he retired to the Natal South Coast, where he lives with his wife and family. In fact, his son Denis, who was on the Hampshire staff for a short period, is now also retired and living nearby.

Neil had an outstanding playing record as opening batsman and wicket-keeper. It was a tribute to his dedication and fitness that he was able to carry out this role with so much success over many seaons. In fact, his record number of dismissals has only just been surpassed by Bobby Parks during the 1992 season.

# MALCOLM MARSHALL

Born: 18 April 1958 St Michael, Barbados
Played: 1979–1992

FIRST-CLASS HAMPSHIRE RECORD

| Matches | Innings | NO | Runs | HS | Ave | 100s |
|---|---|---|---|---|---|---|
| 197 | 253 | 35 | 5597 | 117 | 25.67 | 5 |

| Runs | Wkts | Ave | Best |
|---|---|---|---|
| 14542 | 798 | 18.22 | 8-71 |

NOTABLE FEATS

● In 1982, he took 134 wickets for Hampshire at 15.73 runs each.
● He performed the hat-trick v Somerset at Taunton in 1983.
● In 1986, he took 100 wickets for Hampshire at 15.08 runs each.
● One of the leading all-rounders in the country in 1990, he scored 962 runs at 45.81 and took 72 wickets at 19.18.

Malcolm Marshall has been consistenly whole-hearted for Hampshire since making his debut against Glamorgan in 1979. He has served the county better and for longer than might have been expected of one on whom enormous demands were placed by his country – when he eventually ends his county career, he will leave Hampshire a deservedly popular man.

He was born in the village of St Michael, Barbados on 18 April 1958. A right-arm fast bowler, he first played for his island team in the final match of the 1977–78 Shell Shield and took six Jamaican wickets. He was chosen for the West Indies' World Cup squad in 1979, although he did not play and in the same summer, he began his county career with Hampshire. The Hampshire secretary noted: 'He is an opening bowler and useful lower-order batsman and comes with a good reputation as a fielder. Although he may take time to settle to English conditions, Hampshire have high hopes that he will develop quickly with experience.'

On the day that Malcolm Marshall made his debut for Hampshire in early May of 1979, flurries of snow blew in to his face, as he ran into bowl. It was certainly a strange introduction to English cricket for one brought up on the year-round sunshine of the Caribbean, but it failed to bother the 21-year-old – Marshall took seven wickets in the match and was firmly set on a course of terrorising English batsmen at both Test and county level. In fact, he topped the county bowling averages, as he did in 1981 after a year playing international cricket.

Initially, he wasn't particularly successful at Test level, for after seventeen Tests he had taken 55 wickets at 28 runs apiece. Three of those Tests had been in India in 1978–79 when he had to be elected for the tour after one game for Barbados, as all the established bowlers had signed for the W.S.C; and at the end of that series, he had three very expensive wickets. In fact, he didn't really fit into the West Indians' scheme until given the new ball by Clive Lloyd and made leader of his attack – someone in the know had already appreciated the extraordinary pace he could develop. In 1982, he came second to Richard Hadlee in the national average though he took twice as many wickets, 134 – the highest return since the county programme was reduced in 1969. It was a tip from Denis Lillee after a match in Melbourne during the West Indies tour of Australia which helped Marshall develop and perfect a delivery he thought had earned him between 40 and 50 wickets for Hampshire that season in fact, he took 44 more wickets than the next bowler, Nick Cook – a phenomenal performance that might well not be repeated this century. He was without doubt, the fastest bowler in England and took five wickets in an innings for Hampshire on twelve occasions – a figure not recorded in the county since the days of Derek Shackleton. It was the season too, in which he produced his best ever figures with the ball, taking 8 for 71 against Worcestershire at Southampton. He also came fourth in the Hampshire batting averages, hitting his maiden Championship century, 116 not out against Lancashire at Southampton.

In county cricket, Marshall was carrying out experiments on Hampshire's opponents. He developed an inswinger and more importantly, reduced his run-up with no loss of lethalness, whilst accumulating notes on every batsman for his mental file. Although for some years he was widely thought to be the fastest bowler in the world, he can now call upon more subtle weapons. Marshall is a master of changes of pace, slight enough to be concealed, but also distinct enough to confuse.

Marshall's success is not the product of natural ability. He keeps himself superbly fit and never gives less than 100% for any team. He sees county cricket not just as a means of the all-year round employment, but as a way to sharpen his skills both as a bowler and as a serious batsman. Like all West Indians, he is stylish and loves to hit the ball. He does not, as some fast bowlers do, worry about receiving a dose of his own medicine and when he broke a bone in the field against England at Headingley in 1984, he not only bowled better than ever (seven wickets for 53) but batted one-handed with great courage.

Marshall himself has broken many a bone with a nasty skidding bouncer – such injuries give him no pleasure – but he obviously believes that cricket is a tough game and as such, it should be played by tough men. Of all the great fast-bowlers in the history of the game, Malcolm Marshall is probably the least spectacular. For him, there is no gradual acceleration just a sharp stutter of the feet before he breaks into a direct sprint, smooth and swift.

When he delivers the ball, the right arm comes over with great rapidity, having used a high left arm as a sighter. Marshall runs past the stumps like a world-class sprinter breasting the finishing tape – such is his superb athleticism that he achieves blistering pace, formidable accuracy and movement off the seam.

In 1986, he took 100 wickets at 5.08, though his 35 wickets during the West Indies' 4–0 victory in 1988, was arguably the high point of his career – No West Indian has ever taken more wickets in a series. Anyone who saw him at work in 1990 will have been in no doubt that they were watching the complete bowler. He reached his full pace only when the pitch's response demanded it and such occurences were rare. During Portsmouth week, Hampshire's championship challenge was nourished by two victories. In both, Marshall's bowling was influential and in the second, it was decisive as he took 7 for 17 in a memorable spell against Derbyshire. Marshall has always believed that he had it in him to become an all-rounder and has in recent years, moved up the order in the Hampshire side. It was during this season that he hit his highest first-class score, 117 against Yorkshire at Headingley.

In 1990, Marshall's contract had a year to run and he made no secret of the fact that it would be his last. At the age of thirty-two, fitness worries begun to niggle at him and he even looked tired and overweight. Hampshire went so far as to register a potential successor, on Marshall's recommendation, the Guyanese Linden Joseph.

In June 1992, Malcolm signed to play Currie Cup cricket with Natal later in the year. His signing followed South Africa's return to the cricket fold and their historic Test match against the West Indies in Barbados. In July, he finally savoured the Cup Final win he wanted as Hampshire took the Benson and Hedges cup with a 41-run win over Kent (Marshall taking 3 for 33). The West Indies paceman has twice missed Lord's finals – in 1991 when Hampshire won the Nat West Trophy and in 1988 when the County won their first Benson and Hedges Cup.

However, though he has ended his Test career, he has been encouraged to assume more responsibility and has agreed to a new three-year deal that will keep him at Hampshire to the end of 1993.

A golden era in Hampshire cricket will end when Malcolm Marshall ends his association with the club, for to most Hampshire followers, he is irreplaceable.

# ROY MARSHALL

Born: 25 April 1930 St Michael, Barbados
Died: 27 October 1992
Played: 1953–1972

FIRST-CLASS HAMPSHIRE RECORD

| Matches | Innings | NO | Runs | HS | Ave | 100s |
|---------|---------|-----|-------|------|-------|------|
| 504 | 890 | 49 | 30303 | 228* | 36.03 | 60 |

| Runs | Wkts | Ave | Best |
|------|------|-------|------|
| 2403 | 99 | 24.27 | 6-36 |

NOTABLE FEATS

- He was Captain of Hampshire from 1966 to 1970.
- His best season was 1961, when he scored 2,607 runs – he topped the two thousand run mark on three other occasions.
- He hit three double-centuries for Hampshire, with a highest of 228* v Pakistanis at Bournemouth in 1962.
- In 1968, he added 227 with B L Reed v Bedfordshire at Goldington to establish the Hampshire first wicket record in the Gillette Cup.
- In 1970, he added 263 for the fourth wicket with D A Livingstone in the match v Middlesex at Lord's to set a new Hampshire record.

No cricketer who had ever appeared for the County had been able to attract crowds to Hampshire grounds as did Roy Marshall.

He was born in Barbados on 25 April 1930 and in January 1946, when he was still under sixteen years of age, he made his first-class debut for Barbados against Trinidad.

It was in 1950, when we were being dazzled by the batting of Weekes, Worrell and Walcott, that Roy Marshall came to England as one of the lesser lights of a powerful West Indies side. At nineteen, he was the youngest member of the party and almost as soon as they arrived, he fell ill. Despite that setback, he scored 1,117 runs – with three centuries and a 99 – on the tour without being picked for a Test. To begin with, he struggled, but an innings of 135 against Hampshire at Southampton, one of the most brilliant played on the ground, was an innings which clearly shaped his destiny!

The following English season, he returned as professional for Lowerhouse in the Lancashire League and set a club aggregate record of 969 runs. He then gained selection for the 1951–52 West Indies team to Australia. On that tour, Marshall appeared in two Tests against Australia and a further two when the side went to New Zealand, but his best innings was a splendid century against New South Wales. Marshall spent a second year in the Lancashire League in 1952, but in September of that year, he was offered a contract with Hampshire and decided to take a chance and stay in England to qualify by residence.

Although he wasn't available for Championship matches, he made top score – 81 – in the pre-season match with Somerset, 122 against the Army and in the Australian game on an unusually difficult Southampton wicket, a most spectacular 71 in less than an hour-and-a-half. The next time he could play for the county during his qualifying period was against the 1954 Pakistanis. He was lbw to Fazal Mahmood for 0 in both innings – the only 'pair' he ever suffered in his life! In 1955, his first season after qualifying, he scored 1,890 runs at 36.34 in an attractive manner that gave confidence to the rest of the side. He scored 71 out of the first 94 runs made, making the Lancashire attack, including Statham, look quite ordinary. At Bournemouth that summer, when Hampshire needed 71 in thirty-four minutes to beat Leicestershire, he made 47 to finish it with seven minutes to spare. In 1956, after a poor start on wet wickets, when he found the ball coming through slower, he won the Middlesex match at Lord's almost single-handed with 112. The following year, he scored the fastest century of the season – in sixty-six minutes – with twenty fours, twelve of them from consecutive strokes.

Roy did not seem to mind much if he got out. He batted as though there was always tomorrow and plenty more runs to be picked up. He enjoyed making them and liked to experiment – he could not resist a challenge. He scored most of his runs square of the wicket, cutting or hooking, but he could drive superbly.

Everyone who ever watched Roy Marshall, remembers different achievements of his batting. There were two savage blows with which on an awkward, lifting pitch, he hit Ron Archer, a pace bowler of the 1953 Australian tourists back over his head into Northlands Road; there was the superb uppercut with which he hit Ted Dexter over third man at Portsmouth and then there was the stroke which cost him his wicket when Bob Blair, the New Zealand fast bowler, set two third men to him, and Marshall attempted to late cut him for a six and was caught on the boundry behind second slip!

Roy Marshall was also a very capable off-spinner, but could bowl medium-pace and an adequate leg-break. In 1956 when Hampshire won in Yorkshire for the first time for twenty-three years, he took nine wickets and had his best analysis, 6 for 36 against Surrey, the County Champions at Portsmouth.

One of his more memorable seasons was 1961 when Hampshire won the Championship for the first time.

He scored 2,607 runs for the county that summer at an average of 43.45 and a highest score of 212, after Hampshire had been more than 100 behind on the first innings against Somerset at Bournemouth. The pitch was helping the spinners, but Marshall set about Langford, who was expected to have the winning of the match in his hands – Hampshire won in the end by 63 runs. His 153 in the second innings enabled Hampshire to score 310 in four hours twenty minutes to beat Surrey. Yet, he can never have played a better innings than he did against Yorkshire at Dean Park at the end of the season. The championship was already won and Yorkshire, the reigning champions, had been beaten into second place. Yorkshire won the toss and finally set Hampshire 245 to win in two hundred minutes. The pitch was responsive to Trueman's cut and even more so to the spin of Close and Illingworth. Marshall scored 109 out of 170 in a total of 186 and although he scored at 45 an hour, it was for him a care-laden innings. Indeed, he was only out when Fred Trueman's direct throw hit the stumps to run him out, as he was hogging the bowling. As he walked in, a wise Hampshire follower, long-informed in cricket, turned and said: 'If Roy Marshall cared to bat like that every day, he would make 4,000 runs every season.' He paused and then added, 'But then he wouldn't be Marshall.'

He hit three double-centuries, all for Hampshire, the highest being 228 not out against the Pakistani tourists in 1962. His last double century came in his final season of 1972, when he hit 203 in mid-August against Derbyshire and was 69 not out when play ended Hampshire's final match of the year against Yorkshire at Southampton.

Following his retirement in 1972, he continued to live in Southampton: he played for Deanery and in 1974, produced two fine innings for MCC against Ireland in Dublin. He later moved to Somerset to coach at King's College, Taunton, where he was happy, with happy customers in charge of the Westgate Inn in the same town. To clutter up an appraisal of Roy Marshall with statistics would be superfluous, just to see him bat was proof enough of singular talent.

He became involved in the game as Chairman Cricket Committee, Somerset CCC, before his untimely death in a Taunton hospice in October 1992.

# PHILIP MEAD

Born: 9 March 1887, Battersea
Died: 26 March 1958
Played: 1905–1936

FIRST-CLASS HAMPSHIRE RECORD

| Matches | Innings | NO | Runs | HS | Ave | 100s |
|---|---|---|---|---|---|---|
| 700 | 1171 | 170 | 48892 | 280* | 48.84 | 138 |

| Runs | Wkts | Ave | Best |
|---|---|---|---|
| 9252 | 266 | 34.78 | 7-18 |

NOTABLE FEATS

- He scored 1,000 runs in a season for Hampshire on twenty-seven occasions.
- He carried his bat on three occasions with a best of 120* out of 234 v Yorkshire at Huddersfield, in 1911.
- He scored a hundred in both innings of match on three occasions with a best of 113 and 124 v Sussex at Horsham in 1921.
- He scored eleven double centuries for the county with a best of 280* v Nottinghamshire at Southampton in 1921, when he also topped the national averages with 2,438 runs at 67.72.
- He topped the national average again in 1933, scoring 2,478 runs at 68.83 and a top score of 227 v Derbyshire at Ilkeston.
- In 1927, he added 344 with G Brown v Yorkshire at Portsmouth to set a new Hampshire record for the third wicket partnership.
- He topped 2,000 runs in a season on nine occasions, with a best of 2,854 in 1928.
- He held 629 catches in his career with Hampshire – a county record.
- His final career total of 48,892 runs at 48.84 with 138 hundreds is likely to remain the record for all time.

Philip Mead must be numbered among the major batsmen in the history of cricket. A massively competent and consistent left-hander, he scored 55,061 runs – more than anyone else except Sir Jack Hobbs, Frank Woolley and Patsy Hendren. His 48,892 runs for Hampshire though, is the greatest aggregate of anyone for a single club in the history of the game. He was born in Battersea, was ony ten when he scored the first century in South London School League cricket and played in the London schools match. At fifteen, he was taken on the ground staff at The Oval, primarily as a slow left-arm bowler. During that time, he formed a friendship with a team mate, Jack Hobbs, that was to last a lifetime; but he was one of a group of players not retained at the end of the 1903 season. The circumstances in which he left Surrey have never been fully explained. One theory was that he upset the stuffy Surrey Committee when, on being told to remove his rolled-up sweater before he commenced bowling, he refused because he had no shirt on underneath!

Soon afterwards, Surrey changed their minds and offered him fresh terms, but it was too late; two days after leaving the Oval, Mead had accepted an invitation to qualify for Hampshire.

He made his debut in 1905 against the Australian touring team, taking 2 for 56 in a total of 620 and scoring 41 not out against 'Tibby' Cotter, whom Jack Hobbs reckoned the fastest bowler he ever faced. In 1906, Mead appeared for the first time in a Championship match and, opening against Surrey, scored a duck and 3. In his next game against Yorkshire, he scored 60 and 109. Wisden noted that 'his 109 as regards sound judgement and hard hitting, was such an admirable innings, that everyone, including the Yorkshire bowlers thought that a first-rate left-handed batsman had come to the front.'

Between 1906 and 1910, Mead learnt the craft of batsmanship. He was a natural batsman who timed the ball to perfection and was always severe on any loose deliveries. During those years he never averaged fewer than 1,000 runs per season and occasionally, such as when he took 7 for 18 against Norhamptonshire, as they were bowled out for 60 in 1908, he proved a valuable second-string bowler.

By 1911, he had established himself as the soundest left-handed batsman in England, scoring 1,706 runs in the championship at an average of 58.82, including six centuries. In all cricket, he became the first Hampshire player to score 2,000 runs, helped by a magnificent 223 on his debut for the Players against the Gentlemen at Scarborough, but perhaps his greatest feat was against Yorkshire at Huddersfield when he carried his bat through an innings of 234 for a score of 120 not out. His achievements led to his inclusion as one of Wisden's Five Cricketers of the Year, and an invitation to tour Australia with MCC under Pelham Warner.

That side was one of the strongest ever sent out by MCC, but Mead's contribution to the 4–1 series victory was meagre. Only in the Third Test, when he made 46 out of 63 for the fifth wicket with Jack Hobbs did his batting rise above the mediocre.

Back in England, Mead shrugged off the disappointments of the winter and together with Fry and Johnston, he formed a trio from Hampshire that topped the national averages. The side's greatest triumph was over Australia – Mead making 160 and 33 without being dismissed from either innings. In 1913, he scored 2,495 runs at an average of 51.91, achieving an ambition by heading the National averages, narrowly beating his old friend and rival Jack hobbs. Both men toured South Africa in the winter of 1913–14, Mead scoring solidly with two centuries in the second and fifth Tests – it was in many ways his best tour.

For the second year running in 1914, Mead scored over 2,000 runs for Hampshire, coming third in the national averages behind Hobbs and J T Hearne. He scored seven centuries, with a best of 213 against Yorkshire. Wisden commented 'Only 27, he should prove a tower of strength to Hampshire for many seasons to come.' But of course, Mead was to lose the next four years of his career to the Great War.

Philip Mead was a man of superstition and ritual, who despite his large total of centuries, experienced attacks of nervousness in the nineties. He had one odd mannerism; before settling into his rather cramped stance, he would undergo a lenthy routine, involving looking round the field, touching his cap peak four times; next grounding his bat, he tapped it four times in the crease before finally shuffling his feet up to it. If any impatient bowler attempted to bowl before he had completed the ritual, he simply held up his hand, stopped him and began it all over again.

Mead was the county batsman in form in 1921, scoring 3,179 runs in all matches at 69.10 and topped the county's averages, but he was not picked for England until the fourth Test. However, it was in the fifth and final Test at the Oval that he made his mark. He scored 182 not out, a record for England against Australia at home that was to stand until Len Hutton.

In the six weeks from the beginning of June to mid-July, he scored 1,601 runs in nineteen innings. His 280 not out against Nottinghamshire at Southampton remains a record for the ground, although the Notts captain was convinced that Mead had simply stonewalled for five hours! He was so ill during the winter of 1921–22 with pneumonia that the doctors had despaired of his life, but he returned the following summer to score 2,270 runs at 63.05 and a top score of 235 in 185 minutes againt Worcestershire as Hampshire won by an innings and 115 runs. His appearance as he came waddling to the wicket caused more bad language among bowlers than any other batsman! Yet, for a man of his build, he was impressively quick on his feet. He took no risks, but he never missed scoring off the loose ball and he would invariably score one off the fifth ball or failing that the sixth, in order to get to the other end!

On the 1922–23 tour of South Africa, after the other four of the first five batsmen had made only 41 between them in the Durban Test, he shored up the innings with a score of 181. Although he continued to be one of the most consistently heavy scorers in the country, he was not called back to an England side until the first-Brisbane Test of 1928–29. Then he scored 8 and 73, was dropped and left international cricket with a batting average of 49.37 from only seventeen Tests.

Any bat which happened to be in the dressing-room would do for him to pick up and use to make a hundred. Often he did not go to the nets for weeks on end. 'You lead in May, but I'll catch you in June' he used to say. It was certainly true in 1927, when between the end of May and the latter half of June, in 14 consecutive innings, he totalled 1,257 runs at an average of 125.7. On July 19th that season, when he scored 100 not out against Northants, Mead became the first left-hander to score 100 hundreds and only the fourth batsman ever to achieve the feat. As F S Ashley-Cooper noted at the time, Mead's average when he passed the 100 mark was 202.87!

The following year at the age of forty-one, he enjoyed another glorious summer, scoring 3,027 run in all matches at 75.67 – a season when he was amused to find himself on paper, also top of the county's bowling table (14 wickets at 17.5 each). It was on the strength of this form and the recommendation of Jack Hobbs that he was picked for the MCC party to tour Australia.

It was often said that Philip Mead was a slow scorer. Yet for the MCC Australian side against Lord Hawke's XI at Scarborough in 1929, against bowlers of the calibre of 'Gubby' Allen and Wilfred Rhodes, he scored 233 in a few minutes over five hours; and Wisden records such other innings as 180 in three-and-a-half hours, 213 in four and a quarter and 110 in two and a quarter.

Most of the other outstanding batsmen of his time played in strong batting sides and carried less responsibility than Mead did – he had to carry an uncertain Hampshire batting side for many years and as Altham and Swanton wrote, 'if Mead took root the odds against a finish automatically became considerable'. Alec Kennedy once said of Mead, 'Sometimes I used to think he made more runs on turning wickets than on good ones.' Jim Langridge, a major slow left-arm bowler, shared that opinion. 'Many a time I've been bowling at Philip when he wanted one for his fifty or hundred and spun a lifter in to his hip and he's gone up on his toes and wristed it through the short legs and almost before it was off his bat, he's off down the wicket saying "There that's another ton of coal for the winter".'

With an innings of 104 not out against Derbyshire at Southampton in 1932, he achieved the feat of having scored a century against every first-class county. In May 1934, he was part of the Hampshire team that gave the Australian tourists something of a shock when they scored 420 in their first innings. Mead's contribution was 139, described by Bradman as a truly great innings. Mead returned the compliment by catching Bradman at slip before he had scored.

Stiffened by rheumatism and failing in eyesight, he left Hampshire at the end of 1936. He had appeared in exactly 700 matches for the county, scoring 48,892 runs at 48.84 and 138 centuries. Statistics however, cannot clearly show how, year after year he carried the Hampshire batting – a cricketer's cricketer; not only bowlers, but also his fellow batsmen, respected his skill.

He joined Suffolk in 1938 at the age of fifty-one, was top of their averages in the Minor Counties with a figure of 76.80 and a year later not only was their most successful batsman, but finished second in the second-class averages with 71.23.

Before the end of the Second World War, Philip Mead had gone blind. After the War, he went to Hampshire's matches to talk with the players and his old friends at the club whilst the play was described to him. In 1949, he was elected an Honorary Life Member of the MCC, a tribute that meant a lot to him. He died in Boscombe on 16 March 1958 – an immortal of his game.

# DICK MOORE

Born: 14 November 1913, Bournemouth
Played: 1931–1939

## FIRST-CLASS HAMPSHIRE RECORD

| Matches | Innings | NO | Runs | HS | Ave | 100s |
|---|---|---|---|---|---|---|
| 129 | 225 | 7 | 5885 | 316 | 26.99 | 10 |

| Runs | Wkts | Ave | Best |
|---|---|---|---|
| 978 | 25 | 39.12 | 3-46 |

## NOTABLE FEATS

- He was captain of Hampshire in 1936 and 1937.
- He scored 316 in 380 minutes on the first day of the match against Warwickshire at Bournemouth in 1937 – Hampshire's highest individual score.

Dick Moore was a magnificent batsman, whose bold and positive captaincy caused him to be remembered with great admiration by those who played under him.

Almost Dick Moore's first association with Hampshire cricket was a visit accompanied by his father, a baker, to 'Mead and Toomers' sports shop, where a bat was solemnly purchased and Dick was required by Phil Mead to demonstrate some shots, which seemed to meet with the great man's approval. Little did Dick Moore realise that within five years, he would be playing in the same Hampshire team as Phil Mead or that ten years later, he would be captain of the county team in which Mead was still playing.

A former Bournemouth schoolboy, he was one of the most promising batsmen the county had found for some years. Essentially orthodox, with a full back-lift and free swing of the bat, Moore was a competent puller and cutter, but a tremendous vertical bat-stroke maker off front or back foot. He was already a fine fast-wicket player, but whatever the strengths or weaknesses of his technique, they cannot have been particularly apparent on his debut for the County in 1931 at the age of seventeen-and-a-half.

Two years later, whilst he was working for his father in his bakery business in Bournemouth, a message came through that Phil Mead's varicose veins were so bad that he was unable to play in the final home game of that 1933 season against Essex. It wasn't too long before Moore was out there, facing Kenneth Farnes, one of the fastest bowlers of all time. He began to bounce the ball at the young apprentice batsman, but to no avail, for Dick Moore refused to depart. That most flamboyant of characters, Leonard Crawley was fielding at cover in golf shoes and he showed his disapproval of Farnes' tactics. In fact, Dick Moore had to return to the pavilion during this initiation in order to hammer out his box, which Farnes had turned inside out! Moore went on to score 159 – it remained his highest score in first-class cricket until his epic innings at Bournemouth four years later.

In 1934, he appeared in every match and scored 1,536 runs, adding to the power of the Hampshire batting line-up. The following summer, Moore was ill with scarlet fever and was only able to play in five matches. At the end of that season, the County finished second from bottom in the Championship and so Moore was given the captaincy. Of all the captains that Dick Moore had played under, Lionel Tennyson occupied an especial place in his affections. He always made him feel comfortable and in fact, treated him like a son. Phil Mead was also a great help to the young cricketer, who was often called upon to lead 10 seasoned professionals. Moore recalls that Mead once said to him: 'When you get a bad ball, skipper, don't always try and hit it for four. Place it for two and nine times out of ten, it'll go for four!' His friend and contemprary, O W 'Lofty' Herman writing in the very readable 'One Hundred Years at Southampton' and coupling him with Lionel Tennyson and Geoffrey Lowndes refers to ' . . . Dick

Moore, who also set off with a win in mind'. Yet the brochure does not do justice to Dick Moore's stature as a batsman. The fact that his triple hundred, still the highest individual score for Hampshire is not listed under 'A Century of Statistics' compiled by Vic Isaacs, the county scorer is quite understandable, since the list deals only with the County ground.

In his first game as Captain of Hampshire at Southampton in 1936, he made a hundred against Derbyshire.

His great innings came at Bournemouth in July 1937 when he made 316 in 380 minutes – it was the highest score made for Hampshire, overtaking Poore's 304 in 1899. Hampshire's opponents that day were Warwickshire, the occasion also proving to be the County's best win of the season as well. Moore was the last man out, lbw to a very weary Eric Hollies off the last ball of the day, hitting 43 fours and 3 sixes as Hampshire totalled 509. Herman and Creese then dismissed the opposition twice and Hampshire won by an innings and 143 runs. Moore continued as captain this season, providing the public with the most enterprising cricket in the championship, he accepted each and every challenge and on several occasions, this led to the defeat of the County. Moore led by example, and opening the batting he attacked the bowling, often to the point, where on occasion he could be accused of being reckless !

Owing to the pressure of work, Dick Moore was compelled to give up the cataincy in 1938 with Paris replacing him. He was only able to appear in a few matches, but with the aid of two hundreds, topped the County averages by a large margin, scoring 770 runs at 45.29. This only emphasized what a loss he was from the regular strength on sheer figures, regardless of his desirable pace of run-making.

Like most cricketers of his generation, some of Dick Moore's best years were lost to the war, but he did represent the Gentlemen against the Players. Though he was a competent batsman against all types of bowling, he admits to not getting too many runs against Harold Larwood and cites one occasion when he was caught at slip off him by Arthur Carr halfway to the boundary! Also in those days, there wasn't the same array of protective gear as there is today and when Moore's team-mate George Brown went out to bat, he wrapped three towels round his leg. Larwood struck him on the towel and Brown waved to his skipped cheerily, then when he was ready to face the next one, he fell flat on his face! On leaving Hampshire, he played for Colwyn Bay; representing North Wales against an Australian Professionals XI, which included Bruce Dooland, Cec Pepper and George Tribe, three magnificent wrist spinners, he scored 44 runs of his sides total of 70 odd by means of a superb exhibition of batsmanship on a wicket well-suited to wrist spin.

# JACK NEWMAN

Born: 12 November 1884, Southsea
Died: 21 December 1973
Played: 1906–1930

## FIRST-CLASS HAMPSHIRE RECORD

| Matches | Innings | NO | Runs | HS | Ave | 100s |
|---|---|---|---|---|---|---|
| 506 | 786 | 121 | 13904 | 166* | 20.90 | 9 |

| Runs | Wkts | Ave | Best |
|---|---|---|---|
| 48305 | 1946 | 24.82 | 9-131 |

## NOTABLE FEATS

- He scored 1,000 runs in a season for Hampshire on six occasions.
- He took 100 wickets in a season for Hampshire on nine occasions.
- In 1909, he performed the hat-trick v Australians at Southampton.
- His best season with the ball was 1921, when he took 177 wickets at 21.56, including his creer best of nine for 131 v Essex at Bournemouth.
- In 1926, he scored 1156 runs at 28.90 and captured 145 wickets at 23.82, including match figures of 14 for 148 v Gloucestershire at Bournemouth.
- In 1927, he scored 1281 runs at 32.02 and captured 105 wickets at 21.46 including match figures of 16 for 88 v Somerset at Weston-super-Mare.

One of the finest all-rounders who ever played for Hampshire, Jack Newman in all matches, scored 15,333 runs and took 2,032 wickets. In 1927, when well past forty, he was the first player to complete the 'double' – a feat he achieved five times. In spite of his remarkable ability, Newman never played for England, but his consistency for his county was truly amazing.

He was born in Southsea, but when he was quite young, his parents moved to Bitterne, not then a suberb of Southampton, but a village with a character and identity of its own. There was no school cricket, but as a self-taught player, he became a member of the local Sunday School cricket team. One Saturday morning of his last year at school, just before he was fourteen, he went to watch a match at the County Ground. Watching the Hampshire players at net practice, he picked up a ball that was hit towards him and asked if he might bowl. He was given permission and after a few minutes, Tom Soar, a senior professional fetched the secretary, Frank Bacon to look at him. The same morning, Bacon took Newman into his office and offered him an engagement on the ground staff.

Primarily, Newman was an off-break bowler who spun the ball hard and had natural flight and pace off the pitch. Unfortunately, he could never bring himself to bowl round the wicket so that frequently, on responsive wickets, he turned the ball too much. Often too, he ran eagerly across the line of the wicket as to unsight the umpire when he appealed for l.b.w; his colleagues thought that habit cost him many wickets. He varied his off-breaks with a well concealed quicker ball which went with his arm. Perhaps in his early days, he used it too often so that batsmen were not taken by surprise, but it constantly took wickets by means of slip catches: 'caught Mead bowled Newman' was a frequent entry in Hampshire scorebooks.

Jack Newman was a sensitive man and cricket could often irritate him – sometimes he would point to the bent places in the pavillion railings at Southampton and say: 'Look at those dents – all from batsmen edging my quickie for four.'

In 1909 against the Australian team that won the Ashes from England, Hampshire who were without Fry and Sprot had the distinction of dismissing their opponents for 83 – this was a great triumph for Jack Newman, who took eight for 43 and did the hat-trick with the last three balls of the innings.

In taking 156 wickets at 18.45 each in 1910, he jumped right to the front among English bowlers and indeed, only four in the country exceeded his number of victims. Though he still lacked something in consistency of length, he was a bowler of lively pace and aggression. Sir Pelham Warner in an article in that year's Wisden singled him out as a young cricketer of outstanding promise.

Tennyson grossly overbowled the willing Newman and Kennedy, putting them on at the start of an innings and leaving them on for hours on end. In 1921 for instance, they sent down between them 14,792 balls and captured 340 wickets. When they got the opposing side out, they would often be told to put their pads on and open the innings – Jack enjoyed this total involvement!

He performed the 'double' five times beween that season of 1921 and 1928, being the first to do so in 1921, when he also achieved his best-ever figures of nine for 131 against Essex at Bournemouth.

He fell from grace just once in 1922, when he did something which has become fashionable in recent times, he kicked the stumps down. Hampshire were playing Nottinghamshire and the

Trent Bridge crowd were up to their familiar goading chants as Newman was at pains to re-arrange his field before trying the experiment of bowling round the wicket. The bowler could not refrain from showing his contempt. His captain Hon. Lionel Tennyson sent him from the field, made him apologise, told him not to do such a thing again and gave him a fiver, knowing what a fundamentally good chap he was!

At Hove in 1923, he dismissed three Sussex batsmen in the course of four balls. In 1926, he had his best all-round season, typified by his scores of 66 and 42 not out and 14 for 148 in the match against Gloucestershire. The following season, when approaching the veteran stage, he took 16 for 88 in the match against Somerset at Weston-super-Mare and scored 102 and 102 not out from the Surrey bowling at the Oval, when Jack Hobbs also hit two separate hundreds in the same match.

His fellow players loved to play practical jokes on him. They would alter the position of his marker between the overs and convince him that he had lost his run up; they would suggest when he was in a bad batting seam that he was dropping his right hand and he would spend hours in front of a mirror in his hotel bedroom, trying to eradicate an imaginary technical flaw!

Jack backed horses even more heavily and less successfully than Philip Mead and lost his entire benefit fund to the bookies before he collected it!

After the 1930 season, his health broke down and he was advised that the strain of six-day cricket was too much for him.

There are only ten performances of the all-rounders double of a hundred wickets and a thousand runs in a season in the county's records – five of them by Jack Newman. Only Derek Shackleton and Alec Kennedy have taken more wickets for Hampshire than he did; only fourteen men have scored more runs; and only nine fielders have held more catches.

Jack soon reappeared as an umpire, for the game was his life. He became a legendary figure as coach – in India and New Zealand, but above all in South Africa, where he settled. No one did more for Western Province cricket and when his health gave way, they made him a life member at Newlands, staged a benefit for him, and with the proceeds gave him an annuity for life. When he said he would like to pay one more visit to his homeland to watch Hampshire play, they clubbed together and sent him back to England for the summer of 1966.

Greatly resenting the fact that Wisden knocked three years off his age, a fact they later corrected, this rare character died in Cape Town, six weeks after entering his 90th year.

# MARK NICHOLAS

Born: 29 September 1957, London
Played: 1978–1992

FIRST-CLASS HAMPSHIRE RECORD

| Matches | Innings | NO | Runs | HS | Ave | 100s |
|---|---|---|---|---|---|---|
| 305 | 503 | 72 | 14091 | 206* | 32.69 | 27 |

| Runs | Wkts | Ave | Best |
|---|---|---|---|
| 3126 | 69 | 45.30 | 6-37 |

NOTABLE FEATS

- He scored 206* v Oxford University at The Parks in 1982.
- In 1983, he added 290 with D.R.Turner for the 2nd wicket v Oxford University at The Parks.
- In 1984, he scored 108 v Gloucestershire at Bristol in the Sunday League.
- He has captained Hampshire from 1985.

An inspirational leader of men, Mark Nicholas, Hampshire's captain since 1985, has never captained let alone played for the full England side, despite proving an immensely capable and popular skipper of England A and B tours to Sri Lanka, Zimbabwe and Kenya. He also captained M.C.C against the touring Australians in 1985, scoring an unbeaten century. An attractive right-handed batsman, Nicholas was three years in the eleven at Bradfield, being captain of the school side in 1976, and he led a Public Schools side to South Africa in 1976–77. In 1977, he played regularly for the Hampshire Second Eleven, whilst the following summer, he played his first matches for his adopted county, impressing both opponents and spectators. A Championship debut at Trent Bridge produced an entertaining innings of 26 not out, in which he nonchalantly flicked off-spinner Bob White for six in a successful quest for an extra batting point.

He spent the winter of 1978–79 in Australia as captain of Southern Lakes C.C. but the following summer saw him make little advance towards a permanent place in the County side, despite a maiden century in The Parks on a green wicket, where more established players failed – it was a commendable effort after only six first-class innings.

In his opening seasons, Nicholas was predominantly a leg-side player and he practised hard to eradicate defensive frailties to

121

discover that a straighter bat pays dividends against the more experienced professional bowlers. His confidence completely returned in 1980 and in mid-June his attacking stroke play was much admired – Nicholas scoring his maiden Championship hundred, 112 off the Somerset attack at Bournemouth. His reward was a place in the M.C.C side to Bangladesh in 1980–81. Nicholas scored almost 1,500 runs over the seasons of 1980 and 1981, during a transitional period for Hampshire cricket. It was a frustrating time for Nicholas, for while he batted regularly at No.3 in Championship cricket, he found his position fluctuating for one-day matches.

Nicholas was awarded his county cap in 1982, a season in which he scored 1,312 runs at an average of slightly under 40. He hit a double century at the Parks off Oxford University – the score of 206 not out remains his highest so far. Hampshire ended the summer third in the Championship as their fortunes began to change, a position they held the following season as well. Nicholas consolidated his No. 3 spot and was becoming a serious candidate for international honours. He also did a little more bowling, although a chronic back injury limited his contribution over the full season.

Standing up with the bat held high, he achieved a more positive approach and a consistent supply of runs. Solid practice in the back garden of the Smith residence, sometimes under the watchful eye of Barry Richards reaped its reward in 1984 when he had his best season with 1,482 runs and a highest Championship score of 158 against Lancashire at Portsmouth. In 1985, he was appointed Hampshire captain, having a hard task in following Nick Pocock, who within a happy atmosphere received whole-hearted support from all the players. He was then given the task of leading the England 'B' side to Sri Lanka the following winter. On this tour his best innings were played in the third one-day international and the third unofficial Test, but like most of the English players, he found the standard of cricket in Sri Lanka higher than expected; his selection for the tour though was an indication that the England selectors regarded him as a future Test cricketer – but it has yet to happen.

He led Hampshire to the championship of the Sunday League in 1986 and returned the following summer to score 1,626 runs in all matches at an average of 40.65, including four centuries, two of which were not out. It was also a summer in which he passed 2,000 sunday League runs – his best innings probably being an unbeaten 79 against Glamorgan at Bournemouth.

In 1988, and in fine batting form, Nicholas was very close to the highest honour in the game as the England selectors changed captains for almost every Test. Though he is obviously disappointed not to have played Test cricket and captained England, he has not given up hope.

After years of recurrent exasperation, he led Hampshire to success at Lord's in the 1988 Benson and Hedges Final, though his character was severely tested in 1991 when a short ball from Surrey and Pakistan fast bowler Waqar Younis broke his finger two days before the Nat West Trophy Final against Surrey at Lord's. Confined to the players' balcony rather than plotting a Hampshire victory from mid-on – he saw his side overcome the absence of their injured captain to gain their first title in this competition with two balls to spare. He shared in the team's triumph, but his personal ambition was cruelly thwarted. He was however, back at Lord's in 1992 as Hampshire defeated Kent, to give the County their second success in the Benson and Hedges Cup.

The great South African and Hampshire opening batsman, Barry Richards believes that Nicholas would have been better suited to playing for the County in the early 1960s under Colin Ingleby-Mackenzie, when people enjoyed their cricket! 'Mark has always been one of my favourite cricketers, brash to the point of arrogance, which doesn't always sit comfortably with either establishment or some fellow players of quieter disposition. I think him an outstanding player, who should have played for England.' He still might, but if he doesn't he most surely will go into the record books as England's finest 'Unofficial Test match' captain.

Hampshire have been well served by Mark Nicholas – he hopes to bring more success to the County and I believe he will do so.

# BOBBY PARKS

Born: 15 June 1959, Cuckfield
Played: 1980–1992

### FIRST-CLASS HAMPSHIRE RECORD

| Matches | Innings | NO | Runs | HS | Ave | 100s |
|---------|---------|-----|------|-----|-------|------|
| 253 | 282 | 82 | 3936 | 89 | 19.68 | 0 |

| Runs | Wkts | Ave | Best |
|------|------|-----|------|
| 166 | 0 | – | – |

*Number of dismissals:* 630 caught; 70 stumped.

### NOTABLE FEATS

- In 1981, he helped to dismiss 6 batsmen in an innings (10 in the match – a Hampshire Record) v Derbyshire at Portsmouth.

- He also helped dismiss 6 batsmen in an innings v Essex at Colchester in 1984 and v Nottinghamshire at Southampton in 1986.
- His best season behind the stumps is 1986 with 81 victims (73 caught and 8 stumped) in 25 matches.
- In 1992, he overtook the County's wicket-keeping record of 688 dismissals previously held by Neil McCorkell.
- Took exactly 1,000 dismissals in all cricket (700 first-class 300 1-day).

Bobby Parks was born in Cuckfield, Sussex on 15th June 1959 into a cricketing family – his father Jim Parks, who played for Sussex and England, as did his grandfather J H Parks and his uncle, H W Parks, who played for Sussex.

Initially, it was Bobby's studies which caused him to leave his home county, but also, he had a desire to find personal satisfaction from the sporting ability he had obviously inherited that led him to move counties.

The opportunity to break family ties occurred late in the 1976 season when, after appearing for the Somerset Second Eleven against Hampshire, he was invited to come to Southampton on trial. The Somerset connection had been the result of his father's involvement with the County between 1974 and 1976. The events of that summer culminated in both Somerset and Hampshire offering him professional terms for the following season. Whilst the choice was a difficult one, he decided to opt for Hampshire, which meant that he had the chance to start a first-class career away from many of the pressures and influences of the Parks' cricketing tradition.

Though it was a decision he never regretted, there were occasions when he felt despondent, as his Second Eleven colleagues got their call-up to the first team ahead of him. But, he remained confident that the chance for him to prove his worth at first-team level would come. When the opportunity did arise, fate seemed to be against him. The occasion was a John Player League match early in June 1980 and played at the County Ground at Southampton. Overnight, Hampshire's regular wicket-keeper, Bob Stephenson had fallen ill, which meant that Parks was due to play. But, unknowingly, he was back in Sussex visiting relations and could not be contacted. Fortunately for Bobby, the bitterness of knowing that he had been so close to his first game for the County was short-lived for he learnt that he was to appear in a County Championship match two days later. Bob Stephenson had announced his intention to retire at the end of the season and so the Hampshire Committee decided to blood some youngsters.

Bobby Parks made his first-class debut against Sussex – a fitting way for him to start his career with Hampshire.

In 1981, Bobby Parks made real strides behind the stumps – it was his first full season and he only missed the Sri Lankans match, when he was rested. Evidence that he had 'arrived' came at Portsmouth in mid-July when he broke the County record with ten catches in the match against Derbyshire. He held six catches in the first innings – another record – both of which were recognised by the presentation of the ball suitably mounted and inscribed a month later. He was a clear winner of the Hampshire Young Cricketer of the Year Award, chosen by members of Hampshire Exiles and Hampshire Cricket Society. In all, he claimed 52 victims in his 23 Championship and first-class matches and 21 in one-day matches. His neat competent style pleased his famous father Jim, who was often there to watch him in his first season, but like most Hampshire followers, Parks senior wished his son would score more runs! For the record in 1981, he scored 330 runs at 15.71.

The following summer, he was the leading wicket-keeper in the country with 76 dismissals.

He toured Zimbabwe in 1985 with the English Counties XI and must have felt that he was close to winning his first cap at Test level. In 1986, he helped to dismiss 81 batsmen and won his first Man-of-the-Match award in that season's Benson and Hedges Cup. It was the summer when Bobby Parks actually did appear in the England team.

The first Test at Lord's against New Zealand saw a little bit of history made when England fielded four wicket-keepers in one innings. Bruce French was struck on the helmet by a bouncer from Hadlee in his first innings which left him groggy and dazed when England took the field. England captain Mike Gatting was given Coney's agreement to use Bob Taylor (then 45, retired from cricket and on duty as the Cornhill liaison officer) as temporary substitute. While Taylor gathered together a collection of borrowed clothing and equipment, Bill Athey went behind the stumps for the first two overs. Taylor then took over for the next 76 overs and was replaced by Bobby Parks for almost the remainder of the innings. In 1987, a broken finger in early June ended Parks' run of 131 consecutive Championship matches over six seasons. He also missed a Sunday League match, but was quickly back in action and keeping wicket as well as ever.

It was a great disappointment to him that this form didn't catch the eyes of the England selectors, but he did himself no harm in having his best season with the bat, though his top first-class score of 89 was made against Cambridge University some three seasons earlier. In spite of limited chances and not getting a chance to bat on the very best ptiches, he still averaged 33.63 in first-class cricket and headed the Sunday League averages at 56.00 – figures more impressive than his national rivals – his top score was 38 not out against Essex at Portsmouth, while he also passed

100 catches in the Sunday League. Losing his place to Adrian Aymes, he was recalled to the side for the odd game in 1992. He overtook Hampshire's wicket-keeping record of 688 dismissals previously held by Neil McCorkell, during the Britannic Assurance County Championship match against Essex at Bournemouth in June. Later that month, in the county match against Sussex at Arundel, Parks provided Malcolm Marshall with his 1,500th first-class wicket when he caught David Smith.

Released by Hampshire at the end of the 1992 season, he finished with exactly 1,000 dismissals for his county (700 first-class 300 1-day).

# NICK POCOCK

Born: 15 December 1951 Maracaibo, Venezuela
Played: 1976–1984

FIRST-CLASS HAMPSHIRE RECORD

| Matches | Innings | NO | Runs | HS | Ave | 100s |
|---|---|---|---|---|---|---|
| 127 | 186 | 22 | 3790 | 164 | 23.10 | 2 |

| Runs | Wkts | Ave | Best |
|---|---|---|---|
| 396 | 4 | 99.00 | 1-4 |

NOTABLE FEATS

- He was Captain of Hampshire from 1980 to 1984.
- He held five catches in an innings v Oxford University at Oxford in 1979.
- He hit his highest score, 164 v Lancashire at Southampton in 1982.

Born in Maracaibo, Venezuela on 15 December 1951, (a fact well known to cricket quiz students) Nick Pocock's appointment as captain of Hampshire in 1980 was among the more surprising items of news to break from the English county scene during the winter recess.

A master, inevitably alerted Desmond Eagar, then the Hampshire secretary, to the talent of a boy who was five years in the school cricket XI, captaining it for two. As a fourteen-year-old, Pocock was drafted in for the two-day match against Uppingham and made an early mark with 60 not out in that main school match.

Hampshire pursued him and eventually got their man. Along with Gordon Greenidge, Pocock played for the youth team run by Arthur Holt and 'Holt's Colts'. When the County offered him terms in 1970, Pocock declined because he was aiming to qualify as a surveyor and because cricket prospects were not so inviting then. However, over the next few years, the influence of one-day cricket made the game both more attractive to watch and in career terms, so Pocock became happy to devote himself to cricket.

By 1975, he was scoring heavily for the Second Eleven, though still an unregistered player – scoring 1,164 runs at 50.60 to top the averages. His top score was an unbeaten 100 against Glamorgan, whilst he also topped the county bowling averages with 25 wickets at 18.04 and held 18 catches for good measure. The following season, he was registered and made an enjoyable first-class debut at Bournemouth, scoring 68 against Leicestershire. But at that time, Hampshire had an established side doing well and it was hard for someone like Nick Pocock to break into the team. The pressure was reflected in two seasons of occasional appearances and minimal achievement.

On 21 August 1977, playing for Shrewsbury Saracens in the Cricketer Cup Final, he took the game by the scruff of the neck. His bowling analysis of:

| O | M | R | W |
|---|---|---|---|
| 12 | 5 | 16 | 4 |

and fielding might have won him the Man-of-the-Match, but when he followed these excellent performances with an innings of the highest quality, the game could only be known as 'Pocock's match'. Set to make only 118 to win, Pocock cut the Oundle Rovers' attack to ribbons and when he hit the winning run, he had taken his score to 96 off only 81 balls in eighty-two minutes.

Though he hit his maiden first-class century, 143 against Middlesex at Portsmouth, 1979 was still not a season of high achievement for him. Yet, he matured enough for the Hampshire committee to put their faith in his coming good, both as a player and captain. Appointed to lead the County in place of Bob Stephenson, he had only played in twenty-seven first-class matches spread over the previous four seasons. But Hampshire are concerned more with potential and personality than statistics and were prepared to underwrite the judgement of Desmond Eagar who saw in him when he brought him to the County, a likely leader in the making. After the disappointments of his first season as Hampshire captain, Nick Pocock had good reason to enjoy much of 1981, as he experienced the thrill of his unfancied side storming to the head of the County Championship with a sequence of wins. The county's first defeat was at the hands of Surrey at Portsmouth when the enterprising captain had his hand broken by Sylvester Clarke. It was a season when his own form produced his best-ever season's average – 28.07 – it would have been even better but for his admirable unselfishness on occasions, sacrificing his wicket in the quest for quick runs. Also, his frustration was heightened by a series of injuries which kept him out of the side for five weeks.

During the close season of 1981–82, he spent three weeks in the Far East with M.C.C. and a week on The Cricketer tour to Dubai, before returning to his normal close-season pursuits – working in an insurance business fronted by another Hampshire captain, Colin Ingleby-Mackenzie and following National Hunt racing.

The break must have done him good, for in 1982, he hit the highest score of his first-class career, 164 against Lancashire at Southampton.

Playing his last game for Hampshire in 1984, Nick Pocock played well enough to enjoy his own cricket and help others enjoy theirs.

# 'SAM' POTHECARY

Born: 1 March 1906, Southampton
Died: 21 May 1991
Played: 1927–1946

FIRST-CLASS HAMPSHIRE RECORD

| Matches | Innings | NO | Runs | HS | Ave | 100s |
|---|---|---|---|---|---|---|
| 271 | 445 | 39 | 9477 | 130 | 23.34 | 9 |

| Runs | Wkts | Ave | Best |
|---|---|---|---|
| 2140 | 52 | 41.15 | 4-47 |

NOTABLE FEATS

● He produced his best bowling figures, 4 for 47 against Surrey at the Oval in his debut match.
● His top score with the bat was 130 made against the 1937 New Zealanders at Bournemouth.

Arthur Ernest 'Sam' Pothecary played 271 matches for Hampshire between 1927 and 1946 as a middle-order batsman and slow left-arm bowler. He scored 9,477 runs, including over 1,000 runs in a season four times and nine centuries, plus 52 wickets.

Mervyn Burden 1953–63

Henry Horton 1953–67

Roy Marshall 1953–72

Malcolm Heath 1954–62

Peter Sainsbury 1954–76

David White 1957–71

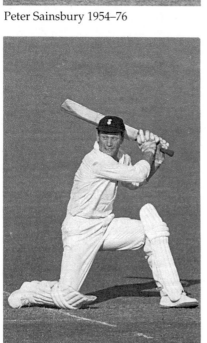

Bryan Timms 1959–68

Danny Livingstone 1959–72

Bob Cottam 1963–71

Trevor Jesty 1966–84

Richard Gilliat 1966–78

David Turner 1966–89

Bob Stephenson 1969–80

Barry Richards 1968–78

Gordon Greenidge 1970–87

John Rice 1971–82

Mike Taylor 1973–80

Andy Roberts 1973–78

Nigel Cowley 1974–84

Nick Pockock 1976–84

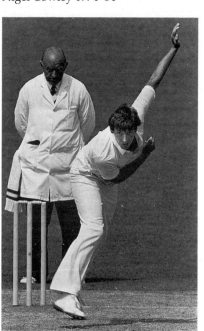

Tim Tremlett 1976–91

Mark Nicholas 1978–(93)

Paul Terry 1978–(93)

Malcolm Marshall 1979–(93)

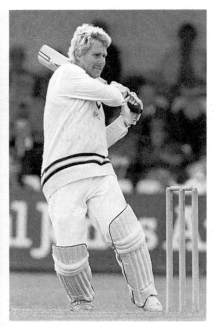

Chris Smith 1980–91

Bobby Parks 1980–(93)

Robin Smith 1982–(93)          Cardigan Connor 1984–(93)

Malcolm Marshall bowling with arm in plaster to David Gower

A Southampton professional, he was given an extended trial by the County, replacing Norman Bowell, the son of Alec on the groundstaff. Always known as 'Sam' after his uncle who had played a dozen times for Hampshire on either side of the first World War he was one of the first post-war colts to attain a fairly regular place in the Hampshire side.

As a left-handed batsman, his favourite strokes were the cut and the cover drive, though his leaning towards strokes outside the off stump made him vulnerable to fast bowling. Slightly built and nimble, he was an attractive batsman to watch and usually made his run quickly. In his early years however, he was still below County standard as a batsman but in 1933 he topped the 1,000 run mark and scored two centuries. The highest of his nine centuries was 130 against the 1937 New Zealanders at Bournemouth, whilst the summer of 1938 saw him score more runs for Hampshire – 1,357 at 27.14 – than he had ever done before, as he played with much more confidence.

He did on occasions bowl the left-arm off-break – the 'Chinaman' – but rarely did he get any success with it in county cricket. In fact, his best figures were 4 for 47 against Surrey at the Oval in his debut match.

One of the best cover fielders in the country, he found being naturally left-handed, the normal cover stroke spinning to his throwing hand and he had a quick, low return – always over the top of the stumps. Less than two weeks after VE day, Hampshire under the captaincy of 'Sam' Pothecary were back in the field once more as the Southampton Police were beaten by six wickets in a one-day game at the county Ground.

At the end of the Second World War, he was appointed groundsman at Southampton, but still represented the County during the first season of cricket after the hostilities. After a season as groundsman, he was released from his duties after being offered a good coaching appointment at a school in Somerset.

He wasn't there too long, before he became a first-class umpire – a position he held until 1957 when he started an eighteen-year spell as head groundsman at the RAF cricket ground at Vine Lane, Uxbridge. Here, he produced pitches of the highest quality and was intrumental in preparing the ground for the county cricket that Middlesex now play there. In the 1960s, 'Sam' was a well-respected coach at the Chiswick Indoor Cricket School.

No friendlier cricketer ever lived than 'Sam' Pothecary who died at a nursing home in Iver after a long term of illness during which his leg was amputated in 1991.

# JOHN RICE

Born: 23 October 1949, Chandlers Ford
Played: 1971–1982

FIRST-CLASS HAMPSHIRE RECORD

| Matches | Innings | NO | Runs | HS | Ave | 100s |
|---|---|---|---|---|---|---|
| 168 | 271 | 22 | 5091 | 161* | 20.44 | 2 |

| Runs | Wkts | Ave | Best |
|---|---|---|---|
| 7707 | 230 | 33.50 | 7-48 |

NOTABLE FEATS

● He took 7 for 48 v Worcestershire at Worcester in 1977.
● He hit his highest first-class score, 161* v Warwickshire at Edgbaston in 1981.
● He performed the hat-trick v Northamptonshire in the 1975 Sunday League game.

Born in Chandlers Ford on 23 October 1949, John Rice grew up in Surrey and played Schools and Second Eleven cricket there until returning to his native county after not being re-engaged on the Oval staff. Making his Hampshire debut in 1971 as an opening batsman and medium-pace bowler, Rice played for the county until 1982.

An outstanding one-day player, he had a very successful 1975 season in the Sunday League. He took 5 for 14 against North-amptonshire at Southampton as the visitors were shot out for 44 in the ten over per side game – achieving the hat-trick in the process. Against Derbyshire at Darley Dale, he took 4 for 14 from his eight overs and ended the season at the top of the county John Player League averages with 27 wickets at 11.48 each.

In the Benson and Hedges Cup match against Somerset, he completed the rout of the tail-enders with three wickets in four balls. Also in 1975 in the County Championship match against Somerset at Weston-super-Mare, Hampshire won in convincing fashion despite losing half of their first innings wickets for 101. John Rice was unfortunately left on 96 not out, in sight of his maiden century. It was the summer in which was he awarded his county cap – 619 runs at 22.10 and 49 wickets at 26.65.

The following summer, he was promoted to open the innings with Barry Richards for the last few matches and ended the season with 548 runs at an average of 16.60.

In 1977, he produced some good bowling performances, but none better than his 7 for 48 against Worcestershire at New Road.

The summer of 1981 ended far too soon for John Rice. Recalled to the Hampshire side when Tim Tremlett broke his wrist, he did at the age of thirty-one, score his maiden hundred and in the next match, the penultimate fixture, follow up by celebrating with another. Everyone connected with Hampshire cricket rejoiced for this keen student of the game who had been stricken with injuries over the previous two seasons.

His maiden century came gainst Sussex at Hove, after the Hampshire innings had opened in rather bizarre fashion. The County lost their opening batsman Tremlett, run out off the first ball without even facing. Rice came in next to play an heroic innings, staying put for six hours with an obdurate unbeaten 101 in a total of 241. He saw his maiden century arrive with last man Steve Malone at the other end; indeed, he was 97 not out when Malone came into face Imran Khan, but Malone loyally stood firm as Rice reached his first century in eleven seasons. After his 344 minutes at the crease, he had only ten minutes between innings before opening with Greenidge in the follow-on that same evening. Sussex chasing their first Championship, won easily enough by nine wickets, but Rice had proven himself and broke a mental barrier. In the next match, Rice made his second-ever century and highest score only a week after scoring his maiden century – taking an unbeaten 161 off Warwickshire at Edgbaston.

He made a brilliant slip catch in a vital Benson and Hedges Cup match against Sussex at Hove that season, but it cost him a broken finger and crucially deprived the Hampshire side of his bowling. However, more frustrating was a long period out of the side with the finger and then knee injuries and a struggle to regain his first team place.

Though he only managed to play in 11 first team games that summer, his maiden century had given him much needed confidence and he went on to finish second in the averages to Gordon Greenidge with 639 runs at 39.93. The qualification of Chris Smith and the development of Paul Terry brought about John's release from the staff in 1982 and he took up the position of Cricket coach at Eton College (which he still holds today), following the retirement of another Hampshire player, Vic Cannings.

John Rice's intense loyalty and willingness to serve Hampshire in any capacity, probably had an unsettling effect on his form, for he undertook various roles with bat and ball and in the field.

# BARRY RICHARDS

Born: 21 July 1945 Durban, South Africa
Played: 1968–1978

FIRST-CLASS HAMPSHIRE RECORD

| Matches | Innings | NO | Runs | HS | Ave | 100s |
|---------|---------|-----|-------|-----|-------|------|
| 204 | 342 | 33 | 15607 | 240 | 50.50 | 38 |

| Runs | Wkts | Ave | Best |
|------|------|-------|------|
| 1675 | 46 | 36.41 | 7-63 |

NOTABLE FEATS

- In 1968, he scored 2,314 runs for Hampshire.
- In 1972 playing for Natal, he was the first player to score 1,000 runs in the Currie Cup.
- During the summer of 1972, he held five catches in an innings in the match against Gloucestershire at Gloucester.
- He scored three Gillette Cup hundreds, with a highest of 129 v Lancashire at Bournemouth in 1972.
- He hit nine John Player League hundreds, with a highest of 155* v Yorkshire at Hull in 1970, carrying his bat in the process.
- In 1974, he scored 129 v Gloucestershire at Bristol in the Benson and Hedges Cup.
- He carried his bat on two occasions, with a best of 225* out of 344 v Nottinghamshire at Trent Bridge in 1974.
- He hit three double-centuries for Hampshire, with a highest of 240 v Warwickshire at Coventry in 1973.
- Took 264 catches for Hampshire.

Probably the greatest batsman ever to come out of South Africa, Barry Richards was born on 21 July 1945, in Durban. He went to Clifton School and then to Durban High, where rugby and cricket were the two major sports. A complex weakness in both ankles prevented him from playing much rugger and even in cricket, he found that a long innings would produce an unbearable tiredness in his ankles, while a day in the field always meant rubber soles replacing his spikes.

He was seventeen when he first came to England as captain of the visiting South African Schools team of 1963. It was plain for all to see, that here was a player of unusual talent, for against a number of adult sides, he averaged 49.87 for the tour. An innings of 70 at run a minute against Hampshire Seconds caused county coach, Leo Harrison to say : 'That is the best young batsman I have ever seen.'

He made his first-class debut for Natal in 1964–65 and spent 1965 in England, playing for Gloucestershire Second Eleven, but to many observers it was already obvious that he would ultimately play Test cricket and to ensure this, he had to play in his own country. Wilf Isaacs included him in his 1966 touring side and when the team returned to South Africa, Barry stayed on in England, sharing a room in Earls Court with Mike Procter and Lee Irvine and living on anything they could earn by casual employment. At the Oval, they each made two pounds a day as dressing room attendants for the West Indians and they were happy to play cricket for any side who offered them a game!

Back home, he scored a century for a South African XI against the 1966–67 Australians, but most surprisingly, was not given a Test place against them.

The registration of overseas players by county teams led to him signing for Hampshire after turning down an initial offer from Sussex, 'I did'nt mind which team I played for, so long as it was a Southern side, as I thought the batting wickets would be better in the south'.

Interviewed on his arrival in England, Richards announced that he was determined to hit 2,000 runs in the season – he came second to Geoff Boycott in the national averages and was chosen as one of Wisden's 'Cricketers of the Year' – the writer ending with 'Richard's horizons seem limitless and it will be fascinating to see how far his talents will take him. Few anywhere in the world, have his possibilities,' In fact, in a dismally wet season, Richards scored 2,395 runs in all matches at an average of 47.90 and with a top score of 206 against Nottinghamshire at Portsmouth. Yet Richards rebelled against the day-to-day slog of county cricket and after his first year, told Wisden that he didn't know how the players kept it up from year to year. The strain is immense,' he said. 'I used to wake up in the mornings and say to myself "Surely not another day's cricket!"' There were times when he could scarcely hide his apparent fatigue, and there were times when he arrogantly rose to heights few could aspire to reach down the ages. Some declared Richards was in such a class apart that he became bored with mediocrity and lacked the incentive of challenge with the passing of time.

He could not be kept out of the 1970 South African side against Australia and in his mere four Test appearances at the age of 24, he scored 508 runs at an average of 72.57. Because South Africa ceased to play test cricket after 1969–70, he had little opportunity to play at the highest level. Yet, in that Test series, Richards showed both sides of batting in compiling two centuries of marked contrast. His first Test hundred in Durban was the most perfect exhibition you could wish to see – the 100 reached four balls after lunch on the first day after a glorious array of quick-footed strokes – the second in Port Elizabeth, was part painstaking, part risk-taking and extravagantly brilliant – something of the moods of the man himself.

Australians were anxious to see the player who had slaughtered their attack in South Africa and so in September 1970, fresh from a successful season with Hampshire, Barry Richards arrived in Adelaide for his season with South Australia. Six months later, it was a very satisfied Richards, who in his initial first-class season in Australia, had rewritten the record books with his dashing batting. Richards' deeds as an opening batsman for South Australia were astronomical. He topped the Australian batting aggregates and averages with 1,538 runs at an average of 109.90. He eclipsed Sir Don Bradman's record as the highest rungetter for South Australia in a first-class season. He also became South Australia's biggest scorer in Sheffield Shield cricket with 1,145 runs, beating Bradman's record of 1,062 set in 1939–40. He hit a century against all the State sides, including an unforgettable innings of 356 against Western Australia, 325 being reached on the first day!

Richards' driving was frequently compared with Wally Hammond and Sir Len Hutton, whilst he possessed a brilliant knack of square cutting anything short of a length. A sure sign of his greatness was that when he was well set, he could offer more than one stroke to a delivery. He was good on the eye as he 'stood up' and made full use of his height as he made his shots. He also stood perfectly still and calmly until he decided what stroke to employ - and he had them all. Equally good on either front or back foot, he showed the full face of the blade, always came down straight from his back lift and did not hit across the line of the ball.

In 1974, he was in prolific form and hit 609 runs in seven innings and averaged over a hundred. Batting for five hours, he carried his bat for 225 not out from Hampshire's total of 344 against Nottinghamshire at Trent Bridge, whilst eight of his colleagues failed to reach double figures.

Nine times he scored a century before lunch, though he was particularly volatile in the limited-over competitions. He would perpetrate strokes of an unparalleled extravagence. Stepping away to leg to an off-break pitched on, or outside the leg stump and play it, against the spin, for four through the covers; or he would pick up a left-arm breakaway from outside the off-stump and smack it over mid-wicket for six. He hit hundreds in all the one-day competitions and was particularly brilliant as I recall when scoring 129 against Lancashire at Bournemouth in the 1972 Gillette Cup Competition.

He returned to Australia for Packer's World Series Cricket,

playing for the World XI. He hit 207 against Australia at Perth in 1977–78 and was one of the leading batsmen for the World side.

Though it is true he fell away in his last two seasons and left with fourteen matches to go in 1978, his contribution to Hampshire until then had been vast. First with Roy Marshall and then with Gordon Greenidge, he formed, fashioned and made a spectacular start to many a Hampshire innings. He had said at the beginning of the 1978 season: 'When I walk off a county ground for the last time, it will be with a sense of relief.' He continued to play for Natal with success until 1982–83, and there can be little doubt that had he played at Test level regularly, his achievements would have matched everything he accomplished in the best grades in three separate countries.

Peter Sainsbury once stated: 'If I wanted a batsman to make a hundred for my life, it would be Barry Richards.'

# ANDY ROBERTS

Born: 29 January 1951, Urlings Village, Antigua
Played: 1973–1978

## FIRST-CLASS HAMPSHIRE RECORD

| Matches | Innings | NO | Runs | HS | Ave | 100 |
|---|---|---|---|---|---|---|
| 58 | 65 | 23 | 583 | 39 | 13.88 | 0 |

| Runs | Wkts | Ave | Best |
|---|---|---|---|
| 4076 | 244 | 16.70 | 8-47 |

## NOTABLE FEATS

- In 1974, he took 119 wickets for Hampshire, including a best of 8 for 47 against Glamorgan at Cardiff in his first Championship season.
- In 1983, he scored 68 (his highest first-class innings) when sharing in a West Indies record ninth wicket stand of 161 with Clive Lloyd in Calcutta.

One of a fisherman's family of fourteen, Anderson Montgomery Everton Roberts did not play his first game of cricket until he left school at the age of sixteen. Until then, the only games he had taken part in were improvised affairs, played with his friends in the cornfields, when he had nothing more lethal to bowl with than a tennis ball.

Even in those early days, the young Roberts liked to bowl fast, and after playing for his village and parish teams, he won a place in the Antigua side, which included former West Indies captain, Viv Richards. Representative honours with the Leeward Islands followed and at twenty, he won a place in the Combined Islands side for their Shell Shield match with Barbados. However, despite taking four wickets including that of Gary Sobers on his first-class debut, he was dropped for the next match against Trinidad.

Although again taking most wickets in the trials of the 1972 season, Roberts found himelf left out of the combined Islands side for the fist two matches of the Shell series.

That season however, brought him the break which led ultimately to his joining Hampshire. He and Viv Richards were sent over to the Alf Gover Indoor Cricket School in London by the Volunteers Cricket Committee in Antigua.

Hampshire heard that. he was coming and the county who felt that a pace bowler was their most important need, sent Captain Richard Gilliat to take a look. Gilliat liked what he saw and recommended to the Hampshire Cricket Committee that they should invite Roberts over for a trial. Returning home for the 1973 season, he suffered a serious knee injury in the opening Shell Shield game which threatened not only the arranged trial with Hampshire, but his whole career. Told he would never play again, he was determined to prove everyone wrong, and after just two months out of action, he left for England and his trial with Hampshire. It didn't take the county long to realise that they had found a winner in Roberts, who took 40 wickets in the Second Eleven matches of that season.

At that time though, Roberts was unregistered and had played in only one county match – against the West Indian touring team, when he took 1 wicket for 144. The Hampshire committee had to choose between Roberts and David O'Sullivan, the New Zealand slow left-arm bowler, who had played his part in the county's Championship success that summer. In spite of the objections of some experienced members of the committee, they took Roberts. Perhaps ten years earlier, they would have made the opposite choice, but with three of the four county competitions being limited-overs matches, a fast bowler can put out a couple of early batsmen and sweep aside the tailenders.

Back home in Antigua for the winter, Roberts played for West Indies against England in the third Test at Bridgetown, Barbados, when he took 3 for 124 and was not chosen again in the series. He returned to these shores barely recognisable as the bowler who had left six months earlier. Within a few weeks, he had lifted

Hampshire by way of a series of two-day innings wins to the top of the Championship table, and was recognised – indeed hailed – as the fastest bowler in England and probably the world. In truth, he hardly had any right to be allowed to play Second Eleven cricket, so dangerous did he prove to be – he knocked Colin Cowdrey over his stumps and out cold when Kent were beaten inside two days at Basingstoke. One county player referred to Roberts as 'a cold killer' in awe rather than revulsion. Brian Luckhurst and Alan Knott both said Roberts was the fastest they had seen since Dennis Lillee.

Seldom can a young fast bowler have made as big an impact on an English summer as Andy Roberts did in 1974. On generally slow pitches, he took 119 wickets at 13.62 to head the English national averages.

Like all West Indian bowlers of authentic pace, he began with the physical advantages of height and strength. His bowling action began with a bustling run-up, not overlong, the power building up every step of the way. His arm was not textbook high in delivery, but everything else about the delivery was perfect. He had the ability to slant the ball either way and backed this with an explosive bouncer delivered without any apparent extra effort. His bouncers had a range of speeds and angles and the ugly short-of-a-length delivery such as he hurled at Greg Chappell at Adelaide early in 1980 was probably the worst possible greeting for any batsman who ever lived!

He was devastating in his first Test series in India, with 32 wickets, including 12 at Madras, the first time a West Indian had reaped so many in a Test. He routed Australia with 7 for 54 at Perth, his best Test figures and had 28 wickets in his first series in England. In India, he showed the extent of his talent by virtually winning the series single-handed, whilst under the handicap of being a fast bowler operating on slow pitches.

After 1974, opposing counties began to pay him the compliment of preparing slow wickets, yet he could still bring a whistle of surprise from spectators who were seeing him for the first time.

After this, he calculated that he would be better off cutting down his run and prolonging his career. He didn't take kindly to being overbowled in county matches and there were some differences of opinion between himself and Richard Gilliat on this question, but it was the cold English summers which finally persuaded Roberts to quit Hampshire at the end of the 1978 season, though he did play later on a part-time basis for Leicestershire.

World Series Cricket was a turning point in helping cricketers to realise their own value – and it worked, for Roberts remained in test cricket until he was thirty-three, in spite of the intense demand for fast-bowling places. In his forty-seven Tests, he scored 762 runs at 14.94 (including hitting 24 runs off an Ian Botham over in 1981 – a world Test record; and took 202 wickets at a cost of 25.61 each.

He may have appeared moody, sullen and colourless, but he was actually a deep thinker about the game, which his radio commentaries on the Antigua Test of 1985–86 served to confirm.

On retirement, Andy Roberts set himself up as a fisherman in Antigua with his own motor-boat, though he had always been a fisherman of batsmen – a thoroughly dedicated wicket-hunter, never allowing the batsman one moment of peace.

# NEVILLE ROGERS

Born: 9 March 1918, Oxford
Played: 1946–1955

## FIRST-CLASS HAMPSHIRE RECORD

| Matches | Innings | NO | Runs | HS | Ave | 100 |
|---------|---------|-----|-------|-----|-------|-----|
| 285 | 506 | 25 | 15292 | 186 | 31.79 | 26 |

| Runs | Wkts | Ave | Best |
|------|------|-----|------|
| 37 | 0 | – | – |

## NOTABLE FEATS

- He scored 1,000 runs in a season for Hampshire on nine occasions.
- In 1950, he scored a century before lunch in the match against the West Indies at Southampton.
- His best season was 1952, when he scored 2,020 runs.
- He carried his bat on four occasions, with a best of 172* against Gloucestershire at Bristol in 1954.

Despite coming into the game late and retiring prematurely, Neville Rogers was Hampshire's regular opener for eight years, scoring 16,056 runs in all matches at 32.04, with 28 centuries.

Born in Oxford, he was working there as a clerk for a meat importing firm and had given up the idea of playing cricket for a living when his big break came in 1939. While playing club cricket for Oxford City, he had been recommended to Hampshire by their former player Alec Bowell. Neville having just turned twenty-one, arrived at the county ground to serve a one-year residential qualification. But the outbreak of war a few months later wrecked his cricketing dreams.

He quickly made up for lost time, as he made his belated Hampshire debut at the age of twenty-eight in an exciting victory over Worcestershire at Southampton. Hampshire totalled 346 as Bailey (133) and Rogers put on 209 for the fifth wicket – Rogers scoring 90 on his first appearance.

The next season, he opened the innings for the first time and in the first match scored 99 against Sussex at Portsmouth, before being given out lbw! It was a season in which he showed himself to be a class batsman making 1,722 runs at an average of 36.63. He had to wait until 1 July before making his century. Prior to this, he had scores of 90, 99, 91 and 90. His consistency deservedly earned him the second county cap to be given to a Hampshire professional since the war.

After a disappointing start to the 1950 season, he improved to have his best season to date. He hit 137 out of Hampshire's total of 229 in the match against Sussex at Eastbourne as Hampshire won a remarkable match by 59 runs, Knott taking 5 for 5. Against the touring West Indians, he hit a very good 100 before lunch as the Southampton crowd saw some delightful cricket. He ended the summer with 1,857 runs at 35.54 – being the only Hampshire batsman that season who was undisturbed by opposing pace.

In 1951, he came very close to playing for England, being twelfth man against South Africa at the Oval. In the Springboks' next tour match he took 118 off them for Hampshire at Southampton. He went on to have a magnificent season, scoring 1,934 runs, for the highest aggregate of his career. Yet the following season, he hit over 2000 runs in Championship matches alone, being the first to total the number since Arnold and Mead achieved the feat in 1934. That he only made two hundreds and for the first part of the season had no satisfactory opening partner, makes his performance even more praiseworthy. Rogers' consistency was admirable and in mid-June he completed his 10,000th run for Hampshire in post-war cricket – a great achievement.

He had started the season in tremendous form by scoring 600 run by the end of May at an average of over 50. He had been batting so well that he fully earned a place in the Test trial, but whilst at Bristol in the following match, he had injured his thumb so badly, that he was out of the game for some time. When he returned to the Hampshire side, he could not get going again.

In 1954, he started the season in great style, hitting a magnificent unbeaten 172 as Hampshire beat Gloucestershire at Bristol by an innings. Yet, he didn't show his best form again until the month of August, when he batted as well as he had ever done. It was hard to believe that until 10 July, he had only once made over 50, yet at the end of the season, his final record was to show that throughout the land, only five players had made more runs than he had in 1954. He carried his bat through an innings on four occasions that season, including an unbeaten 101 in a total of 182 on a difficult wicket, when playing for an England XI against the Pakistan tourists at Hastings. Though essentially a resistant batsman, Neville was always a skilful player of off-spin and in that same season, carried his bat for MCC against Surrey at Lord's when Jim Laker was at his most destructive.

Before the 1956 season started, the County learned that Rogers would play no more for them. Though he hadn't been quite as prolific as in other seasons in 1955, he had played many fine innings at the unaccustomed position of No. 5 as he unselfishly tried to bolster the middle-order. The county hoped that his business commitments would allow him time to play for at least a few weeks each year, but it was not to be.

Neville, who later played for Southampton club Trojans, joined a paint company. As area manager, he travelled throughout the south and was too busy to follow Hampshire's fortunes first hand. His circumstances changed and he is now on Hampshire's cricket committee. Hampshire have never had a more technically and temperamentally complete and reliable opening batsman - he was at his best when his side was in trouble – and was one of the best post-war batsman never to play for England.

His record in that decade after the war ensures that Neville Rogers will always hold a place among the immortals in Hampshire's cricket history.

# PETER SAINSBURY

Born: 13 June 1934, Southampton
Played: 1954–1976

## FIRST-CLASS HAMPSHIRE RECORD

| Matches | Innings | NO | Runs | HS | Ave | 100s |
|---|---|---|---|---|---|---|
| 593 | 913 | 189 | 19576 | 163 | 27.03 | 7 |

| Runs | Wkts | Ave | Best |
|---|---|---|---|
| 30060 | 1245 | 24.14 | 8-76 |

## NOTABLE FEATS

- In 1965, he took 7 for 30 v Norfolk at Southampton in the Gillette Cup.

140

- He added 154 with Leo Harrison for the eighth wicket v Worcestershire at Worcester in 1957.
- He took 601 catches for Hampshire, with a best of 56 in 1957.

Peter Sainsbury, a true son of Hampshire, symbolized all that is the best in the English county cricketers: hard work, integrity and a consistently high level of performance.

From his early school days, Peter Sainsbury has been a cricketer, playing for Bitterne Park School, Southampton Schools, Hampshire Boys County side and twelfth man for South of England Schools. His evenings in the nets at Southampton were not overlooked by Desmond Eagar and when Peter was leaving school, he was offered a position on the ground staff. This was a difficult decision to face, for Peter was the only one from three boys to play sport and his father, who was in ordnance survey, regarded a cricket career with apprehension,. They talked over the prospects and decided to give it a trial, a decision that neither son nor father regretted.

He was only just sixteen when he joined the Hampshire ground staff in 1950 as a slow left-arm bowler who was also a brilliant field. Two years later, he was promoted to the club and ground staff which certainly gave him more cricket. He spent nearly three seasons with the county Second Eleven before his career was interrupted by National Service, with a Royal Artillery battery stationed at Southend from 1952 to 1954. He made a great impression when he turned out for the Army against the RAF at Lord's in 1954, before returning to his native county. His County Championship debut came in the same summer against Notts. Jimmy Gray, the Hampshire batsman was trying to protect the inexperienced Sainsbury from the spin attack of Bruce Dooland and he spent forty minutes at the wicket before he was bowled off his pads by Arthur Jepson without scoring. He modified his tactics in the second innings and played confidently for 63 not out.

In 1955 under Desmond Eagar, the young Sainsbury, fresh from his National Service, enjoyed his first full season for Hampshire. His twenty-first birthday coincided with Hampshire's visit to play Yorkshire at Bradford. Hampshire batted first, and with Roy Marshall scoring freely, they totalled 224 on a good wicket. Bradford wickets can be difficult and when Yorkshire batted on Monday morning they were soon in trouble. Bowling with a change of pace and varying the flight, young Sainsbury had Len Hutton bowled for 17 and went on to take 5 for 19 in 18 overs. Batting again in the follow-on, Yorkshire did little better with Sainsbury again dismissing Hutton for four. He had captured the wicket of Len Hutton twice in a day, to end with match figures of 9 for 62. No sooner had the match finished than Hutton was in the Hampshire dressing-room, presenting the embarrassed youngster with the ball and a signed copy of his book *Cricket is my Life* in appreciation of a fine spell of bowling.

He took 102 wickets that summer and was invited to tour Pakistan in the winter with an MCC team.

Peter however excelled at both cricket and football and with regard to the latter was to receive an invitation from Ted Drake to join Chelsea in the mid-50s. This invitation to tour Pakistan interfered with his footballing plans, and he had to settle for turning out for Alton Town, speeding down the left flank in a purely amateur capacity.

With Tony Lock in the party as senior spin bowler, he did not get a great deal to do, but he learnt a lot from him. However, on his return to England, he altered his bowling style, changing from flight to spin and becoming a batsman who could bowl rather than vice versa. It was this alteration that dented his prospects of playing international cricket, for as a bowler, it appeared he might develop into a Test player.

As a batsman, Peter Sainsbury will be remembered as a retriever of lost causes rather than an entertainer in the purest sense. The right hand would soon be working the ball away for ones and twos, squeezing his runs out of tight corners. He used to relish those situations, because they made fewer demands on his limited repertoire as a batsman – he could do it his way. His love affair with the leg-side brought much amusement to the Hampshire side. One member of the county side told of a friend who had to go to work in the North for the summer – his parting words were: 'Send me a postcard if Sainsbury plays a cover drive this season . . . .'

As a bowler, he admits that he was never a big enough spinner of the ball to challenge the likes of Laker, Lock, Titmus or Wardle for a place in the England team, but he certainly had his days when there was something in the pitch. One of these was in 1971, when he took 12 for 127 against Gloucestershire at Portsmouth. This was his best season, for he just missed performing the 'double' with 959 runs at 33.82 (no centuries) and 107 wickets at 17.51 to head the Hampshire bowling.

Peter Sainsbury was a man who had to be in the game all the time. His all-round performances have earned him three 'Man of the Match' awards in the Gillette Cup and one gold award in the Benson and Hedges Cup. Against Norfolk in 1965, his 76 runs and 7 for 30 left the adjudicator with no alternative. At his peak, Sainsbury was in a class of his own as an all-round fielder. Of his contemporaries, Lock, Vic Wilson and Ken Grieves were perhaps his equal in holding catches in the leg trap, but they did not have Sainsbury's fleetness of foot and sureness of aim away from the wicket.

By the time he retired in 1976, he had played in 593 matches for

Hampshire, hitting 19,576 runs, as well as taking 1,245 wickets and 601 catches, testifying to the immense contribution that he made to Hampshire cricket.

On his retirement, be became county coach and though he emigrated to South Africa at the end of the 1989 season, he continued his job as long-standing coach by returning in the summer from his new home in Durban until the close of the 1991 season.

The only Hampshire player to have played in two Championship winning sides, he gave a great deal to the game of cricket both on and off the field.

# DEREK SHACKLETON

Born: 12 August 1924, Todmorden
Played: 1948–1969

FIRST-CLASS HAMPSHIRE RECORD

| Matches | Innings | NO | Runs | HS | Ave | 100s |
|---------|---------|-----|------|-----|-------|------|
| 583 | 773 | 177 | 8602 | 87* | 14.43 | – |

| Runs | Wkts | Ave | Best |
|-------|------|-------|------|
| 48674 | 2669 | 18.23 | 9-30 |

NOTABLE FEATS

- He took 100 wickets in a season in each of twenty consecutive years, failing to achieve this target only in his first and last seasons in County Championship cricket, with a best of 163 in 1958.
- In 1953, he took 9 for 77 v Glamorgan at Newport.
- He took five wickets in nine balls v Leicestershire at Leicester in 1950.

- He had figures of:

| O | M | R | W |
|------|----|---|---|
| 15.4 | 12 | 5 | 5 |

v Somerset at Bournemouth in 1956.

- In 1958, he took 9 for 59 v Gloucestershire at Bristol, followed by 9 for 81 in the same match in 1959.

- He took 14 for 29 v Somerset at Weston-super-Mare in 1955, including a bowling analysis of:

| O | M | R | W |
|---|---|---|---|
| 11.1 | 7 | 4 | 8 |

- His best figures were 9 for 30 v Warwickshire at Portsmouth in 1960.

Derek Shackleton, an adopted son of Hampshire, was claimed proudly by the people of Todmorden, a manufacturing town on the river Calder, set in the midst of the lofty moorlands of Yorkshire, not Lancashire, as has sometimes been suggested.

He had been a useful club player, mainly as a batsman with the Todmorden club before Sam Staples, then the Hampshire coach, spotted him playing Services cricket and brought him for trial at Southampton. So, at the age of twenty-two, he joined the Hampshire staff – as a batsman – in 1947. He played correctly straight in defence and his scoring strength lay in front of the wicket; his bowling in the nets consisted of slow leg-breaks which were not treated seriously by his colleagues.

'Shack' became a bowler by accident. At the beginning of the 1948 season, the County were so desperate for opening bowlers, that the club chairman ordered the entire playing staff into the nets to bowl as fast as they could. It emerged that Shackleton had bowled 'seam up' in club cricket. Though he had an easy action, his pace was no more than a fair medium and his appearance hardly suggested the stamina he was to reveal. Playing in sixteen matches in 1948, he made 228 runs at 11.40 and took 21 wickets, average 29.57. The figures were not impressive, but it was significant that he played better as the season wore on.

In 1949, he emerged as a county cricketer – as opposing batsmen found that they had a new problem to tackle in Derek Shackleton. He took 100 wickets at 26.16, though on figures, he was an all-rounder, for he missed the 'double' by only 86 runs and hit the highest score of his career – 87 against Derbyshire. However, it was quite clear that he would not be asked to bat seriously, but to reserve his strength for more and more bowling.

In his early days, 'Shack' bowled almost solely inswing, but he soon added the outswinger, evolving every possible variation on 'seam up' while the height of his arm gave him baffling movement off the seam when there was any greenness in the pitch. There is one ball that 'Shack' did not bowl and that was the half-volley – except after a winter's lay-off and then only in his opening spell!

He made his Test debut for England against the West Indies at Trent Bridge in 1950 – the first Hampshire player to be picked for England since Johnny Arnold in 1931 – he ran into Weekes and Worrell and emerged rather scathed, although he did top score in

England's first innings with 42, after Johnson and Worrell had wrecked the early batting. He did not play another Test until the fifth against South Africa in 1951. He went on the Commonwealth tour of India in 1950–51 and with MCC to India and Pakistan in 1951–52, taking a hundred wickets in the tours combined. His outstanding bowling performances in terms of figures are his five wickets in nine balls against Leiestershire in 1950, whilst in 1955, he was virtually unplayable on a green Weston-super-Mare wicket. Somerset were put out for 37; Shackleton's share of the spoils was eight wickets for 4 runs. Only one player stood his ground against him – Stephenson who scored 18 not out, leaving a paltry 13 for the other ten players; there were six leg-byes (quite obviously when Shackleton had beaten the bat). In the second innings, Somerset did substantially better; they reached 98. This time, 'Shack' took 6 for 25 for a match aggregate of 14 for 29.

In 1959, he topped the bowling averages with 140 wickets at 21.48, nearly twice as many as the next man. In 1960, he shot Warwickshire out by taking 9 for 30 at Portsmouth, yet perhaps 'Shack's' most valuable piece of bowling occurred in the last afternoon of the game against Derbyshire at Bournemouth in the following season – by which Hampshire became County Champions for the first time. On a slow, easy Bournemouth pitch, Derbyshire needing 252 to win, were 11 for one wicket with 170 minutes remaining for play. A draw seemed the likeliest outcome. 'Shack' broke the back of Derbyshire's innings in the thirty minutes after lunch when he took four wickets for eight runs to reduce Derbyshire to 24 for four. He came back later to take two more wickets and finish with 6 for 39 as Hampshire won by 140 runs. He ended the season with 158 wickets at 19.09 runs each.

To prove his prolific output, if indeed proof was necessary, he bowled no less than 10,303 balls in the summer of 1962 – only four bowlers have done better in the history of the game.

'Shack' never appealed without good cause, and accepted his punishment phlegmatically – applauding anyone who hit him for six.

There were countless occasions when his bowling figures were not as good, but when he contained strong batting on a batsman's wicket and then extracting from the pitch some assistance no one else could find, hammered away to win a match against all cricketing odds.

Through the years of bowling over after over, no day was ever too long for him; there was no deviation in his perfect rhythmic approach to the wicket, the delivery stride and the complete follow-through – poise and balance personified.

During the Club's centenary year 1963, he took 116 Championship wickets at 14.83 – this inspite of him playing in four Test matches, while the following season, he was the first in the country to 100 wickets, which he reached just short of his fortieth birthday – his 138 championship wickets costing him 19.98 runs each. He topped the bowling averages again in 1966 with 117 wickets at 17.84 – whilst he took 114 for 16.84 in 1967.

The summer of 1968 was 'Shack's last full season, at the end of which he announced his retirement, though he was recalled for one Championship match the following summer, taking seven wickets at a cost of 13.57 – he seemed as good as ever.

During the summer of 1969, the first year of the Sunday League, he bowled his opening spell without having to return for the slog and only had 168 runs taken off his 80 overs – quite remarkable when one considers he was forty–four going on forty-five!

His 2,669 wickets (at 18.23) for Hampshire is a County record. Nobody else has clocked up a hundred wickets in twenty consecutive seasons as Derek Shackleton did without fail from 1949 to 1968 – in fact, only Wilfred Rhodes reached this landmark more often.

'Shack's' astonishing consistency became even more remarkable when he revealed after his retirement that he was blind in one eye!

He combined coaching at Canford (1969–78) with appearances for Dorset (1971–74) before becoming a first-class umpire (1979–81).

The sight of Derek Shackleton wending his way to the pavillion with his sweater slung across his shoulder as the shadows lengthened at the end of yet another long day, is something all followers of Hampshire cricket cherished.

# CHRIS SMITH

Born: 15 October 1958 Durban, South Africa
Played: 1980–1991

FIRST-CLASS HAMPSHIRE RECORD

| Matches | Innings | NO | Runs | HS | Ave | 100s |
|---|---|---|---|---|---|---|
| 222 | 383 | 48 | 15287 | 217 | 45.63 | 41 |

| Runs | Wkts | Ave | Best |
|---|---|---|---|
| 2366 | 44 | 53.77 | 5-69 |

NOTABLE FEATS

- In 1983, he added 321 with T E Jesty for the third wicket v Derbyshire at Derby.

- In 1985, he scored over 2,000 runs for Hampshire in all matches.
- In 1987, he added 347 with V P Terry for the first wicket v Warwickshire at Edgbaston – a Hampshire record, hitting his top score of 217.
- He carried his bat for 140* out of 304 v Dorset at Southampton in the 1987 Nat West Trophy.

Chris Smith is the first to admit that he was not as naturally talented as younger brother Robin, but he proved beyond all doubt, that practice can be a passport to success. Even as a young boy he would spend half-an-hour every morning in the net in the garden of his family home; every Sunday summer and winter, he was in the nets by eight o'clock in the morning, working with former Natal player Grayson Heath, the coach his father John had brought in to channel Chris's youthful enthusiasm. The elder son of a Walsall raised father and Scottish mother, his grandfather Vernon Shearer had represented Edinburgh University at three sports, before emigrating to South Africa, playing for Natal and becoming mayor of Durban.

A successful career as a batsman at Northlands High School, Durban, led to Smith's selection for South African Schools in 1975–76 and from there at Natal 'B' for which team he made an unsuccessful debut in February 1978. He first came to England in 1976 with the Kingsmead Mynahs and returned in 1979 to play for Gorseinon in the South Wales League as well as appearing for the Glamorgan Second Eleven.

He won a place in the Glamorgan team against the Sri Lankans and in contrast to his failure on his Natal debut, he hit the highest score for the Welsh county – 67 – he also hit 124 in the match against Hampshire Second Eleven.

Chris Smith's earliest ambitions revolved around playing cricket in England, unshackled by the stricture of overseas regulations. This meant satisfying the requirements of qualification. So for two summers, he had to be content with just the odd first team appearance, spending the rest of his time making runs in the Second Eleven, though there were times when boredom threatened. But the presence of younger brother Robin helped – especially the brotherly rivalry that cropped up when Robin was making a lot of runs. Chris never made any bones about his ambitions: 'I want to be known as a good batsman . . . My ambition is to score as many runs as I can . . . I would be quite happy to bat for two days if there was a century at the end of it.'

Joining Hampshire in 1980 he held together a Hampshire side that was in the early stages of re-building after the days of Richards and Roberts and one deprived of the services of Greenidge and Marshall by the West Indies tour. In his maiden season, he scored 1,048 runs – the only Hampshire batsman to reach a thousand runs. In fact, he scored three hundreds in his first five championship matches, including 130 against Kent at Bournemouth – a typically painstaking effort which provided evidence of his unflappability since a bouncer removed the face guard from his trademark white helmet when he had scored 26. Yet, he was still a totally-unknown quantity when he reported to Northlands Road that April. People who met him for the first time, met a broad-shouldered young man, with a resolute face and were immediately struck by his assured self-confidence.

He missed most of the 1980–81 South African season with a chipped thumb and although Greenidge's return blocked his opportunities during the next two summers, he celebrated becoming qualified for England in May 1983 by scoring 1,000 runs before July.

In his first innings of the 1983 season, he scored 129 at Leicester – and that set the pattern. He hit a career best 193 at Derby and exactly 100 in the next match at Bournemouth against Lancashire. In that same innings at Bournemouth, his nineteen-year-old brother Robin scored a century championship debut. In that summer of 1983, the County's most satisfactory game was against the eventual Champions, Essex at Southend in July. After a low-scoring first innings on both sides, Essex declared at 340 for six, setting Hampshire a target of 410 – the target was reached in the penultimate over, with Chris Smith making 163 – Hampshire thus becoming the first side since the war to score 400 in the fourth innings of a Championship match and win it.

In the end, it came as no surprise to most people when he was elected to replace Graeme Fowler for the third Test against New Zealand at Lord's. His test baptism produced the traumatic experience of a first-ball dismissal by Richard Hadlee. Chris admits that was the worst moment of his life, followed by the most depressing two days. He overcame that horrific start with a 204-minute vigil in the second innings to score 43.

The summer of 1983 ended with 'Kippy' (thus known because of his fondness for sleeping in dressing-rooms) having scored more runs in all competitions than anyone else in England.

He was included in the England touring team to New Zealand and Pakistan the following winter, playiny in five Tests on the tour and had his most impressive innings at Auckland, when he batted 459 minutes for 91 runs to force a draw.

Though he lost form in the Championship in 1984 and with it his Test place, he could do no wrong in the Sunday Legue, hitting 720 runs to replace Barry Richards as the County's heaviest Sunday scorer. He had an outstanding year in 1985, topping the Championship batting averages with 1,720 runs at 53.75, winning the summer race to 1,000 runs, getting to the landmark in his sixteenth innings in mid-June. The following season, he twice broke a finger and missed six matches, though he still scored 1,027 runs at 51.35. He was recalled for the second Test against India at Headingley, but it was his last appearance for England, though there have been occasions since, when a player of Smith's calibre has been missing.

In 1987, Chris Smith was the County's leading run-scorer in all competitions except the Benson and Hedges Cup. His first-class aggregate of 1,519 runs at 46.03, included a maiden double-century during which he and Paul Terry set a new county record opening partnership of 347 in the match against Warwickshire at Edgbaston. In the Refuge Assurance League, he hit five half-centuries in scoring 476 runs and in the Nat West Trophy, he scored a century against Dorset. Another 1,000 runs came inevitably in 1988 and the seventh in succession in 1989.

In 1990, he again finished as the leading run scorer. His single-minded professionalism made that almost inevitable – he had set himself a pre-season target of 1,800 runs and hit that mark with a Championship match and the Sri Lankans to go. He then bowed to his benefit calls by sitting out what little of the season remained: otherwise , he may have topped the 2,000 run mark.

He began the 1991 seaon with an indulgent double-century against Oxford University, two fifties in friendlies, a half-century in the opening Sunday League match and a total of 342 runs, dismissed just once in the first three Benson and Hedges Cup group games. Adapting his sound technique most effectively to one-day cricket, his 121 not out against Nottinghamshire on a bleak Southampton Tuesday, included some stunning back-foot blows.

Those who watch the county on a regular basis and like to get to the ground early will be familiar with Smith's routine. Once the toss had been made and he knew he would be batting first thing, he would stroll out to the centre and for five minutes or so, would stand batless but in his stance position and play imaginary defensive strokes, as he concentrated on the direction from which the bowler would attak. Always the possessor of a business brain, it was no surprise to anyone in the game when his benefit year produced more than £181,000. His marketing skills were employed sucessfully at the Hampshire club.

In the summer of 1991, while in the best form of his life, he took up a marketing position with the Western Australian Cricket Association. He had just taken Hampshire into the last four of the Nat West Trophy with his tenth century of the season, knowing that he would be unable to play in the final if, at long last, Hampshire were to get there – which they did, beating Surrey by four wickets.

# ROBIN SMITH

Born: 13 September 1963 Durban, South Africa
Played: 1982–1992

FIRST-CLASS HAMPSHIRE RECORD

| Matches | Innings | NO | Runs | HS | Ave | 100s |
|---------|---------|-----|------|------|-------|------|
| 149 | 248 | 44 | 9235 | 209* | 45.27 | 24 |

| Runs | Wkts | Ave | Best |
|------|------|-------|------|
| 630 | 12 | 52.50 | 2-11 |

NOTABLE FEATS

- In 1987, he scored 209* v Essex at Southend.
- He was one of Wisden's Five Cricketers of the Year in 1989.
- He has hit centuries in all three one-day competitions: 125* v Surrey in the 1989 Nat West Trophy; 155* v Glamorgan in the 1989 Benson and Hedges Cup and 131 v Nottinghamshire in the 1989 Sunday League.

A major force in Hampshire and England cricket, Robin Smith's determination to succeed can be traced back to his early days in South Africa. Robin Smith and his brother Chris grew up in Durban, where their father is a very successful saddler to the South African racing industry. So successful in fact, that he expected his sons to take over the business! As a boy, Robin would rise at 4.30a.m. to practise his sports – cricket, rugby, and athletics. As a kicker during one rugby season, he broke the school record for the highest amount of points scored – 218, the next highest being 13. During the athletics season, he managed to break thirty-two records – including two Springbok records – ranging from the shot putt through to the 400 metres. Many of these were records that had stood for eighty years!

In his final year at school in Durban, he scored six centuries and an aggregate of 1,780 runs at an average of 85, breaking the Natal school records previously held by another distingushed Hampshire old boy, one B A Richards. Robin Smith was only ten when Richards, then with Hampshire, produced a batting book for boys in which all the pictures featured the younger Smith. His career has virtually been mapped out since then. Robin left school a year early, because he wanted to make cricket his profession. He wanted to play Test cricket and realised that his only real chance lay in England. Robin's decision to qualify for England owed a lot to family persuasion. Brother Chris had come over to England when he left school and had a season with Glamorgan Second Eleven. He enjoyed it so much, that when he went home to South Africa, he kept going on to Robin about how great it was to play county cricket for a living. When Robin left school in 1980, he came straight over with brother Chris – Hampshire acting quickly to offer a four-year contract on seeing his performance in the nets fully supporting Robin's remarkable record-breaking feats in Natal and South African Schools' cricket.

Whilst he was waiting to play county cricket, he played club cricket for Ickenham in the Middlesex League – in his first innings, he scored almost 300 runs and he was not once dismissed !

For Hampshire Second Eleven in 1981, he batted with a power and maturity that belied his years; he averaged 52.61 and his 206 against Gloucestershire was the highest Second Eleven score in the championship – it was a magnificent innings, containing three sixes and 31 fours. His brief sorties into the county game, brought him instant success – a Championship debut hundred, followed by two more hundreds in the space of ten innings in 1983, were ample proof of his class and temperament.

He qualified as an English player at the beginning of the 1985 season and proved most successful – he hit a swift 85 against Kent and followed that with his first century of the season against Oxford University, when he shared a century partnership with his brother 'Kippy'. It was the Smith brothers too with a stand of 161 in 130 minutes who saw Hampshire to a stiff target of 379 in 79 overs against Derbyshire. Robin made a then career best of 140 in 165 balls, finishing the match with two massive sixes off Geoff Miller. Known as 'Judge' a nickname given to him because of his wig-like hair and not because of his deep knowledge of the legal system, he ended the season with 1,351 Championship runs at an average of 39.73. A broken thumb in early May 1987, effectively kept him out of the side for about two months. On his return, a natural impatience to make up for lost time occasionally caused his downfall, but he did record his maiden double century, 209 not out against Essex at Southend.

Hampshire supporters found it difficult to understand the prior claims of some of the other young batsmen who were preferred to Smith in the England side, but one innings played in the quarter-final of the Benson and Hedges Cup on a hazardous pitch at Worcester removed all doubts. His 87 out of 170 for seven was a masterly display of courage, tenacity and technical maturity against an attack including Dilley, Newport and Radford. His resolute batting in the last two tests against the 1988 West Indians provided a much-needed source of cheer for English cricket followers in a season of national despair.

He worked hard at his technique during the winter of 1988–89 after the tour of India was cancelled and began the 1989 season in prime form. In the years leading up to this season, Robin had failed on his own admission to do justice to his own outstanding natural ability, but he progressed in this one summer to become England's number one middle-order batsman. His emergence in the 'Ashes' series won him a regular Test place and international prominence for his lone defiance of the Australians – hitting two centuries in a total of 553 runs at 61.44. He ended the summer top of England's Test and Hampshire's batting averages and was the highest placed English qualified player in the national averages. England calls restricted Robin Smith to just 12 matches in 1990 and in those, he scored 941 runs, including four hundreds. His highest innings came at Southampton, as he hit 181 in 188 balls off the Sussex attack, including 127 before lunch on the second day.

His decline during the disappointing winter of 1990–91 in Australia was only temporary, returning for the 1991 season to score 852 runs at 42.60 for Hampshire and 416 Test runs against the West Indies at 83.20. Man-of-the-Match in Hampshire's 1992 success in the Benson and Hedges Cup Final win over Kent with a hard-hitting innings of 90, his acquisition of a regular England place has inevitably reduced the amount of his cricket for Hampshire, but not the quality or quantity of his runs.

# EDWARD SPROT

Born: 4 February 1872, Edinburgh
Died: 8 October 1945
Played: 1898–1914

FIRST-CLASS HAMPSHIRE RECORD

| Matches | Innings | NO | Runs | HS | Ave | 100s |
|---------|---------|-----|-------|-----|-------|------|
| 267 | 452 | 28 | 12212 | 147 | 28.80 | 13 |

| Runs | Wkts | Ave | Best |
|------|------|-------|------|
| 1856 | 54 | 34.37 | 5-28 |

NOTABLE FEATS

- He was Captain of Hampshire from 1903 to 1914.
- In 1910, he added 159 with C B Fry for the seventh wicket v Worcestershire at Bournemouth.
- He scored 125 in forty-eight minutes v Gloucestershire at Bristol in 1911, completing his century in only forty-five minutes, the

fastest century ever scored for the county. Most of the runs came in a last wicket stand of 147 in forty minutes with A E Fielder.

Born in Scotland, Edward Mark Sprot was educated at Harrow before making his name in Army cricket.

A remarkably versatile man, Sprot was an excellent pianist, about the best dry-fly fisherman in Hampshire and a first-class billiards player – on a strange table in Cairo, he won a 200 up game from the opening left by his opponent on starting the play! He had also won the Army rackets doubles with Col J Spens whilst serving with the Shropshire Light Infantry in 1899.

He had first played for Hampshire in the previous summer in the company of many other noted solidiers, namely Captain E G Wynyard, Major R M Poore an Colonel J G Greig.

In 1900, the old Harrovian was available on a regular basis and made his maiden first-class hundred off the Warwickshire attack. The following season saw him make a great advance as a batsman, scoring 932 runs for an average of 34.51, with two hundreds. Againt Somerset at Taunton, Hampshire made 642 for nine, with Sprot scoring his highest ever score of 147, as he and Greig (113) made 148 for the second wicket and then he and Webb (56) 127 for the third in fifty minutes. As a batsman, Sprot was a natural hitter of the ball, with a variety of strokes, who believed that attack was the best form of defence – putting plenty of power into his strokes, he accumulated his runs in quick style when at the crease, even if he did have a tendency to launch into it as soon as he came in to bat which often cost him his wicket. At the end of the 1902 season, Charles Robson handed over the captaincy to Sprot. He was to captain the side until the outbreak of World War One.

In the opening fixture of 1903, Sprot's first in charge, he scored 96 to lead by example, as Hampshire defeated Derbyshire at Southampton. Barratt, Hill and Wynyard, who all averaged over 40, were only able to play eighteen innings between them throughout the season and in their absence, Sprot had little support. One of the few amateurs who had played regularly for Hampshire in the Boer War period, he played well that season to average 36.30 from twenty-six Championship innings.

In 1904, the county struggled to dismiss the opposition (in five out of six consecutive matches, Hampshire's opponents scored over 500 runs in an innings) and in four games, the county failed to make a hundred in either innings. It says much for Sprot that throughout this discouragement, he almost made 1,000 runs and set his side a splendid example in the field.

Slim, strong and athletically built, Sprot was a fine field, especially in the slips, where he very rarely missed a catch.

As a captain, he was not Robson's equal in terms of tactics, but played every game with an optimism and zest that was proof against constant disappointment. He made the game extremely enjoyable for both his own side and the opposition.

In fact, he helped to raise Hampshire County Cricket Club to such a good standard, that they reached fifth place in the County Championship in 1914.

In 1905, Sprot was the most consistent Hampshire batsman, averaging 41 for an aggregate of 1,206 runs – no matter the state of the game, he played attractive and aggressive cricket. Again he led by example in the field and though this was an asset to his leadership, no captain could really master conditions under which thirty players appeared for the county and twenty-four of them bowled !

After a disappointing season in 1906, he returned to his best form the following season, doubling his average. Against Kent in 1907, he scored 111 before being run out as Hampshire beat the men from the hop county by five wickets after being asked to get 306 in the last innings.

In the 1908 match against Northamptonshire, Sprot created quite a sensation, when to the disbelief of the Southampton crowd, he declared Hampshire's innings closed when with a wicket to fall, they were 24 runs behind their opponents total. By this action, he saved the interval between the innings, for rain had continually interrupted the progress of the match. Philip Mead then took 6 for 18 with his left-hand slows and Hampshire required only 86 for victory. Sprot then hit 62 in less than an hour – an innings containing two sixes and 8 fours. It was a victory that Wisden summed up as 'without parallel, which makes unique incident in the history of the game.' That was one of seven Championship wins for Hampshire and maintained the county's position in mid-table. At the 1909 AGM, Charles Fry 'speaking as a kind of semi-outsider', paid a very warm tribute to Sprot's leadership and described the side as the most promising in England.

In 1911, Sprot had a rather moderate season with the bat, though his personality was still a great asset to the side. In June of that season, he had a day of glory, when he scored 125 not out against Gloucestershire at Bristol. Completing his century in only forty-five minutes, it is the fastest century ever scored for the county. Most of the runs came in a last wicket stand of 147 in only forty minutes with A E Fielder. During 1918, Sprot indicated that he did not wish to continue as captain when cricket resumed and the committee elected the Hon. Lionel Tennyson for the post.

The debt which Hampshire cricket owes to E M Sprot in a vital period of its history is indeed deep.

# BOB STEPHENSON

Born: 19 November 1942, Derby
Played: 1969–1980

FIRST-CLASS HAMPSHIRE RECORD

| Matches | Innings | NO | Runs | HS | Ave | 100s |
|---------|---------|-----|------|------|-------|------|
| 263 | 343 | 66 | 4566 | 100* | 16.48 | 1 |

| Runs | Wkts | Ave |
|------|------|-----|
| 39 | 0 | – |

*Number of dismissals:* 570 caught; 75 stumpings

NOTABLE FEATS

- He was Captain of Hampshire in 1979.
- He made 645 dismissals (570 caught, 75 stumped) in his career with Hampshire.
- His best season was 1970 with 80 victims (73 caught, 7 stumped) in twenty-four matches.
- He made six dismissals in an innings v Middlesex at Lord's in 1976.
- He added 168 with M N S Taylor for the eighth wicket v Glamorgan at Southampton in 1978.

Bob Stephenson was a professional soccer player with Derby County, Shrewsbury and Rochdale. He was twenty-six years old when the fourth division outfit told the son of the Derby, Sheffield Wednesday, Aston Villa and England defender, George Stephenson, that he would not make the grade, even at their level.

Stephenson like so many other footballers, had always been proficient, rather than brilliant at the game of cricket and the then long summer break allowed him time to follow this pursuit.

While he was at the Baseball Ground, he played for St Peters CC on Saturdays and Derby Amateurs on Sundays; in Rochdale, he played for Milnrow in the Central Lancashire League.

The verdict by Rochdale not to renew his contract came as no surprise to him. Indeed, he had already begun to plan his future by studying for the extra 'A' Level which would allow him to take up a mature student's place at Loughborough College and a teaching post. However, he was never to fill that place, for Derbyshire knew his qualities and although at that time they were unwilling to offer him a place on their staff, they were happy enough to provide the occasional game as cover for Bob Taylor. He was happy with the arrangement, for it gave him a chance to rub shoulders with players who had previously been names in the press and on television. He understudied Taylor on nine occasions – his appetite had been whetted.

So, when Hampshire, faced by the departure of Bryan Timms, wrote offering a trial, he accepted; yet before the time arrived for that, the county wrote again – this time they offered the almost unknown wicket-keeper a contract – he did not need asking twice. I suppose it was really more of a gamble for Hampshire than for Stephenson, yet he immediately gained a first-team place and appeared in every Championship match the following summer, becoming an integral part of the Hampshire side for the next ten years.

That decade saw Bob Stephenson develop into one of the best wicket-keepers in the business. He was never an extrovert, never flashy, but always capable of blinding flashes of inspiration. His best season was 1970 when he helped to dismiss 80 batsmen.

As a batsman, Stephenson was the traditional tail-ender, always prepared to fling his bat, favouring the arc between mid-on and mid-wicket. Much of his character shone through in his batting. His stance at the wicket was of a man who was never coached. He was almost fully erect as he faced up to the incoming bowler, his cap always slightly askew. Stephenson's fighting nature was often evident when he was asked to open the innings for Hampshire-showing that he could grind the shine off the ball as well as anyone. His one and only first-class hundred, 100 not out came in the match against Somerset in 1976.

Bob Stephenson was above all else, a professional – when he led the county side out for the first time as official captian in his home town of Derby in late April 1979, his promotion still had a dream-like quality about it – as he said at the time: 'it's still a fairly tale to me.'

He was only the fifth Hampshire captain since the end of the war – change for the sake of change had no place in the affairs of life at Southampton. The change was enforced rather than contrived, as he became the County's fourteenth captain since first-class status was achieved in 1895. Bob Stephenson was very different from the many who had preceded him. In the main, these were men with university and public school backgrounds, not the world of professional soccer. He was not a dour stick-in-the-mud captain; he carefully weighed up every decison in the best interests of Hampshire cricket and its players.

Wicket-keepers are quite often over-looked men, yet many a Hampshire bowler was made by Bob Stephenson's performances behind the sticks. Starting late, he had a lot of catching up to do yet he played his last game for the County in 1980, when the teenage son of Jim Parks replaced him. He was Stephenson's understudy and yet in his first ten seasons, the experienced wicket-keeper missed only four of a possible 214 Championship matches – it was quite a surprise when Parks' wait on the sidelines ended so soon.

In his time at Hampshire, he claimed 645 victims in 263 first-class matches. And that puts him statistically speaking at the head of the long list of men who have worn the gloves for Hampshire; it gives Stephenson a record of 2.45 victims per match.

# JAMES STONE

Born: 29 November 1876, Southampton
Died: 18 November 1942
Played: 1900–1914

FIRST-CLASS HAMPSHIRE RECORD

| Matches | Innings | NO | Runs | HS | Ave | 100s |
|---|---|---|---|---|---|---|
| 274 | 468 | 57 | 9167 | 174 | 22.30 | 5 |

| Runs | Wkts | Ave | Best |
|---|---|---|---|
| 104 | 1 | 104.00 | 1-77 |

*Number of dismissals:* 361 caught; 113 stumped

NOTABLE FEATS

● He helped to dismiss 474 batsmen (361 caught 113 stumped) in his career with Hampshire.
● In 1905, he hit the highest score of his career, 174 v Sussex.

James Stone gave valuable service to Hampshire County Cricket Club, both behind the stumps and as a batsman.

A product of the Southampton Parks, he showed great promise as a junior prompting Captain Hoare to take him under his wing at the Training Ship Mercury. Still impoving, he was given a trial in the Hampshire Second Eleven in 1899 and the following year, made his debut for the Hampshire first team, though it wasn't until the summer of 1902, that he began to hold down a regular place.

Played at first for his wicket-keeping alone, James Stone subsequently improved his batting so much, that in later years, he became one of the more consistent scorers in the Hampshire side, in his early days, he had a very sound defence, but scarcely a scoring stroke, though as his career progressed, he still retained his defence, but possessed as many strokes as the average county batsman, whilst his bravery in a crisis was unquestionable. From going in as last man, he was promoted to a regular place as one of the opening pair.

The following figures show very clearly the great advance James Stone made as a batsman since he was first tried for the County:

|  | Innings | NO | Runs | HS | Ave |
|---|---|---|---|---|---|
| 1902 | 22 | 4 | 228 | 31 | 12.66 |
| 1905 | 34 | 3 | 660 | 174 | 21.29 for Hants |
| 1907 | 45 | 6 | 941 | 97* | 24.12 |
| 1911 | 45 | 1 | 1030 | 83 | 23.40 |

His highest first-class score for the county was a sparkling 174 made against Sussex in 1905 and though he never attained any really great distinction, he was a good and tenacious batsman, with a rather curious propensity for hitting the rising ball on his body high to leg over his left shoulder.

After hitting 109 against Worcestershire in 1909 and 105 in the match against Lancashire the following summer, the seasons 1911 to 1913 saw him exceed a thousand runs. James Stone did especially well in 1912, when he helped Hampshire beat the Australians at Southampton by eight wickets – the first victory by a Hampshire team over an Australian team. It was directly after this match, that the Hampshire committee allotted James Stone the fixture against Yorkshire at Southampton for his benefit.

The committee of Hampshire were very keen to impress upon the paying public that Stone was the first Southampton-born player to be given a benefit by the Club and they hoped they would respond by rewarding him with the recognition he deserved for his unswerving loyalty, consistency and ability.

It was the most successful benefit of any Hampshire professional up to that time James Stone being rewarded with a sum of £500. In his benefit match, he went in first and helped by C B Fry added 109 for the third wicket. Yorkshire were hard pressed until Haigh and Hirst caused a second innings collapse.

A smart and unobtrusive wicket-keeper, James Stone was instrumental in disposing of 474 opponents in his career with Hampshire.

After the First World War ended his fifteen years on the Hampshire staff, he joined Glamorgan, where his experience of first-class cricket was an important factor behind his signing. His presence in the Welsh side certainly bolstered the batting. An example came in the match with the West Indies at Cardiff Arms Park over the August Bank Holiday of 1923. The Welsh county celebrated their first-ever win over a touring team, with Stone making an invaluable 108 to see Glamorgan to 324. Ryan and Mercer bowled out the tourists for 195 to give Glamorgan a 43 run win. He played 48 innings for Glamorgan, scoring 1,047 runs at 22.66. From 1925 to 1934, he acted as a first-class umpire.

One of a number of players to have represented both Hampshire and Glamorgan, James Stone died in Maidenhead on 18 November 1942, aged nearly sixty-six.

# MIKE TAYLOR

Born: 12 November 1942, Amersham
Played: 1973–1980

FIRST-CLASS HAMPSHIRE RECORD

| Matches | Innings | NO | Runs | HS | Ave | 100s |
|---|---|---|---|---|---|---|
| 145 | 198 | 39 | 3646 | 103* | 22.93 | 2 |

| Runs | Wkts | Ave | Best |
|---|---|---|---|
| 7458 | 308 | 24.21 | 7-23 |

NOTABLE FEATS

- In 1965, whilst playing for Nottinghamshire, he performed the 'hat-trick' v Kent at Dover.
- In 1977, he produced his best bowling figures, seven of 23 v his former county at Basingstoke.
- In 1978, he added 168 with G R Stephenson for the eighth wicket v Glamorgan at Southampton.

Hampshire's announcement in the winter of 1972–73 that they had recruited the services of Nottinghamshire's Mike Taylor, possibly generated little excitement among their supporters, for Taylor had soldiered on for Notts for nine seasons without becoming much more than a run-of-the-mill all-rounder.

Yet in a way, the signing of Mike Taylor was one of the shrewdest moves in the county's history.

Mike had started his career in the Minor Counties with his native Buckinghamshire, playing alongside his twin brother Derek, the wicket-keeper – batsman who was to become an important member of the successful Somerset side of the early 1970/1980s, before emigrating to Australia. While brother Derek went off to Surrey and then Somerset, Mike was recommended to

Trent Bridge by Alf Pope, one of three Derbyshire brothers and made his first-class debut for Nottinghamshire in 1964. The following season, he performed the 'hat-trick' in the match against Kent at Dover and in 1967 hit his highest ever first-class score, 105 against Lancashire at Trent Bridge

The following summer, he turned in his best ever season with the ball taking 99 wickets at 21.00. In the last match of the season against Glamorgan at Swansea, it was Mike Taylor who was Nottinghamshire's match-winner, though the record books of course will tell of Sir Garfield Sobers, then captain of Nottinghamshire, hitting six sixes off one over from Glamorgan's Malcolm Nash. Sobers did in fact score 76 not out, including those six sixes in the first innings and 72 in the second, whilst Brian Bolus made 145. Eventually, Glamorgan had to get 280 to win in four hours, but good bowling by Taylor (five for 47), who made the most of a damp pitch caused by overnight rain, resulted in the Welsh side being dismissed for 113 and Notts pipping Hampshire for fourth place in the county championship!

An upheaval at the end of the 1972 season led to his release – Nottinghamshire's loss was to be Hampshire's gain. In 230 matches for Notts, he scored 4,377 runs at an average of 18.01, whilst his 522 wickets cost 27.86 runs each.

When Mike Taylor played for Notts, he used to spend hours of their matches with Hampshire studying Derek Shackleton's method. He applied, in effect for Shackleton's place in the Hampshire side – got it – bowled resourcefully throughout his career with the southern county, at medium-pace, with new ball or old and played some valuable innings. In fact, he had arrived at Hampshire at a time when the county were in a transitional period; Shackleton had retired, Andy Roberts was yet to arrive and Hampshire needed a stock bowler to relieve Peter Sainsbury of some of the load of carrying the attack's main responsibility. After years of labouring at Trent Bridge without reward, he sensed a chance of finally sampling some of the games glory, yet even he could scarcely have dreamed that within five months he would be sharing in the glory of bringing the County Championship title to Northlands Road for the second time.

By the end of that first summer, he had taken 63 Championship wickets at 19.33, scored 441 runs at 24.50 and snapped up 14 catches, mostly at gully and short leg.

Against Worcestershire at New Road, he took four for 17 as the home side fell 191 runs short of their target of 316, whilst in the match against Gloucestershire he took 7 for 53, bowling with superb control and accuracy. In fact, Gloucestershie were 74 for 0 when Taylor struck, taking three wickets for one run and the score was 75 for three. In 1974, he had his most productive season for the county, taking 72 (63 championship) wickets at 17.48 to finish sixth in the national first-class averages. He had a good all-round match against his former county, taking 5 for 29 and then hitting 68, as Hampshire overwhelmed Nottinghamshire inside two days to win by an innings and 101 runs. Three years later, he produced his best bowling figures for the county in the match against his former county at Basingstoke, taking 7 for 23. It was also the season when he hit his first century for the county, 102 against Essex at Portsmouth.

After helping the county to their first Sunday League title in 1975, he played his typically yeoman part in the second three years on. This was particularly satisfying for him, because the victory was clinched at Bournemouth, when his twin brother Derek was attempting to snatch the title away from him at Taunton. It was also the season when he scored his second and highest century for Hampshire, 103 not out against Glamorgan at Southampton finishing the season with 770 runs at 38.50 and second in the Hampshire batting averages! In fact, I know he won't thank me but at the end of the season, his batting and bowling averages were virtually identical.

His bowling began to fall away as he finally admitted that years had blunted his edge. His 145 first-class matches for the county yielded 308 wickets at 24.21 and 3,646 runs at 22.93, before he retired to serve Hampshire as Assistant Secretary – an area in which his vast experience was invaluable.

His efforts for the County were broadened by his increasing involvement as Marketing Manager – a crucial part of the game's future.

In 1989, Hampshire showed their appreciation of all Mike Taylor has achieved both on and off the field by granting him a Testimonial Year – a wonderful spontaneous gesture, though without doubt, Mike Taylor has made an indelible mark on the affairs of the county which offered him a second chance when Nottinghamshire showed him the door.

# LIONEL TENNYSON

Born: 7 November 1889, Westminter
Died: 6 June 1951
Played: 1913–1935

FIRST-CLASS HAMPSHIRE RECORD

| Matches | Innings | NO | Runs | HS | Ave | 100s |
|---|---|---|---|---|---|---|
| 347 | 553 | 20 | 12626 | 217 | 23.68 | 15 |

| Runs | Wkts | Ave | Best |
|---|---|---|---|
| 2374 | 43 | 55.20 | 3-50 |

NOTABLE FEATS

- He was captain of Hampshire from 1919 to 1933.
- He scored 94 out of 112 in eighty minutes in his combined innings v Lancashire at Old Trafford in 1925.
- Against Kent at Southampton in 1921, he hit one ball for 139 yards 1 foot 8 inches from hit to pitch.
- He scored 217 v West Indians at Southampton in 1928, adding 311 with J A Newman for the sixth wicket in the process.

Lionel Tennyson known and loved in turn as the Hon. L H Tennyson, Lord Tennyson and just 'Lionel' . . . was the grandson of the poet. His posterity rests well on his cricket and his ripe human nature. He was, as man and sportsman, fashioned in the image of a Regency 'buck', living well, uninhibited, spreading around him the flavour of carefree relish of the world's good things, a rare friend and a gallant opponent.

He started his cricket life as fast bowler good enough for Eton, but not for Cambridge University and was in his twenty-fourth year before he attracted any attention. He had joined the Army and had scored runs for the Household Brigade and Greenjackets before making his first-class debut for MCC against Oxford University in July 1913, when he and Meyrick Payne opened the second innings with a stand of 175 in an hour- and-a-half. Though he was dropped three times in his innings of 100, it was good enough to alert Hampshire and a little over two weeks later, he made his debut for them in the game against Worcestershire at Dudley. In only his second match against Essex at Leyton, he scored 116 in 105 minutes out of 198 for six. In his next game at Trent Bridge, he hit a magnificent 111 and shared in a thrilling stand of 132 in just over an hour with Edward Sprot. In his first four matches in first-class cricket, the Hon Tennyson had scored three centuries and came close to making it four in five, when he scored 96 against Yorkshire in the next match. He finished the summer with 832 runs from 19 innings and an average of 46.22 – the fifth best in England – though he he was never to reach those heights again.

On the strength of his first season's performance in county cricket, he was included in a strong MCC touring party to South Africa the following winter and was chosen as one of Wisden's Five Cricketers of the Year for 1914. But his performances on tour – he was fortunate to keep his place for all the Tests while scoring a total of only 116 runs – tended to support Wisden's view that 'he may or may not have the qualities to make for permanent success'.

He took over the captaincy of Hampshire after the First World War, during which he was wounded three times and mentioned in dispatches twice, and his qualities of leadership more than atoned for any drop in batting average.

Receiving a telegram, Tennyson read it, rolled it into a ball, tossed it into the air and caught it, remarking: 'Good gracious they've asked me to captain England.' That was in 1921 when Tennyson displayed the pluck that was to be a mark of his play. He scored 74 not out in the Lord's Test, relishing the challenge of Gregory and McDonald. He scored 63 and 36 at Headingley despite a badly injured hand and got another half-century at the Oval after being hit over the heart and being nearly knocked out. That summer of 1921 was a good one for Tennyson as he led Hampshire to sixth place in the Championship. He scored three centuries, 152 against Leicestershire at Portsmouth, 131 not out against Lancashire at Southampton and 101 in 110 minutes against Yorkshire at Sheffield. His keen sense of sportmanship was evident in the game which ended in a six-wicket win for Yorkshire, but ended with Edgar Oldroyd 99 not out. The game was over, but Tennyson bowled another ball which Oldroyd hit for four to get his century. Tennyson hit the ball with such power that during the game against Kent at Southampton that summer, he drove a ball from Bill Fairservice over the pavilion and into a garden, a distance of almost 140 yards.

When he was captain, there was never any doubt as to who was in charge, as Jack Newman found out at Trent Bridge in 1922. His was an inspirational captaincy that helped Hampshire up the championship table and produced some unlikely results, the most noteworthy beiing the match at Edgbaston in 1922.

Bowled out for 15 by Warwickshire, Hampshire followed on 208 runs behind. Before Hampshire's second innings started, Calthorpe (who had taken 4 for 4; suggested that the amateurs should play golf at Stourbridge on the following afternoon, as the match would be over in the morning. Tennyson always with an eye to a wager at the longest odds, bet the Warwickshire captain that Hampshire would emerge victorious. Hampshire totalled 521 thanks to Brown and Livsey and then Kennedy and Newman carried the county to victory. His winnings were enormous and the celebratory dinner he put on for the team during the train journey back to Southampton was an occasion that was long remembered.

One of Tennyson's longest innings came at Southampton in 1925, when in the match against Middlesex, he stayed in 165 minutes and hit three sixes and 27 fours in his 184.

With the death of his father in 1928, Lionel Tennyson succeeded to the title and henceforth became 'Lordship' to his players. Also in that year, he hit the highest score of his career – 217 in four hours against the touring West Indies side. Hampshire were 88 for 5 when Tennyson joined Jack Newman. They were 399 for six when he left, with Newman scoring 118.

One of Tennyson's pleasant little habits was to send telegrams to his batsmen on the field. H L V Day was trying to cope with the Notts fast bowlers and was flattened by a very short long hop. As he sat on the ground, recovering his composure, he got a telegram which read, 'What do you think your ———— bat is for,' signed Lionel. Another young amateur striving to find his touch, received an encouraging message: 'For God's sake, get out and let someone else take a hundred off this jam.'

In his last year as captain, when he was forty-two years old, he still possessed the ability to get quick runs when needed, though again his only century of the season came for the Gentlemen v Players at the Oval. He was by no means the most illustrious batsman in the Gentleman's XI and indeed there were 'comments' on his selection! He confidently predicted that he would score a century, though it was three years since he had scored a hundred in first-class cricket, and was prepared to wager bottle of champagne – the challenge was accepted. Tennyson scored 112 on a wicket that was difficult after overnight rain and Wisden said: 'he was very lucky to begin with' but he scored at almost a run a minute and when the lunch interval interrupted his innings at 73, he confidently ordered his bottle of champagne then drank it – and scored 39 in twenty-five minutes after lunch!

As he himself said, he was born with great physical strength, a most robust constitution almost insensible to fatigue, the highest of spirits and a superabundance of energy. Which was just as well, since he lived life twice as hard as most poeple. He might when Hampshire were playing in London, go from play to dinner and a night of cards and talk, then, without sight of bed, on to breakfast and back to the match!

Cricket for him was fun – he neither sought nor accepted advice. At the prompting of a whim, he would all but reverse the side's batting order. He continued to play for Hampshire until 1935 and two years later sponsored and captained a strong team to India, where they won three of the five unofficial Tests. Tennyson played one innings of any note, hitting two sixes and 13 fours in a century at Sind.

On that trip to India, the team stayed as guests of the Jam Sahib of Newanagar, an independent state in the Bombay area. A ceremonial panther shoot was arranged in their honour at three different lodges where a goat was tethered on the platform. Several goats had been sacrificed to lull the panther into feeling secure and another was there, the bait for the panther, when the party including Tennyson arrived. After thirty minutes or so, the panther arrived and after what seemed a lifetime, a shot rang out (it had been arranged that only Lord Tennyson would shoot). The panther looked about and then vanished into the dark. Alf Gover sitting behind Tennyson exclaimed: 'Good lord my Lord, you've shot the goat!'

Almost certainly the only county captain who employed his wicket-keeper as butler, the Lord Lionel Tennyson died at Bexhill-on-Sea in 1951 at the age of sixty-one. His funeral took place while the opening Test between England and South Africa was being played at Trent Bridge. Play was stopped for a few moments as a tribute.

# PAUL TERRY

Born: 14 January 1959 Osnabruck, Germany
Played: 1978–1992

### FIRST-CLASS HAMPSHIRE RECORD

| Matches | Innings | NO | Runs | HS | Ave | 100s |
|---|---|---|---|---|---|---|
| 223 | 372 | 37 | 11988 | 190 | 35.78 | 26 |

| Runs | Wkts | Ave | Best |
|---|---|---|---|
| 58 | 0 | – | – |

### NOTABLE FEATS

- In 1984, he added 302 with T E Jesty for the second wicket v Cambridge University at Fenners.
- In 1987, he added 347 with C L Smith to establish a new Hampshire record for the first wicket v Warwickshire at Edgbaston.

- He has scored three Sunday League centuries, with a highest of 142 v Leicestershire at Southampton in 1986.
- He has scored four Nat West centuries, with a highest of 165* v Berkshire at Southampton in 1985 – carrying his bat in the process.
- He has scored two Benson and Hedges Cup centuries, with a highest of 134 v Combined Services at Southampton 1990.

Born in Osnabruck, Germany, Paul Terry went to Millfield, from where he was chosen to lead England Schools on their 1977–78 tour of india. Having played for the Hampshire Second Eleven since 1976, he made his first-class debut for the county in 1978, playing in two first-class matches and one John Player League match.

Over the next four seasons, he only made seventeen appearances and a top score of 31 against Worcestershire at Bournemouth in 1980. However, his cover fielding and speed around the outfield made him a most valuable member of the Hampshie side. I well remember his boundary catch at Old Trafford in the John Player League match of 1981, to end Clive Lloyd's innings – it was an incredible piece of fielding. In fact, Hampshire's exciting victory that day owed much to Paul Terry, who not only held two magnificent boundary catches, but batted coolly for 26 not out as Hampshire nearly wasted their victory chance. However, in terms of the county Championship, it was a frustrating season for him with but a few first team opportunities, though he showed in the very last match of the season against Norhamptonshire with an unbeaten 94, what a fine batsman he is. In 1983, Paul Terry, who had been in and out of the Hampshire team for several seasons, gained a regular place and reached a thousand runs (1,096) for the first time and with the impressive average of 40.59.

He seized his chance in 1984, while Gordon Greenidge was absent with the West Indies tour to score 1,192 runs at 54.18 and top the County's batting averages, and the England selectors chose him for two Tests.

Normally a correct and confident player of fast bowling, the West Indies' extra pace immediately exposed a weakness outside his off stump. When he was given a second chance, he appeared to lose sight of a short ball from Winston Davis and suffered a fractured left ulna. He amazed everyone by appearing at 278 for 9, when the fall of England's ninth wicket had left Allan Lamb on 98. Paul Terry's injured arm was in a sling under his England sweater – when he was advised to bat left-handed, he declined saying, 'No thanks, I don't want my right arm broken as well!' Fortunately Allan Lamb went on to complete his hundred before Terry had to face a ball. When he did, Joel Garner produced a perfect Yorker at his second attempt. In 1985, the tall square-shouldered opening batsman was appointed as Hampshire vice-captain. It certainly didn't affect his batting, as he had his most successful season, with the bat to date, 1,284 runs at 32.92. In 1984 he hit his then highest score of 175 not out against Gloucestershire at Bristol as well as taking the Man-of-the-match award in the Nat West Trophy tie with Berkshire, by hitting a superb unbeaten 165.

He had a disappointing summer in 1986 in terms of championship matches, but hit a magnificent 142 against Leicestershire at Southampton in the Sunday League.

In the close season of 1986–87, Paul Terry had been breaking records in district cricket in Australia – at the end of the 1987 season, he had almost more or less doubled his batting average. He hit form against Worcestershire with scores of 74 and 83 not out, but the highlight was his innings of 122 as he and Chris Smith shared in a new Hampshire record 1st wicket partnership of 347 against Warwickshire at Edgbaston. His century took 315 minutes, but he faced less bowling than Smith. The following summer saw him take 190 off the Sri Lankans at Southampton, to register his highest first-class score.

Paul Terry fully justified his reputation as one of the outstanding fielders in modern cricket with thirty-nine catches in first-class games in 1989 – a seasons total only five times bettered for Hampshire (by players appearing in more matches than Terry's twenty-three). During the match against Warwickshire, he equalled Hampshire's record with five catches in an innings. At Derby, he hit a championship best 180 and though he hit thirteen other scores of fifty in first-class and one-day cricket, it was his only hundred – though he was dismissed four times in the nineties.

In 1990, he began to show again the ability that brought him England selection some six years earlier with five first-class centuries and two more in one-day cricket. His 113 not out against Somerset at Taunton in the Refuge Assurance Sunday League was his second century of the weekend and helped him pass 3,000 Sunday League runs. Against Combined Universities at Southampton in a Benson and Hedges Group match, he hit 134 as he and Chris Smith put on 252 for the first wicket in 165 minutes. He continued his fine form the following summer, hitting 1,226 runs at an average of 40.86.

Terry topped the Hampshire averages in 1992, scoring 766 at 51.06, but a serious back injury curtailed his season to just eleven FC matches. Unlucky not to have added to his two Test appearances, he has at the time of writing, scored 11,988 runs for Hampshire.

# BRYAN TIMMS

Born: 17 December 1940, Ropley
Played: 1959–1968

FIRST-CLASS HAMPSHIRE RECORD

| Matches | Innings | NO | Runs | HS | Ave | 100s |
|---------|---------|-----|------|-----|-------|------|
| 208 | 273 | 67 | 3236 | 120 | 15.70 | 1 |

NOTABLE FEATS

- He dismissed 462 batsmen (402 caught 60 stumped) in his career with Hampshire.
- His best season was 1965 with 79 dismissals (73 caught 6 stumped; in thirty-one matches.
- In 1964, he helped dismiss six batsmen in an innings v Leicestershire at Portsmouth.
- In 1964, he added 153* with P H Sainsbury for the seventh wicket v Northants at Southampton.

Bryan Timms succeeded Leo Harrison as Hampshire's regular wicket-keeper in 1963, though he had made his first-class debut some four seasons earlier.

During the summer of 1960, the County's regular wicket-keeper chipped a bone in his right hand and so Timms from Ropley came in to play for the rest of the season. Though he gave a good account of himself behind the stumps, he didn't really do anything to bolster the batting – 224 runs at 16.00.

He became a supremely efficient wicket-keeper and was equally good standing up or standing back.

In that summer of 1963, Timms helped to dismiss seventy batsmen (57 caught 13 stumped) and was awarded his county cap.

The following season, he helped to dismiss seventy-seven batsmen (58 caught 19 stumped) with his best performance coming in the match against Leicestershire at Portsmouth, where he claimed eight victims (including six in one innings to equal the Hampshire record). He ended the season second only to Roy Booth of Worcestershire in the national list of leading wicket-keepers. His batting too improved – 595 runs at 22.03 – though a large number of incompleted innings produced an average which was rather flattering. One of these incompleted innings came in the match against Northamptonshire at Southampton, as he and Peter Sainsbury added 153 for the sixth wicket. A useful late order batsman who worked hard for his runs, he and Derek Shackleton put on 105 for the ninth wicket in the away fixture with Leicestershire that season.

The summer of 1965 was his best behind the wickets in terms of the number of victims – 79 (73 caught 6 stumped) yet he didn't figure in the country's top two at the end of the season!

In 1966, he hit his one and only first-class hundred against Oxford University his 120 coming out of Hampshire's first innings total of 328, as the students were beaten by five wickets – yet his highest score in the County Championship was only 36. The following season, he almost came to his side's rescue in the third round of the Gillette Cup, as Hampshire chased Sussex's target of 234 off 60 overs. The county didn't seem to have much chance of winning, until Timms whirlwind innings of 55 in a handful of overs brought them within grasp of victory – but unfortunately, they fell nine runs short.

The season of 1968 proved to be Bryan Timms' last in Hampshire colours, for at the end of it, he unexpectedly left the county staff. It was a season in which he hit a couple of valuable half-centuries, 53 against Warwickshire at Basingstoke and an unbeaten 81 against Gloucestershire at Bristol, to give Hampshire victory in both matches.

His career with Hampshire saw him dismiss 462 batsmen (402 caught and 60 stumped) to place him eighth in the county's list of wicket-keepers. Within a short period of leaving Hampshire, he played for Warwickshire on a part-time basis, playing his last match for the Midlands side in 1971. Returning to live in his native county, he is now retired and a business entrepreneur.

# TIM TREMLETT

Born: 26 July 1956 Wellington, Somerset
Played: 1976–1991

FIRST-CLASS HAMPSHIRE RECORD

| Matches | Innings | NO | Runs | HS | Ave | 100s |
|---------|---------|-----|------|------|-------|------|
| 201 | 244 | 65 | 3815 | 102* | 21.31 | 1 |

| Runs | Wkts | Ave | Best |
|-------|------|-------|------|
| 10435 | 445 | 23.44 | 6-53 |

NOTABLE FEATS

- In 1980, he carried his bat for 70* out of 182 v Leicestershire at Southampton.

- In 1985, he added 227 with K D James v Somerset at Taunton, setting the county record for the eighth wicket and hitting his highest first-class score, 102 not out.
- His best bowling figures of 6 for 53 came in the match v Somerset at Weston-Super-Mare in 1987.

The son of Maurice Tremlett, a Somerset player for fourteen seasons and arguably the county's best captain, County cricket as a career seemed to have an inevitability about it for Tim, even though Dad regularly paraded the pitfalls.

Born in Wellington, Somerset, Tim captained his school and sixth-form College teams, before he made his debut for Hampshire in 1976. During 1978 he appeared in six games and looked a promising all-rounder who could deliver a useful ball at medium-pace, and was voted Hampshire's Young Cricketer of the Year.

In those early years, he quietly and realistically faced up to the special demands of etablishing himself in the county team.

The county were rocked in 1980 by David Rock's announcement just before the season got underway that he was retiring. This, plus Gordon Greenidge's involvement with the West Indian tour meant that the County were struggling for a partner for John Rice. He couldn't get going and after weeks of experiment, an unlikely opening pair of Chris Smith and Tim Tremlett evolved. In fact, Tremlett was mainly responsible for Hampshire's only Championship win of a disappointing season. He scored 76 not out from Hampshire's first innings total of 236 and an unbeaten 67 from 142 for 6 as Worcestershire were beaten by four wickets.

Tremlett assumed new discipline at the top of the order, refusing to be rushed or goaded into foreign strokes – ending the season with 717 runs from his seventeen matches for an average of 25.57.

The following season was one of mixed fortune for him, for he consolidated his advance of 1980, with a highest score of 88 against Lancashire at Old Trafford in one of his four half centuries. He and Mark Nicholas (94) shared in a second wicket stand of 153 as Hampshire won by two wickets.

However, in the Nat West match at Cardiff, he suffered a broken hand which kept him out of cricket for a while. Returning to the side after the birth of his son Christopher, he marked the event by wearing a helmet for the first time and was run out first ball without facing! Tim Tremlett had obvious assets as a medium-pace bowler, particularly in the one-day games. A straight and accurate bowler, his main hope was 'To hit the deck with the ball as hard as I can and hopefully get it away off the seam.' It certainly worked in 1984, for in the absence of Malcolm Marshall, Tremlett topped the county's bowling averages with 71 wickets at 20.33, being both consistent and economical.

The summer of 1985 saw Tremlett making the highest score of his career, an unbeaten 102 against Somerset at Taunton, setting the County record for the eighth wicket in a stand of 227 with Kevan James.

After being hampered by injury in 1986, he returned the following summer to enjoy one of his most successful seasons. He finished as the leading wicket-taker in the Club with 103 wickets in first team matches and 72 at 19.54 in first-class matches, to edge Malcolm Marshall out of top place in the County averages. It was a season in which he reproduced the sort of bounce and accuracy which won him a place on the England 'B' tour of Sri Lanka and the distinction of being the leading English-born bowler in sixth place in the national averages – producing his best-ever bowling figures of 6 for 53 against Somerset at Weston-super-Mare.

In 1989, he displayed some early season form, notably at Lord's in the match againt Middlesex, but again his cricket was disrupted by niggling little injuries.

A thinking cricketer, always analytical and often self-critical, it was announced at the end of the season that he was being appointed Cricket and Coaching Administrator and would lead the Second Eleven – an appointment which gave plenty of scope to his considerable administrative and coaching skills. There is no doubt that the future of Hampshire County Cricket club is in good hands as many of Tremlett's charges have progressed into the first team.

'Trooper Tim' delighted his many admirers when he returned to play in a number of championship and Sunday League games during 1990. He hit 78 against Kent at Bournemouth in the Championship (his highest score since 1985) and took 12 wickets in the Sunday League at 13.91.

Tim played his last game for the first team in 1991 – the only consolation for his fans is that the talents of this marvellously reliable team bowler are still making a notable contribution to Hampshire cricket, and is to be rewarded with a testimonial in 1993.

# DAVID TURNER

Born: 5 February 1949, Chippenham
Played: 1966–1989

FIRST-CLASS HAMPSHIRE RECORD

| Matches | Innings | NO | Runs | HS | Ave | 100s |
|---|---|---|---|---|---|---|
| 416 | 678 | 73 | 18683 | 184* | 30.88 | 27 |

| Runs | Wkts | Ave | Best |
|---|---|---|---|
| 357 | 9 | 39.66 | 2-7 |

NOTABLE FEATS

- In 1983, he added 290 with M C J Nicholas for the second wicket v Oxford University at Oxford.
- He enjoyed his best-ever batting average (49.18) in 1987 and hit a new career-best 184* at Gloucester.
- His 100* v Dorset in the Nat West Trophy of 1987 saw him join Barry Richards, Gordon Greenidge and Trevor Jesty as the only players to score a century for Hampshire in each of the four major competitions.
- In 1988, he became the sixth batsman to score 6,000 runs in Sunday League cricket.

David Turner was born and bred in Wiltshire. Encouraged by a fanatical headteacher, he was opening the batting for Chippenham High School at thirteen, besides playing for the Chippenham Club's Second Eleven. A year later, his progress had been so rapid, that he was elevated to the first team, and scored his maiden century against Wiltshire Queries.

In his four years with Chippenham, Turner topped 1,000 runs in each season and so his selection for Wiltshire in 1965 at the tender age of sixteen came as no surprise.

News travels fast along the cricketing grapevine and by the end of his first season in minor county cricket, he had had trials with no fewer than five counties: Gloucestershire, Northants, Somerset, Warwickshire and Hampshire – all of whom offered him a contract. Hampshire have always prided themselves in their encouragement, recruitment and development of local talent. Arthur Holt and Leo Harrison were two outstanding coaches, so it was thus no surprise when David and his parents were persuaded that he should make the short journey to Hampshire to further his cricketing ambitions. Also Hampshire had impending retirements and he thought this might allow him more opportunities than elsewhere, so at the age of seventeen, he joined the staff.

Batting impressively, in 1966 he quickly made several high scores in the Second Eleven and when injuries forced changes, he was brought into the first team in August for a couple of games. He started with a 'duck' against Kent at Bournemouth, but in the second innings, scored an unbeaten 15 out of Hampshire's total of 97. In 1967, he won the County's single-wicket competition, and spent the next few years working hard to consolidate his position. In 1969, he scored 181 not out against Surrey at the Oval and was dropped for the next match at the start of 1970 !

Although small in stature, he always possessed strength of wrist and arm and an excellent sense of timing. He was now being hailed in many quarters as a potential England batsman, especially as on 17 May 1972, he took the cricketing world by storm by scoring a magificent 131 for Hampshire against the Australians at Southampton. The Australian attack, which included Dennis Lillee was savaged by Turner's masterly strokeplay.

His undoing was a most unfortunate accident that occurred soon after this memorable innings.

Always a shrewd judge of length and line, he was quick to seize on to any delivery that was fractionally short of a length. Playing against Gloucestershire at Basingstoke on a wicket of doubtful bounce, he attempted to hook Tony Brown, but only succeeded in top-edging the ball into his face. It broke his nose and caused slight damage to his left eye. He did not play again for over a month – the injury certainly costing Turner the chance of a place in the England touring party to India and Pakistan the following winter – if only helmets had been the vogue in 1972, he would have gone on to represent England! Always an outstanding fielder, his low trajectory returns have sent many a batsman back to the pavilion. The reward for his brilliant fielding was to be selected as twelfth man for England in 1973 and as Wisden records: 'England gave a sketchy display of fielding, an exception being David Turner of Hampshire, who replaced Boycott and saved many runs.'

Probably due to his country upbringing 'Birdie' as he was known to his team-mates always had a shy and retiring personality. From 1973, he spent his winters as player-coach for Paarl in South Africa and it was there that he met his wife Henriette, whom he married in 1977.

In 1981, he was awarded a well deserved Benefit, rewarding his supporters with an heroic innings in the Lord's gloom in the opening Benson and Hedges match, a mature century against Somerset and a magnificent unbeaten 82 in the last John Player League game against Northants at Southampton.

Always willing to have the occasional over, he derived much

pleasure that season from getting four first-class wickets with right-arm medium-pace and in the Lambert and Butler seven-a-side floodlit tournament at Ashton Gate, improbably became the first to achieve a hat-trick (all clean bowled) against Glamorgan. They too were the opponents when he produced his best-ever bowling figures, 2 for 7 at Bournemouth.

His performances in one-day cricket helped to make Hampshire one of the most consistent limited-over sides in the country and if England limited-over teams had been selected purely on merit in that type of cricket, it is hard to explain his absence. On scoring 100 not out against Dorset at Southampton in the 1987 Nat West Trophy, the innings saw him join Barry Richards,Gordon Greenidge and Trevor Jesty as the only players to score a century in each of the four major competitions. David Turner's was perhaps the most surprising name prominently displayed in the 1987 batting averages, for at thirty-eight years of age, he wasn't even expected to start the season in the first team. He scored 1,328 runs at an average of 49.18 and hit his highest-ever score, 184 not out against Gloucestershire – it was his 600th first-class innings and contained 25 fours in his six hours at the crease.

David Turner was a model professional and in his latter years, accepted the disapointment of omission from Hampshire's championship side applying himself to setting a fine example to younger players in the Second Eleven.

Retiring at the beginning of the 1990 season, he went back to his cricketing roots to play for Chippenham, the Wiltshire club where he was discovered – some of the present side not even being born when he first played for the club as a teenager.

David Turner served Hampshire loyally and with distinction – there was no more popular decision than to present him with a silver salver early in 1990. It was a fitting tribute to a solid, reliable and thoroughly competent cricketer – many cricket followers wondering what he might have achieved at international level, but for that unfortunate accident in 1972.

# DAVID WHITE

Born: 14 December 1935, Sutton Coldfield
Played: 1957–1971

FIRST-CLASS HAMPSHIRE RECORD

| Matches | Innings | NO | Runs | HS | Ave | 100s |
|---|---|---|---|---|---|---|
| 315 | 374 | 101 | 2967 | 58* | 10.86 | 0 |

| Runs | Wkts | Ave | Best |
|---|---|---|---|
| 25630 | 1097 | 23.36 | 9-44 |

NOTABLE FEATS

- He performed the hat-trick on two occasions: v Sussex at Portsmouth in 1961 and against the same county at Hove the following season.
- In 1966, he took 9 for 44 v Leicestershire at Portsmouth.

A great-hearted cricketer, 'Butch' White, as he was always known was born in Sutton Coldfield, and in his school days played cricket and football for Boldmere Secondary. Later in the Birmingham League, he bowled for Aston Unity and his performances were watched by Warwickshire who invited him to play as an amateur in the Second Eleven.

His apprenticeship to his father, a master builder, delayed his National Service, where he eventually served the RASC as a driving instructor. Lt-Col Rowley was his commanding officer and cricket was his predominant interest. Of course, a fast bowler in the mould of 'Butch' White was an asset to the battalion team and on the beautiful grounds of Blandford, Wimborne and Sherborne School, he developed the powerful style which was to carry him into the Hampshire side.

His debut for Hampshire came in 1957 at the age of twenty-one, and after Vic Cannings retired, White gained a regular place in the county team. He made a rapid improvement, and in 1960, his first full season in the County team, he took 124 wickets at 18 runs each. If he hadn't been no-balled for throwing, he would most likely have been chosen for the MCC winter tour.

Under Colin Ingleby-Mackenzie, the Hampshire side was enjoying success, the gambled declarations came off, the players were enthusiastic and 'Butch' took another 117 Championship wickets at 24.60 as Hampshire headed the table.

In the match against Sussex at Portsmouth, the visitors were batting steadily as the clock stood at a few minutes to 7.00 p.m. It was the last over when Jim Parks lost his stumps to White; Ian Thomson as nightwatchman was taken behind by Leo Harrison and then there was a wait, for Don Smith had already changed. He need not have bothered, for White knocked over his castle and Graham Cooper came to the wicket. His stay was short-lived for Jimmy Gray just failed to hold a hard chance but the next ball, Henry Horton took one in the gulley. Four wickets in five balls for 'Butch' White, yet up to the time he bowled Parks he hadn't looked like getting a wicket!

As a left-handed batsman, he would thrust his right leg down the pitch and aim an almighty heave towards mid-wicket. If he connected, there was often quite an interval before the next ball was delivered! In fact, in that summer of 1961, he virtually won the match against Gloucestershire single-handed, by hitting some mighty blows. By scoring 33 out of the 37 added for the ninth wicket, he brought success for the County with only two minutes left on the clock.

His reward for this successful season was selection in the MCC team to tour India, Pakistan and Ceylon. On his test debut, he took the wickets of both Pakistan openers, Hanif Mohammed and Imtiaz Ahmed in his first three overs. However, he pulled a muscle in the second test at Karachi and this injury, plus the excessive heat and slow wickets did little to help him and meant that he did not have a very successful tour. He was, quite surprisingly at his most dangerous when he looked as if he was being mastered, and it was again after an uninspiring spell that he collected another hat-trick againt Sussex at Hove in 1962.

A massively built six-footer, he would charge in like a battering ram, giving every ounce of energy for over after over. He could both swing the ball in sharply and break it back off the pitch. On one occasion describing 'Butch's approach to bowling, Trevor Bailey said: 'He's got a heart as big as a lettuce!' – not a bad assessment, for providing his captain didn't rub him up the wrong way, there was never a greater hearted trier.

There is little doubt that 'Butch' was one of cricket's characters, well liked by players and spectators alike. It may have been a bad day or it may have been successful, but when he came off the field tired, the day's play was over and a few pints and some talk in the local or back at the hotel in the company of his fellow cricketers was all he looked for.

'Butch' always believed that the only way to play is to play hard and enjoy the game. An incident that sums up his philosophy occurred on one of those hot and humid days, that takes a fast bowler and drains him, leaving him heavy and tired. As he walked to the third man boundary, a spectator quietly downed a cool beer. 'I could use one of those right now' commented White and when he finished his next over, there in the boundary grass, it was waiting for him!

On many occasions, White was vicious from the first ball and at Middlesbrough in 1965, he took six for 10 (at one time taking five wickets without conceding a run) as Yorkshire were shot out for 23, their lowest-ever score. Also that season when Bob Cottam took 9 for 25 against Lancashire at Old Trafford, it was 'Butch' White that took 6 for 48 in the second innings to give Hampshire victory by 13 runs.

Some of the smaller county grounds struggled to accommodate his long run, but at Portsmouth in 1966, he produced his best ever figures of 9 for 44 against Leicestershire.

He was awarded a benefit by Hampshire in 1969, at which time he spent his winter evenings running the Indoor Cricket School at Southampton. In 1970, he had a nice little freak batting average, for he managed nine not outs in his twelve innings and finished the season with an average of 50.00 to finish seventh in the national first-class averages – he was always very proud of that season!

His bowling seemed to lose its effectiveness the following season, only taking 14 wickets in his eleven Championship matches, and at the end of the season, Hampshire did not renew his contract.

In 1972, he played in just one Championship game for his new county of Glamorgan, but played on a regular basis in the one-day matches. After retiring from county cricket, he became cricket coach at Christ's Hospital.

Hampshire folk appreciated his sincerity and his quiet, dry humour and his approach to cricket, that saw him take 1,097 wickets for the County at an average of 23.36.

# APPENDICES

*Stastical Analysis*

Selecting a best team ever can be a fascinating relaxation, but it can also be highly provocative. For players were at their best in different decades and comparison can be odius, and the more one thinks of all the players who have represented Hampshire, the more difficult the task of selecting the best eleven becomes.

For whilst it is purely a matter of opinion as to how good a player a man is or has been, and it is certainly true that figures seldom tell the true story of any cricketer, I hope the following will go some way to explaining why I have chosen the following eleven players as my team of 'Famous Cricketers of Hampshire' though it wasn't easy to leave out players of the calibre of Neville Rogers, Johnny Arnold, Chris Smith, Stuart Boyes and Andy Roberts.

1. Barry Richards
2. Gordon Greenidge
3. Roy Marshall
4. Philip Mead
5. Robin Smith
6. George Brown (wk)
7. Charles Llewellyn
8. Malcolm Marshall
9. Alec Kennedy
10. Jack Newman
11. Derek Shackleton

# HAMPSHIRE TOP TENS

The following section lists the best performances in each of several categories, showing in statistical form the 'Top Ten' for Hampshire.

## Most Runs

| | | |
|---|---|---|
| 1. | C P Mead | 48,892 |
| 2. | R E Marshall | 30,303 |
| 3. | G Brown | 22,962 |
| 4. | J R Gray | 22,450 |
| 5. | J Arnold | 21,596 |
| 6. | H Horton | 21,536 |
| 7. | C G Greenidge | 19,840 |
| 8. | P J Sainsbury | 19,576 |
| 9. | D R Turner | 18,683 |
| 10. | H A W Bowell | 18,466 |

## Most Wickets

| | | |
|---|---|---|
| 1. | D Shackleton | 2,669 |
| 2. | A S Kennedy | 2,549 |
| 3. | J A Newman | 1,946 |
| 4. | G S Boyes | 1,415 |
| 5. | P J Sainsbury | 1,245 |
| 6. | D W White | 1,097 |
| 7. | O W Herman | 1,041 |
| 8. | V H D Cannings | 834 |
| 9. | M D Marshall | 798 |
| 10. | C B Llewellyn | 711 |

## Most Catches (not W/Keepers)

| | | |
|---|---|---|
| 1. | C P Mead | 629 |
| 2. | P J Sainsbury | 601 |
| 3. | G Brown | 484 |
| 4. | A S Kennedy | 482 |
| 5. | G S Boyes | 474 |
| 6. | J R Gray | 350 |
| 7. | E D R Eagar | 333 |
| 8. | C G Greenidge | 315 |
| 9. | H M Barnard | 313 |
| 10. | J A Newman | 296 |

## Most Matches

| | | |
|---|---|---|
| 1. | C P Mead | 700 |
| 2. | A S Kennedy | 596 |
| 3. | P J Sainsbury | 593 |
| 4. | D Shackleton | 583 |
| 5. | G Brown | 539 |
| 6. | J A Newman | 506 |
| 7. | R E Marshall | 504 |
| 8. | G S Boyes | 474 |
| 9. | H A W Bowell | 473 |
| 10. | J R Gray | 453 |

## Batting Average

| | | |
|---|---|---|
| 1. | B A Richards | 50.50 |
| 2. | C P Mead | 48.84 |
| 3. | C L Smith | 45.63 |
| 4. | R A Smith | 45.27 |
| 5. | C G Greenidge | 45.40 |
| 6. | R E Marshall | 36.03 |
| 7. | V P Terry | 35.78 |
| 8. | H Horton | 33.49 |
| 9. | J Arnold | 32.92 |
| 10. | M C J Nicholas | 32.69 |

## Bowling Average

| | | |
|---|---|---|
| 1. | A M E Roberts | 16.70 |
| 2. | M D Marshall | 18.22 |
| 3. | D Shackleton | 18.23 |
| 4. | R M H Cottam | 20.71 |
| 5. | A S Kennedy | 21.16 |
| 6. | V H D Cannings | 21.69 |
| 7. | D W White | 23.36 |
| 8. | T M Tremlett | 23.44 |
| 9. | C J Knott | 23.53 |
| 10. | G S Boyes | 23.68 |

There are other players with better batting and bowling averages, but they haven't been included as they haven't either played enough matches or performed as a regular bowler to warrant inclusion as a Famous Cricketer of Hampshire.

## Most Hundreds

| | | |
|---|---|---|
| 1. | C P Mead | 138 |
| 2. | R E Marshall | 60 |
| 3. | C G Greenidge | 48 |
| 4. | C L Smith | 41 |
| 5. | B A Richards | 38 |
| 6. | G Brown | 37 |
| 7. | J Arnold | 36 |
| 8. | H Horton | 32 |
| 9. | J R Gray | 30 |
| 10. | D R Turner | 27 |
| | M C J Nicholas | 27 |

## Test Appearances

| | | |
|---|---|---|
| 1. | C G Greenidge | 108 |
| 2. | M D Marshall | 81 |
| 3. | A M E Roberts | 47 |
| 4. | R A Smith | 36 |
| 5. | C P Mead | 17 |
| 6. | Hon L Tennyson | 9 |
| 7. | C B Llewellyn | 8 |
| | C L Smith | 8 |
| 9. | G Brown | 7 |
| | D Shackleton | 7 |

## Highest Scores

| | | | |
|---|---|---|---|
| 1. | R H Moore | 316 v Warwickshire at Bournemouth | 1937 |
| 2. | C P Mead | 280* v Nottingham at Southampton | 1921 |
| 3. | C G Greenidge | 259 v Sussex at Southampton | 1975 |
| 4. | T E Jesty | 248 v Cambridge University at Cambridge | 1984 |
| 5. | W L C Creese | 241 v Northamptonshire at Northampton | 1939 |
| 6. | B A Richards | 240 v Warwickshire at Coventry | 1973 |
| 7. | G Brown | 232* v Yorkshire at Headingley | 1920 |
| 8. | R E Marshall | 228* v Pakistan at Bournemouth | 1962 |
| 9. | J Arnold | 227* v Glamorgan at Cardiff | 1932 |
| 10. | R M C Gilliat | 223* v Warwickshire at Southampton | 1969 |

## Also scored

| | | |
|---|---|---|
| C P Mead | 235 v Worcestershire at Worcester | 1922 |
| | 227 v Derbyshire at Ilkeston | 1933 |
| | 224 v Sussex at Horsham | 1921 |
| G Brown | 230 v Essex at Bournemouth | 1920 |
| B A Richards | 225* v Nottinghamshire at Trent Bridge | 1974 |

The following would normally figure in the 'Top Ten' but haven't been included, as they have not been classed as 'Famous Cricketers of Hampshire'.

| | | |
|---|---|---|
| R M Poore | 304 v Somerset at Taunton | 1899 |
| E G Wynyard | 268 v Yorkshire at Southampton | 1896 |
| | 225 v Somerset at Taunton | 1899 |
| C B Fry | 258* v Gloucestershire at Southampton | 1911 |
| J G Greig | 249* v Lancashire at Liverpool | 1901 |

# BATTING AVERAGES (Up to the end of the 1992 season)

|  | Inns | NO | Runs | HS | Ave | 100s |
|---|---|---|---|---|---|---|
| J Arnold | 701 | 45 | 21596 | 227 | 32.92 | 36 |
| J Bailey | 408 | 35 | 9301 | 133 | 24.93 | 5 |
| H Baldwin | 240 | 65 | 1863 | 55* | 10.64 | 0 |
| H M Barnard | 463 | 41 | 9314 | 128* | 22.07 | 6 |
| H A W Bowell | 806 | 43 | 18466 | 204 | 24.20 | 25 |
| G S Boyes | 677 | 156 | 7515 | 104 | 14.42 | 2 |
| G Brown | 900 | 46 | 22962 | 232* | 26.88 | 37 |
| M D Burden | 191 | 59 | 901 | 51 | 6.82 | 0 |
| V H D Cannings | 294 | 103 | 1888 | 43* | 9.88 | 0 |
| C A Connor | 129 | 38 | 889 | 51 | 9.76 | 0 |
| R M H Cottam | 178 | 65 | 615 | 35 | 5.44 | 0 |
| N G Cowley | 358 | 58 | 6773 | 109* | 22.57 | 2 |
| W L C Creese | 453 | 41 | 9894 | 241 | 24.01 | 6 |
| E D R Eagar | 514 | 34 | 10091 | 158* | 21.02 | 8 |
| R M C Gilliat | 351 | 40 | 9358 | 223* | 30.09 | 16 |
| J R Gray | 809 | 81 | 22450 | 213* | 30.83 | 30 |
| C G Greenidge | 472 | 35 | 19840 | 259 | 45.40 | 48 |
| L Harrison | 593 | 100 | 8708 | 153 | 17.66 | 6 |
| M Heath | 163 | 66 | 569 | 33 | 5.86 | 0 |
| O W Herman | 495 | 105 | 4327 | 92 | 11.09 | 0 |
| A J L Hill | 291 | 17 | 8381 | 199 | 30.58 | 17 |
| G Hill | 595 | 94 | 9085 | 161 | 18.13 | 4 |
| A G Holt | 140 | 13 | 2853 | 116 | 22.46 | 2 |
| H Horton | 723 | 80 | 21536 | 160* | 33.49 | 32 |
| A C D Ingleby-Mackenzie | 513 | 60 | 11140 | 132* | 24.59 | 10 |
| T E Jesty | 538 | 74 | 14753 | 248 | 31.79 | 26 |
| A S Kennedy | 916 | 110 | 14925 | 163* | 18.51 | 10 |
| C J Knott | 235 | 94 | 1003 | 27 | 7.11 | 0 |
| D A Livingstone | 516 | 63 | 12660 | 200 | 27.94 | 16 |
| W H Livsey | 443 | 131 | 4818 | 110* | 15.44 | 2 |
| C B Llewellyn | 341 | 23 | 8772 | 216 | 27.58 | 15 |
| N T McCorkell | 675 | 63 | 15834 | 203 | 25.87 | 17 |
| M D Marshall | 253 | 35 | 597 | 117 | 25.67 | 5 |
| R E Marshall | 890 | 49 | 30303 | 228* | 36.03 | 60 |
| C P Mead | 1171 | 170 | 48892 | 280* | 48.84 | 138 |
| R H Moore | 225 | 7 | 5885 | 316 | 26.99 | 10 |
| J A Newman | 786 | 121 | 13904 | 166* | 20.90 | 9 |
| M C J Nicholas | 503 | 72 | 14091 | 206* | 32.69 | 27 |
| R J Parks | 282 | 82 | 3936 | 89 | 19.68 | 0 |
| N E J Pocock | 186 | 22 | 3790 | 164 | 23.10 | 2 |
| A E Pothecary | 445 | 39 | 9477 | 130 | 23.34 | 9 |
| J M Rice | 271 | 22 | 5091 | 161* | 20.44 | 2 |
| B A Richards | 342 | 33 | 15607 | 240 | 50.50 | 38 |
| A M E Roberts | 65 | 23 | 583 | 39 | 13.88 | 0 |
| N H Rogers | 506 | 25 | 15292 | 186 | 31.79 | 26 |
| P J Sainsbury | 913 | 189 | 19576 | 163 | 27.03 | 7 |
| D Shackleton | 773 | 177 | 8602 | 87* | 14.43 | 0 |
| C L Smith | 383 | 48 | 15287 | 217 | 45.63 | 41 |
| R A Smith | 248 | 44 | 9235 | 209* | 45.27 | 24 |
| E M Sprot | 452 | 28 | 12212 | 147 | 28.80 | 13 |
| G R Stephenson | 343 | 66 | 4566 | 100* | 16.48 | 1 |
| J Stone | 468 | 57 | 9167 | 174 | 22.30 | 5 |
| M N S Taylor | 198 | 39 | 3646 | 103* | 22.93 | 2 |

| | Inns | NO | Runs | HS | Ave | 100s |
|---|---|---|---|---|---|---|
| Hon L H Tennyson | 553 | 20 | 12626 | 217 | 23.68 | 15 |
| V P Terry | 372 | 37 | 11988 | 190 | 35.78 | 26 |
| B S V Timms | 273 | 67 | 3236 | 120 | 15.70 | 1 |
| T M Tremlett | 244 | 65 | 3815 | 102* | 21.31 | 1 |
| D R Turner | 678 | 73 | 18683 | 184* | 30.88 | 27 |
| D W White | 374 | 101 | 2967 | 58* | 10.86 | 0 |

# BOWLING AVERAGES (Up to the end of the 1992 season)

| | Runs | Wkts | Ave | Best |
|---|---|---|---|---|
| J Arnold | 1182 | 17 | 69.52 | 3-34 |
| J Bailey | 12595 | 467 | 26.97 | 7-7 |
| H Baldwin | 14336 | 580 | 24.71 | 8-74 |
| H M Barnard | 563 | 16 | 35.18 | 3-35 |
| H A W Bowell | 1766 | 34 | 51.94 | 4-20 |
| G S Boyes | 33513 | 1415 | 23.68 | 9-57 |
| G Brown | 17857 | 602 | 29.66 | 8-55 |
| M D Burden | 12559 | 481 | 26.11 | 8-38 |
| V H D Cannings | 18091 | 834 | 21.69 | 7-52 |
| C A Connor | 13326 | 405 | 32.90 | 7-31 |
| R M H Cottam | 14354 | 693 | 20.71 | 9-25 |
| N G Cowley | 13979 | 425 | 32.89 | 6-48 |
| W L C Creese | 11141 | 401 | 27.78 | 8-37 |
| E D R Eagar | 937 | 15 | 62.46 | 2-10 |
| R M C Gilliat | 133 | 3 | 44.33 | 1-3 |
| J R Gray | 13543 | 451 | 30.02 | 7-52 |
| C G Greenidge | 387 | 16 | 24.18 | 5-49 |
| L Harrison | 166 | 0 | – | – |
| M Heath | 13237 | 527 | 25.11 | 8-43 |
| O W Herman | 28137 | 1041 | 27.02 | 8-49 |
| A J L Hill | 6213 | 199 | 31.22 | 7-36 |
| G Hill | 18464 | 617 | 29.92 | 8-62 |
| A G Holt | 47 | 1 | 47.00 | 1-24 |
| H Horton | 162 | 3 | 54.00 | 2-0 |
| A C D Ingleby-Mackenzie | 22 | 0 | – | – |
| T E Jesty | 13596 | 475 | 28.62 | 7-75 |
| A S Kennedy | 53950 | 2549 | 21.16 | 9-33 |
| C J Knott | 15224 | 647 | 23.53 | 8-26 |
| D A Livingstone | 68 | 1 | 68.00 | 1-31 |
| W H Livsey | did | not | bowl | |
| C B Llewellyn | 17538 | 711 | 24.66 | 8-72 |
| N T McCorkell | 117 | 1 | 117.00 | 1-73 |
| M D Marshall | 14542 | 798 | 18.22 | 8-71 |
| R E Marshall | 2403 | 99 | 24.27 | 6-36 |
| C P Mead | 9252 | 266 | 34.78 | 7-18 |
| R H Moore | 978 | 25 | 39.12 | 3-46 |
| J A Newman | 48305 | 1946 | 24.82 | 9-131 |
| M C J Nicholas | 3126 | 69 | 45.30 | 6-37 |
| R J Parks | 166 | 0 | – | – |
| N E J Pocock | 396 | 4 | 99.00 | 1-4 |

| | Runs | Wkts | Ave | Best |
|---|---|---|---|---|
| A E Pothecary | 2140 | 52 | 41.15 | 4-47 |
| J M Rice | 7707 | 230 | 33.50 | 7-48 |
| B A Richards | 1675 | 46 | 36.41 | 7-63 |
| A M E Roberts | 4076 | 244 | 16.70 | 8-47 |
| N H Rogers | 37 | 0 | – | – |
| P J Sainsbury | 30060 | 1245 | 24.14 | 8-76 |
| D Shackleton | 48674 | 2669 | 18.23 | 9-30 |
| C L Smith | 2366 | 44 | 53.77 | 5-69 |
| R A Smith | 630 | 12 | 52.50 | 2-11 |
| E M Sprot | 1856 | 54 | 34.37 | 5-28 |
| G R Stephenson | 39 | 0 | – | – |
| J Stone | 104 | 1 | 104.00 | 1-77 |
| M N S Taylor | 7458 | 308 | 24.21 | 7-23 |
| Hon L H Tennyson | 2374 | 43 | 55.20 | 3-50 |
| V P Terry | 58 | 0 | – | – |
| B S V Timms | did | not | bowl | |
| T M Tremlett | 10435 | 445 | 23.44 | 6-53 |
| D R Turner | 357 | 9 | 39.66 | 2-7 |
| D W White | 25630 | 1097 | 23.36 | 9-44 |

# LIST OF ILLUSTRATIONS (In Chronological Order)